The Cosworth Fords

Other books by the same author . . .

ESCORT
Mks 1, 2, 3 & 4
The Development & Competition History
J H Haynes, Second Edition 1990

CAPRI
The Development & Competition History of Ford's European GT car
J H Haynes, Third Edition 1990

RS: The Faster Fords
Motor Racing Publications (MRP), Second Edition 1990

SPORTING FORDS
Volume 3: CAPRI
Including RS2600, RS3100.2.8i & 280
MRP, Second Edition 1990

SPORTING FORDS
Volume 5: FRONT DRIVE ESCORTS
From XR3 to Cosworth 4x4
MRP, published 1993

The author also has marque histories in print covering BMW 3–series, Lotus
Esprit and classic BMWs. The 1984 Haynes title, *Audi Quattro: Competition
& Development History* is out of print.

Patrick Stephens Limited, an imprint of Haynes Publishing, has published
authoritative, quality books for enthusiasts for more than a quarter of a century.
During that time the company has established a reputation as one of the world's
leading publishers of books on aviation, maritime, military, model-making, motor
cycling, motoring, motor racing, railway and railway modelling subjects. Readers or
authors with suggestions for books they would likc to see published are invited to
write to: The Editorial Director, Patrick Stephens Limited, Sparkford, Nr Yeovil,
Somerset, BA22 7JJ.

The Cosworth Fords

A PRODUCTION AND COMPETITION HISTORY

Jeremy Walton

Patrick Stephens Limited

First published in 1994

British Library Cataloguing-in-Publication Data:
A catalogue record for this book
is available from the British Library.

ISBN 1 85260 481 6

Library of Congress catalog card no. 94 77773

Patrick Stephens Limited is an imprint of
Haynes Publishing, Sparkford, Nr Yeovil,
Somerset, BA22 7JJ.

Design & Typesetting by G&M, Raunds, Northamptonshire
Printed in Great Britain by Butler & Tanner Ltd, London and Frome

Contents

Introduction

This is a book I had wanted to write ever since *Autocar & Motor* scooped the existence of an Escort Cosworth to extend the Sierra-Cosworth theme towards the year 2000. I had closed an earlier 1980s edition of the Haynes title *Escort Mks 1, 2, 3, & 4* with the hope that Ford would put respect back into the Escort's sporting reputation, so this '90s combination of compact Escort size with the justly fabled Cosworth and Ferguson 4x4 formula was keenly anticipated.

It was frustrating awaiting the birth of the quickest production Escort, pausing again to let the fully developed factory Ford establish its considerable sporting worth at World Championship level (four factory wins, one privateer in its debut season). I think the enforced delay enabled us to put the complete Sierra to Escort RS Cosworth story into a unique perspective.

After establishing what Ford and Cosworth had to offer each other from their initial '60s sports contacts to their production association, we examine the Sierras that made the earlier programmes possible.

Each of the five Ford Cosworth production cars (all but one carrying an RS badge throughout in the UK, intermittently in some LHD markets) has a production and competition chapter devoted to its career, plus the comments of owners or competition drivers, as appropriate.

The six most exciting production Fords to date appear in the following production order under their UK RHD badges: 1985-86 Sierra RS Cosworth 3-dr (hatch-back); 1987 Sierra RS Cosworth RS500 (modified on original 3-dr base); 1988 to 1990 Sierra RS Cosworth (4-dr, rear drive, sometimes referred to as a Sapphire in Ford on Britain promotional literature); 1990-92 Sierra RS Cosworth 4x4 (4-dr); 1991 to date Scorpio 24v (also available in an Estate body 1993, all with no competition intention and no external Cosworth badge). Finally, we have the 1992 to date Escort RS Cosworth (3-dr, 4x4), as this was written due to be transformed into a better road performer with a smaller turbocharger and Ford EEC-IV engine management.

To put us on the pace at the leading edge of Ford and Cosworth alliances in a production body, I have recorded the fabulous first racing season of the Andy Rouse Engineering Mondeo-Cosworth V6. I regard that car as the spiritual successor to the RS500 racing Sierras. Therefore the Mondeo draws on Ford lineage back to the Anglia, the marque currently totalling an unparalleled 200+ British Championship victories.

Yet the production variants of the Mondeo V6 were destined to be very different, using the American Ford modular V6 rather than the ex-Mazda MX-6/626 unit. Obviously there will be a further performance Mondeo V6 variant for the later '90s and it would be nice to think that the Ford and Cosworth production alliance will be with us to see out the Century.

Jeremy Walton
Wargrave-on-Thames
March 1994

Chapter 1

Pioneer meets modernist

The first contacts between Ford and Cosworth came in competition, but commercial reality was part of the relationship, even in the '60s.

Ford and Cosworth has seemed a natural alliance since Cosworth co-founder Keith Duckworth redesigned the 105E Ford Anglia engine to win Formula Junior (later Formula 3) races. The engine was actually ready for Boxing Day Brands, 1959, but scored its first victory in March 1960. Appropriately, in view of what was to come in Grand Prix, that winner was Jim Clark and the car was a Lotus 18.

Cosworth was then just a couple of years old. September 1958 had seen Mike *Cos*tin (then a Lotus racing mechanic and a fine development driver, brother to aerodynamicist Frank) and Keith Duck*worth* (qualified engineer and determined to set up on his own after also working for Lotus) take an equal share in the formation of Cosworth, then based in North London.

Cosworth was created to serve the competition market, particularly that of single-seater racing cars. Ford in Britain, with a non-competitive product range enlisted Cosworth's help on the production line, Cosworth extracted some 100 bhp a litre, and over 10,000 rpm from a pretty basic pushrod four-cylinder.

The task was to overcome some of Ford's breathing problems on a pre-crossflow 1.3 litre that actually went into production as the 1500 GT unit of Cortina and Capri Classic in 1963.

The Cosworth solution was to become an industry standard: Weber twin choke, downdraught, carburettor, cast alloy semi-circular inlet manifold and a camshaft profile that may just be the most imitated in the converted car. Graham Robson reveals in *Cosworth: the search for power* that Keith Duckworth obtained £750 from Ford for the rights to manufacture that cam profile to his design: a historic decision.

Ford Cosworth co-operation grew around the occasional commercial job and the continuing finesse of Keith Duckworth and company in extracting unreal levels of reliable performance from Ford-blocked racing engines.

The 1964 SCA (Single Cam A-series) was Cosworth's first blooding as creators of a replacement high efficiency (all round, not just power) aluminium cylinder head, a speciality they were to make their own. The

Opposite Spot the Cosworth connection. There are nine 'Powered by Ford' competitors assembled at Brands Hatch in 1993 and more than half of them have a direct Cosworth link. Most obvious is the 3.5 litre Benetton-Ford Cosworth HB V8 for Grand Prix, but there are also Group A and N Escort Cosworths (François Delecour's Portuguese winner is number 5, Robbie Head's is the Michelin Pilot example, 11). The prototype 2 litre rear drive Rouse/Radisich Mondeo-Cosworth V6 was also on hand, whilst the fifth obvious Cosworth-Ford is the ProSport 3000, which uses an uprated Ford Scorpio-Cosworth V6.

Above The Cortina 1500 GT pushrod four-cylinder owed its breathing success to one of Cosworth's first commercial engine consultation links. Most works cars — like this 1964 East African Safari winner for Peter Hughes — utilized the A2 camshaft profile, or developments thereof, which were also sold on to the public after Ford acquired the rights to the design for a further fee. Road cars initially benefited from a semi-circular inlet manifold and twin choke Weber downdraught carburettor that became part of the Ford performance repertoire through the 1960s on many more designs than the Cortina.

Above right The early days for Cosworth were not entirely a magic carpet ride to the top. Here Brian Hart (subsequently a very significant figure in Cosworth Ford engine developments) walks away from his stricken Lotus 22-SCA in 1964. *(Courtesy Cosworth Archive)*

overhead camshaft conversion of a Ford 116E (Cortina crossflow) block yielded 115 bhp from 1 litre initially; more like 140 bhp when Honda started to beat them with a 16-valve DOHC design.

The end of 1964 saw Cosworth finally uproot from the variety of North London premises that had housed their rapidly growing enterprise, and relocate to a 'greenfield' site in Northampton. The site still serves as HQ to the Cosworth group, but the company has now occupied both sides of St James Mill Road, Northampton, and has two other major factory operations in Britain, as well as an American offshoot.

Perhaps *the* landmark Ford Cosworth co-operation was the £100,000 combined programme to design, manufacture and service the 1966 FVA (Four Valve A-series) four-cylinder Formula 2 of 1.6 litres and the 1967 DFV (Double Four Valve) Grand Prix V8 of 3 litres. These efficient four valves per cylinder, DOHC designs, did beat the best, and established Cosworth leadership in the field of DOHC, 16-valve, layouts for both the inline four (136.25 bhp a litre) and the doubled up V8 (135.31 bhp per litre).

Both BMW and Ferrari bowed to the 1.6 litre Cosworth in 1966 onward Formula 2, especially when Jochen Rindt was handing out the medicine. BMW had to abandon their principles and follow the Cosworth route to gain 2 litre Formula 2 success. The Lotus 49-DFV was also a winner on its 1967 Zandvoort debut.

The DFV went on to record the majority (154) of victories credited to V8 Ford Cosworths today and was most successful unit for March, Matra, Tyrrell, Brabham . . . Between 1967 and 1983, practically every chassis save Ferrari came to the grid courtesy of Cosworth Ford in this the British Kit Car heyday of the DFV and DFY motor types.

In 1990 Cosworth continued to supply approximately 50 per cent of the teams contesting the Formula 1 World Championship. Such international trade bought the DFR eight-cylinder descendants of the original 1967 DFV design. These cost more than £45,000 apiece, boosting production of the DF V8 series over 550 kit and completed examples.

In 1991 Eddie Jordan Racing set the precedent for leasing 15 of the later HB engines (the V eight-cylinder design having previously been exclusive to

A still from the Ford-financed film *Nine Days In Summer* records the winning 1967 debut of the Ford Cosworth Grand Prix alliance. Here, a trio of the most influential forces at work in that alliance: Harley Copp, the Ford engineering chief suit, leans on a treaded Firestone; Keith Duckworth recalls the creative angst in amongst the inlet trumpets; and Colin Chapman sports the shades in front of the Team Lotus transporter.

Benetton Ford). Such leasing deals became predominant during the '90s. Leasing allowed Cosworth room for commercial growth whilst preserving their technological advantage. By the end of 1993 Cosworth had manufactured 'over 200' HB family V8s, and more were due out of the door for the following year.

For 1994 only Benetton were allowed a new V8 design Zetec-R, but four other teams contracted to take the HB in both air valve and conventional wire valve formats. The latter team quartet comprised Footwork (Arrows again, by 1994), Minardi, former Chrysler-Lamborghini V12 runners Larrousse, and new boys Simtek.

The '60s DFV programme was particularly relevant in linking Ford and Cosworth commercially once more. The 1970 Escort RS1600 had the first production 16-valve DOHC motor sold by Ford, a belt drive twin overhead camshaft offspring of the Ford Cosworth competition programme, one that had already spawned the FVA and DFV racing motors. (Ford paid £40,000

Much more familiar RS1800 format for the 16-valve motor was as a stretched unit, its aluminium block offering 2 litres and serving the works rally cars under a pair of oversize sidedraught carburettors. Note the simplicity of the roll cage compared to the intricate and beefy scaffolding of the '90s.

The Ford Cosworth alliance continued in the fuel crisis period of the '70s with this 3.4 litre racing version of the 3.0 Essex V6. Equipped with classic Cosworth quad valve technology and DOHC for each cylinder bank, the fuel injected unit began life with more than 400 bhp and was happy beyond 450 bhp after its brief works Capri RS3100 racing life was over. This one was shoehorned into an Escort. (*Norman Hodson, courtesy* Cars & Car Conversions *magazine)*

to Cosworth, plus royalties on each engine made.)

The BDA developed 120 bhp in street trim and displaced 1.6 litres, using both iron and alloy blocks in its production run. At this point Ford could have fairly negotiated to use the Cosworth name, at least on the cam covers of the Escort road cars (there was an RS1800 successor), but it would be another 16 years before the link was so publicly acknowledged.

The BDA evolved into an enormous family of 15 primarily competition variants, the exceptions being the '80s family of BDTs that were destined for aborted RS1700T Escort and then redeveloped for the RS200.

Not so numerous were the 100-off kits based on Ford's Essex V6 in the 1973/4 winter. These transformed the iron pushrod plodder of 138 bhp and 3 litres into a 440 bhp 3.4 litre that lusted after life at 8,750 rpm. The enlarged units were pure racers, designed to power the Capri RS3100 away from BMW's best, and also used in Formula 500, when the fuel crisis reduced touring car racing to a very low key affair for '74.

It was the '80s before Ford and Cosworth co-operated commercially so extensively again, uniting on the YA/YB series of Pinto-block motors discussed in this book. When the Sierra Cosworth was unveiled in 1986, it marked the first formal acknowledgement from Ford of Cosworth's commitment to 'Power by Ford' in the showroom. The companies linked again for the 1991 Scorpio 24v, but this time the Cosworth badge was caged in the engine bay.

On the racing side, 1986 was also the year Ford publicly climbed back under the Northampton duvet, having their name and electronics prominently displayed on the 1.5 litre turbo, the GBA. The twin turbo V6 begun to show its worth by progressing from 600 to 1000 bhp in two seasons at Benetton, when politics swept Ford back into the normally aspirated support of a new Cosworth Ford V8 racing unit.

The 1989 HB family was the Cosworth answer to that commission, but a 3.5 litre, near 600 bhp, DFR development of the DFV had to be used in 1988, whilst Benetton were waiting for the definitive HB family to arrive.

The HB 75° V8 was developed from scratch and was only linked to the

DFV in the principle of providing a compact and comparatively (by GP standards) fuel-efficient package. It started 1989 public life credited with 600 bhp at 10,800 rpm, but was yielding over 730 horsepower and exceeding 13,000 rpm by 1993. It was used to win by both official factory teams at Benetton and Mclaren, the latter deploying the genius of Ayrton Senna so effectively that he won half of the HB's 10 GP wins in *one* season!

The HB was replaced (for Benetton only) by the Zetec R, another 75° V8 design that was due to start the 1994 season with 14,500 rpm capability as this was written. We were assured the Zetec R was not just a Ford ploy to use their commercial engine name alongside an 'R' for racing suffix, but a brand new race eight of such enlarged bores that overall length was measurably up.

By comparison, the often brutal Ford story is over familiar. Ford was and is one of the pillars to the motor industry with a corporate symbol that is recognized by as many of the world's inhabitants as the Coke logo. The first registration of a Ford Company name was 1901, but it was at his third attempt at launching a car company of his own — on 16 June 1903 with $28,000 — that Henry Ford established the multinational we know today, 91 years later.

The Ford brand name would not have existed had Henry Ford not built and raced two competition cars to publicize the name and raise cash. Competition really is in the blue oval's bloodstream!

Ford (1863–1947) came to Manchester in 1911, just three years after the best-selling Model T was launched. The company proved effective enough to become a permanent part of the British motoring scene, but do not imagine today's traditional UK backdrop of Ford leading the market. It would be 1973 before the Cortina overhauled a BMC (now BMW-Rover) product (the front drive 1100) for leadership of the UK top 10.

Since then, Ford has maintained overall market leadership, but sometimes loses the number one slot in the individual car charts to the Vauxhall Cavalier. As this was written the Mondeo led Escort and Fiesta in a company clean sweep of the top three positions.

By the '70s Ford had developed the Dagenham site in Essex (1931),

Above left The other half: Mike Costin (*left*) with the 4-dr Sierra Cosworth and then managing director Richard Bulman.

Above right The 1994 success of the Benetton Ford Cosworth combination traced back further than the consummate skill of Michael Schumacher. Here is a pre-1990 shot of the HBA series that was conceived to race in 3.5 litre trim from the start and evolved from an initial 630 bhp and 11,000 rpm pace to a 13,000 rpm unit capable of generating over 700 bhp in 1993. By then Cosworth were working on another new V8 family that was publicly known as the Ford Zetec-R, a 14,000 rpm wonder of 750 bhp that won six of the first seven Grands Prix of 1994.

Above Ford's beginning in the UK looked like this. Some 60 workers assembled Model T Fords by hand at Trafford Park, Manchester. Just two years later Ford introduced their American-style moving production line and Model T output doubled from 3,000 to 6,000 units a year. Best year was 1922, when Manchester made 46,363 'Tin Lizzies'. In total 300,000 of 16.5 million Model Ts were manufactured in Manchester.

Above right Driving force: Ford Motorsport at Boreham airfield were always a factor in the production alliance of Ford and Cosworth components for ultimate competition abilities. Here's the 1991 Sierra Cosworth that led most of the Monte Carlo Rally for Delecour.

Halewood on Merseyside (1963) and formed the company that represents these Ford Cosworth products most accurately: Ford of Europe. That umbrella company to co-ordinate the sales and manufacturing efforts across Europe was formed in June 1967 and led to products such as the first Transit, Escort and Capri being engineered for production and sale across Europe. The engineering centres for these common assaults were established in Dunton, Britain, in 1967 and Merkenich on the fringes of Cologne, Germany, also in the '60s.

The vehicles would *not* be identical in each market. In particular, engines and gearboxes differed markedly until the late '80s, Ford in Germany being particularly fond of their V4 and V6 power trains. Ford had its eye firmly on the longest production run for the biggest market (on a par with the USA until the Iron Curtain was demolished and transformed the face of Europe). As ever, economies of scale mattered most to a brand name that can truly be said to be global.

Only Ford of Britain and Ford Germany had manufacturing resources then; today the Maverick is made by Nissan in Barcelona, Spain, the Probe in Flat Rock, Michigan. Some Ford German-controlled production plants are outside German borders: Genk, where the Sierra and Mondeo are made, is in Belgium; Saarlouis is right on the Franco-German border, and makes many Escorts.

The front door at Cosworth in 1992, but it's the sprawl of brainpower behind it that sets standards world-wide.

Also relevant to our tale are some other Ford of Britain sites in Essex. They are Boreham Airfield (home of motor sport since the '60s, and an associated specialist parts division), Special Vehicle Engineering (housed within the main R&D Centre at Dunton, and employing between 30 and 50 people, depending on the project) and 'Aveley'. This enormous sprawl is now largely empty save for the Ford photographic unit in one corner, but from 1970 to 1974 it was home to Ford Advanced Vehicle Operations, who made the Escort RS1600, Mexico and RS2000 in their original formats.

As the world's largest manufacturer of racing engines and components, Cosworth Engineering Ltd today is an international leader in the design, assembly and creation of high performance and competition motor car engines. Its links stretch far beyond Ford co-operation and have included profitable work for General Motors in the USA and Europe (including seven road car engine families), Mercedes (three derivatives of the 2.3/16 theme) and many more, who do not like to admit engines engineering is anything other than 100 per cent their own work . . .

Below Honest heritage: Ford Special Vehicle Engineering staff (SVE) line up with the 16 projects that preceded the Escort Cosworth, in left to right date order. Highlights (*left to right*) included the start point (injection Capri 2.8i), the white Sierra Cosworth RS 3-dr (*centre*) and two generations of the Sierra 4-dr Cosworth.

It was with this original Escort outline (here seen in RAC Rally winning trim during a journalists' test day of 1974) that Ford and Cosworth were first wed with complete engine and commercial car. The Escort RS1600 was not a rarity by comparison with some other Ford RS models (notably its RS1800 successor and the Capri RS3100), but public road examples are unlikely sightings a quarter of a century after manufacture begun.

Cosworth employed 770 people at three British locations in 1990, the year that it was acquired by Vickers for £163.5 million. Profits at that time were £14.2 million on sales of £52.7 million. The vendors were Carlton Communications, primarily because they did not understand what they owned: Cosworth just did not fit with the rest of their investments.

Best known for its role in powering generations of Grand Prix World Championship cars, Cosworth racing eight-cylinder engines had motivated the winners of 166 Grands Prix by the end of 1993. That season the company had also won the IndyCar title again, powering Nigel Mansell's Lola with the XB series of V8s that replaced the original turbocharged DFX series of winning eights

Cosworth is now divided into two primary operations at four Anglo-American sites: two in Northamptonshire, one in Worcester and a wholly owned subsidiary in Torrance, California.

The two primary Cosworth divisions are to deal either with racing, or the increasing demand for Cosworth engineering standards to be translated into production road car standards of excellence. Typifying the latter expertise

Just 109 examples of the RS1800 with the Brian Hart development of the Ford Cosworth BDA road engine were registered in the UK between 1975 and 1978. The enlarged capacity and single carburettor could have served a very much wider audience.

was the Cosworth output of 16-valve cylinder heads at Worcester (acquired in the late '70s, redeveloped for mass manufacture in 1983/4) for the Mercedes 2.3 and later 2.5/16 saloon. The expanded Wellingborough, Northamptonshire, facility built in 1984 employed 158 in 1991, and assembled turbocharged 16-valve power units for the Sierra RS Cosworth derivatives.

Cosworth production engine assembly rate was based on 14,000 units predicted for 1991. Motor component output has exceeded some 30,000 high-grade engine pistons annually. The company also has the capability of making 40,000 cylinder head castings per annum. These were theoretical figures at the time of writing, as the European recession had dropped demand considerably. Key Ford and Cosworth contracts were renegotiated, but I think we'll leave the actual production figures agreed as their business: take it as read the ultimate production capacity of the business was not being used in 1994.

By the early '90s, Cosworth Engineering operated 241,000 sq ft of manufacturing, design, storage and administrative space. New buildings were still being commissioned, notably the move for the design staff into new accommodation on the St James Mill Road, site in 1991. There has also been the addition of 29,000 sq ft at Wellingborough. Space was deployed as follows:

St James Mill Road, Northampton	115,000 sq ft
Wellingborough, Northamptonshire	57,000 sq ft
Worcester	62,000 sq ft
Torrance, Los Angeles, California	7,000 sq ft

Wellingborough assembled up to 7,000 Sierra/Sapphire Cosworth road car engines annually in the good years. A similar number of 2.9 litre, 24-valve engines was anticipated for 1991/2 for the Ford Scorpio at this site. The appendices recall numbers actually made, and I repeat that the recession had altered things by the mid-'90s.

The Worcester aluminium castings facility offers only Grade 1 work to the

The freshest Cosworth front door is the face of Cosworth Castings at Worcester. The patented processes manufactured here have been sufficient not just for the Sierra and Escort Cosworth breed, but also Mercedes . . .

Detailing the DOHC 16-valve
principles that lie at the heart of
every Sierra and Escort
Cosworth. In this 1987 study,
the belt drive for the overhead
camshafts (normally beneath a
plastic cover) is displayed, plus
three belt drives from the
crankshaft nose (one to the
heat-shrouded alternator) and
side plus frontal views of the
combustion chamber with inlet
and exhaust porting cutaways.

aerospace, Grand Prix racing and road car manufacturing markets. Chief
aerospace customer was Rolls-Royce at Leavsden.

Cosworth at Worcester has the capability of making up to 40,000 cylinder
heads per annum, and currently has delivered quality production car castings
from a patented process to Ford of Europe (V6 FB type for the Scorpio and
inline YB four-cylinders to fit the Sierra and Sapphire performance variants);
Daimler-Benz (190E saloon, type 2.5/16); General Motors Opel-Vauxhall (six-
cylinder and four-cylinder engines featuring four valve per cylinder
technology); and Maserati twin turbocharger models. The casting process was
also sold for a manufacturing licence fee to Ford in the USA to make their
modular V8 and V6 engine family of the nineties, the V6 for the 1994 Mondeo.

In 1990/91, Cosworth Engineering delivered 25 to 30 engine kits annually
to specialist engine preparation companies for Formula 3000, the senior
European training ground for Grand Prix. At £42,000 each in 1990, 'we were
limited only by our ability to meet demand,' said Cosworth Marketing
Manager Racing Products, Bernard Ferguson. 'Our performances were so
encouraging in 1990 that the engine — a direct 3 litre descendant of the

Top, injection or exhaust side, the DOHC 16-V turbo Ford Cosworth made an instant impression on road and track life for the European enthusiast.

> **DID YOU KNOW?**
>
> • Cosworth Engineering success has included winning the legendary American Indianapolis 500 motor race in every year from 1976–88 with turbocharged 2.65 litre DFX/DFS series of V8s. In 1993 Nigel Mansell used Cosworth Ford V8 power to capture the IndyCar title.
> • For much of the '80s Cosworth supplied racing engine components to the TWR (Tom Walkinshaw Racing) team. The Oxfordshire *équipe* brought Jaguar European (1984) and World Championship titles (1987/8/91). TWR netted a brace of Le Mans victories (1988/90), and valuable American prestige in winning the 1990 Daytona 24 hours. In 1991 TWR Jaguar contested the FIA World Sports Car Championship, replacing their usual V12 and V6 motors with 15 leased Cosworth HB series V8s and won the Team and Driver World titles.
> • Literally climbing to the heights of Britain was Martyn Griffiths. His single-seater Pilbeam Cosworth DFR eight-cylinder won the 1990 RAC British Hillclimb Championship.
> • Cosworth continued their winning ways in 200 mph American 'Days of Thunder' NASCAR stock car racing formula, and midget car oval racing, supplying engine consultancy input for NASCAR and hardware for the Midgets.
> • They secured the only World Touring Car Championship: 1987, Eggenberger RS500.
> • Victory was achieved in both 24-hour races for saloon cars: the Belgian Spa European Championship round and multiple victories at the Snetterton 24-hours in Britain.
> • Multiple wins in the Australian and Japanese Touring Car Championships were backed up by the 1990 Australian Championship verdict: eight of the top 10 used Cosworth products.
> • 1–2 victory for Cosworth powered Sierras in Division 1 of the tough 1990 European Rallycross Championship. The Sierra RS500 won that division for four years (1989–92).
> • Six out of the top 10 finishers in the 1990 Shell Open Rally Championship of the UK utilized Cosworth engine components. The Sierra Cosworth won the UK rallying title in 1988/9, and the Escort Cosworth took both French and Belgian titles in 1993.
> • Cosworth products have traditionally been employed at the leading edge of World Championship car rallying, but their 1990 employment brought a new twist: the first world title in the category for a woman. They also achieved the first rallying world title secured by any Briton. Scottish domiciled Louise Aitken Walker overcame a flight over a cliff and consequent plunge into a river with her Vauxhall Opel during a hectic season.
> • In 1992 and 1993 Cosworth prepared full catalytic convertor versions of the Sierra and Escort YB series to propel Louise Aitken Walker and Gwyndaf Evans in the British Open Rally Championship. Evans won the showroom Group N title easily in 1993, using the Escort version. These engines were not given a unique code, but they were totally the responsibility of Cosworth.
> • Another derivative of the Cosworth BD-prefixed four-cylinder series propelled the 1990 Formula Pacific Champion. The gallant Ken Smith was a former triple bypass heart operation patient.

original DFV Grand Prix design — is seen as *the* one to have in 1991.'

Cosworth engines won the majority of European Formula 3000 titles in the '80s and additionally secured the 1990 British title. They replaced the DFV descendant with a brand new 3 litre F3000 design for the 1992 season, the AC. It drew heavily on HB expertise in a formula that restricts ultimate development via an rpm limiter. At the beginning of 1994 30 such AC Formula 3000 motors had been made and the European Championship of 1993 secured.

Cosworth Engineering single-seater success is more widespread than the creation and field operation of winning Grand Prix motors. The company has prepared inline four-cylinders, V-banked layouts of six cylinders, and turbocharged versions of their legendary V8 to meet the best of world-class opposition in every imaginable kind of automotive competition.

Above The 'Cossie' motor being dyno-tested in 1986: the main problem was how to drop power down to the required 204 bhp so that the hardware outside the engine bay had an easier warranty life!

Above right Busy, busy. In its heyday the Sierra Cosworth spelt big business for Cosworth at Wellingborough. Here the men finally check some of the 13,000 plus units that were shipped to Ford at Genk for Sierra Cosworth 4x4 assembly.

For example, in the years from 1976–88, Cosworth 2.65 litre V8s powered *every* victor in the legendary American Indianapolis 500 motor race. A new and extremely compact turbocharged V8 (XB series) was readied by Cosworth for this premier league of American racing, which is known as CART (Championship Auto Racing Teams) or IndyCar. The new eight-cylinder unit transferred some of the Grand Prix technology that the company acquired in its winning HB Grand Prix unit. It was tested during 1991, making its racing debut the following season, and propelling Nigel Mansell in his glorious debut Championship-winning season of 1993.

Also in America, Cosworth has contributed to the engine efficiency of 200 mph American NASCAR stock car racers, including that of multiple series winner Dale Earnhardt (Chevrolet Lumina). By contrast, Midget car oval racing continues to take complete BDP-coded Cosworth four-cylinder engines that compete effectively against keen competition.

Determined to underline their engineering independence Cosworth Engineering invested 'approaching £1,000,000' in the creation and construction of a World class V6 engine for public road use (the MBA), which made its show debut in 1991; I was able to drive this promising compact V6 in a hack Audi saloon during July 1992 for *Autocar & Motor*.

Ford, loaded down with their own and Mazda V6 engine designs, have not purchased the refined 8000 rpm wonder, although personnel from Special Vehicle engineering teams in Britain and America have experienced its charms. Some of its features, particularly on the unique induction arrangements have made it to production.

The MBA was originally conceived as a member of an engine family that

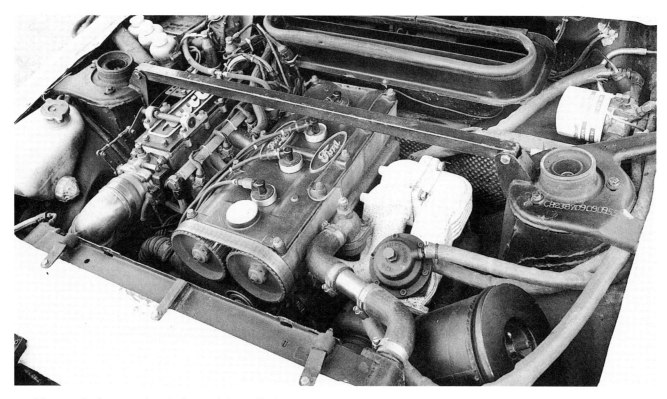

could stretch from a tiny inline triple cylinder to a prestige V12. Just three such engines have been built, one carrying out 'real world' trials in that Audi 80 Quattro saloon; another MBA V6 is seductively employed in a rear drive Escort Cosworth.

Although the engine can squeeze transversely into popular front drive hatchbacks because of its extremely compact dimensions and low weight (120 kg/264 lb), it has been proven for use in rear drive or 4x4 saloons with north–south motor layouts. The lightweight cast alloy unit is a 2.5 litre that

The turbocharged Ford Cosworth combination was previewed by the abandoned Escort RS1700 T with its front mounted BDT motor of RS200 extraction. *(Courtesy Tony North)*

Most unlikely Ford Cosworth racer that I have tried was Supervan II. The transit outline was powered by a 590 bhp version of the oversize Ford DFL V8, which had more noticeable vibration than the smaller DFVs and an extra dollop of torque. Its handling traits through the Craner Curves at Donington remain a vivid personal memory. For those too young to remember, Supervan I was a simpler wild Transit with Ford GT40 motivation that went *everywhere* on two wheels . . .

Unlikely Ford Cosworth origins included the early '80s L 3-dr body and 'Cell Block H' for Henry Ford, otherwise known as the company research and development centre at Dunton in Essex.

offers 'power density' rather than the ultimate horsepower that a company of Cosworth's pedigree could have more easily created. Cosworth senior designer Darren Cairns explained power density as 'getting the best from a total package. The engine is simple enough for a garage mechanic to assemble from a box of bits, yet it exhibits a breadth of ability — from steady 500 rpm tickover to the 8,000 rpm limit — that is simply not available elsewhere. It is absolutely not a racing engine converted for road use, but our unfettered chance to show what we are capable of with no manufacturer constraints at the development stages.'

The MBA was powerful, 220 bhp at 7,000 rpm and 191 lb/ft of torque at 4,500 rpm; enough to fling that converted Audi 80 beyond 140 mph. Electronic timing from reliable sources also showed 0–60 mph covered in 7.6 sec by the heavy test vehicle. Yet outright performance was not the overriding concern for a company that has over 300 wins recorded in Grand Prix and Indycar racing.

Instead Cosworth concentrated on meeting all known emission standards for the mid-'90s, outstanding part throttle fuel consumption (nearly 41 mpg at 50 mph; 31.6 mpg recorded at 70 mph), extended service intervals, a wide range of pulling power (77 per cent of maximum torque is preserved between 1,400 and 7,600 rpm) and a clean appearance.

Cosworth applied for MBA World patents in respect of its EGR (Exhaust Gas Recirculation system) which uniquely reduces both hydrocarbons *and* NOx emissions, plus an integral balancer shaft that keeps things smooth to 8,000 rpm and further patented details of block and cross-bolted bearing construction that provide the massive strength required within such an advanced engine.

The Ford and Cosworth tale continued into the mid-'90s with the winning Andy Rouse Engineering Mondeo. A fitting finale to our Ford-Cosworth tale.

Chapter 2

The Original

The SAS "Who Dares Wins" motto was made for the bold Sierra RS, the first Ford to formally badge the Cosworth alliance.

In the beginning there were Bros, Alison Moyet and the 'Whale tail' Ford Sierra RS Cosworth. From its drooping streamliner snout to the tallest rear wing seen on a production saloon, the first Cosworth-badged Ford was an outrageous motor car, even in an era noted for 'Thatcher's Children' and their company car motoring toys.

The Ford was especially extrovert in the period colour-coded sharp suit of white on white. Unlike the first American Fords, it was also allowed out in magic blue moonstone metallic, besides traditional mean black, and the unavailably gorgeous Ferrari red of one works suspension development prototype.

It was always going to be a fearsome beast! Special Vehicle Engineering prototype RST14, two years before public launch, demonstrates that the correct aerodynamics were quickly established, including the under bumper inlets and additional intake between the headlights. Even the bonnet vents are correct . . .

TIMETABLE FOR THE FIRST FORD COSWORTH

March 1983: Ford Motorsport management Silverstone race attendance; one week later, senior Ford personnel on Cosworth F1 visit; see head casting of T88/16V Pinto, non turbo (coded YAA).

April 1983: Three Ford Motorsport programmes, including turbocharged racing Sierra for Group A, approved.

September 1983: SVE to engineer Sierra Cosworth.

November 1983: MIRA wind tunnel tests, 3-dr (XR4i) body.

December 1983: YBB coded turbo motor runs at Cosworth.

June 1984: First SVE Sierra prototypes running.

November 1984: Wellingborough Cosworth factory officially opened; already making first production YBB motors July 1984; more aerodynamic evaluation, 3-dr (RS) body; need for central bonnet air intake established by later track tests.

March 1985: Static debut, Geneva Show.

December 1985: Spanish press debut, driving 15 P4 (pre-production, sale level) cars, 5 LHD, 10 RHD.

Feb–June 1986: Production build-up: Genk, Belgium.

15 July 1986: 9 am, Sierra RS Cosworth on sale, UK.

1 January 1987: Group A and N homologation: 5,542 built including 500-off stored for 1987 RS500 run. Over 2,600 originals delivered to the UK, nearly 850 to Germany, where most warranty complaints were filed.

The public, press and thieves loved the Ford with the 150 mph tag. The insurance companies — facing an unprecedented spate of stolen Sierra claims almost within minutes of the 15 July 1986 launch — loathed it from the start.

In July of 1986 the performance car world was set on its slick ears by this £15,950 Ford, which made its sales debut alongside another motor sport-inspired project, the £10,028 original Escort RS Turbo. The Cosworth Ford newcomer strutted in the previously exclusive Porsche 911/944 turbo 150 mph zone, slithering from rest to 60 mph in less than the claimed 6.4 sec, and saving more than £10,000 on Porsche prices. Such Porsche-bashing performance was not only (comparatively) easy to buy, but also economical at 21–24 mpg. Looked at from the '90s, it may seem obvious that first there was Sierra Cosworth and then a complete family of descendants to achieve the current Escort RS. But life is never that simple, and Ford had no master plan that swept them through 10 years of the Cosworth Ford road car alliance.

How did it begin? In fact there were a number of coincidental 'great minds think alike' incidents which led to Ford pioneering the most powerful production car (in bhp per litre terms), setting such a standard for racing saloons that the subsequent RS500 found itself strangled or banned out of competitive existence in Britain and Germany.

Fittingly, a former engine builder is a pivotal part of our tale. Retired in 1993 after 20 years as Ford competition manager, Peter Ashcroft knew the value of turbocharged engines in 1983. Ford was already heading down the turbo trail with the Merkur XR4Ti, a turbocharged 2.3 litre that was a winner in the 1985/6 British saloon car races (it took the title in 1985) with more than 350 nose-heavy Andy Rouse Engineering horsepower.

But the XR4Ti had distinct handling and horsepower limits — the SOHC 'Lima' four-cylinder was far heavier than a Rover V8 — and Peter Ashcroft (who was the force behind the '70s Capri's racing reformation) knew there had to be a better answer. There was, and Ford stumbled over it by accident in Northampton. A senior Cosworth executive, speaking anonymously at the start of 1993, told me what led to the original Cosworth a decade ago.

'In 1983, during one of Keith Duckworth's "Thomson Holiday Tours" of our facility, Stuart Turner [then recently returned to the top competitions role in Europe *JW*] and senior Ford executives were up here looking over Formula 1 V8 progress. Legend has it that they tripped over a ready-made 16-valve engine on a Pinto base, which stretches the truth.

'However, those Ford managers did see a part-finished head casting in our prototype shop, one intended for a normally aspirated project on a Pinto base.'

Mr Cosworth (anon) continued: 'Fortunately those Ford executives, who were here on a Formula 1 mission, had the wit to ask what that twin cam head was for.

'We had been playing with the idea of making a 16V, DOHC head for the boys to fit as an aftermarket package to Pinto-engined Fords — rather like Warrior does today. That market might have been 200 units, instead of which we followed a path that has seen over 30,000 engines from this YBB family produced!'

Our Cosworth contact continued. 'Subsequent meetings with Ford Motorsport people like John Griffiths and Peter Ashcroft brought the serious

Some unlikely machinery wore the first pre-production rear wing outlines. Here a 2 litre Sierra GL 5-dr sports the 'Cossie' Whale Tail for late 1983–4 evaluation.

proposal of turbocharging the T88 Pinto block and our 16-valve head into the frame. Ford knew they needed over 300 racing horsepower, and under the Group A rules of the period that meant 200 street horsepower was the final public road target. In the event we had a job to get the engine *down* to that level!' A rich chuckle and our knowledgeable informant retreated into the background.

The output per litre (102.4) was a mass production record of the period, for the legendary 10V/five-cylinder Auto Quattro developed its 200 bhp from a 2.2 litre and the subsequent short wheelbase Sport Quattro of 300 bhp was a limited production (200-off) device. The Escort Cosworth has only been further developed to 227 bhp, 113.9 bhp a litre for 1992 road use. But it was the way that Cosworth conceived that power which proved the Northamptonshire company's genius extended well beyond competition.

The official Sierra Cosworth torque summit was just over 200 lb/ft at 4,500 rpm, but the engine generated such amiable slabs of motivation between 2,000 and 5,000 rpm that even mainstream Ford engineers were astounded by the traffic manners of their cut-price supercar.

Clive Ennos, Director of Product Engineering at Ford (a Jaguar heavyweight by the early '90s) reflected how the original Sierra had changed attitudes, inside and outside the company, when he commented in 1987, 'Anyone who has driven a Sierra Cosworth must get a considerable level of enjoyment from the sheer joy of driving that vehicle. It handles so well, and is so tractable . . . You can take it through the middle of Knightsbridge and it will be tractable. You don't feel like having to go to the osteopath the moment you have arrived!'

I have reported these comments at length because the mainstream of Ford engineers were the most severe critics of the minority interest performance

RST14 suffered an identity crisis: here we see 'OOO OOO' wearing both Sierra XR4i and correct Sierra RS Cosworth identification. Ford management suffered similar schizophrenia over naming the car and approving its wild aerodynamics.

engineering programmes in the '80s, and their words of praise were far more significant to the future of the Ford Cosworth production alliance than the warmest of words from the most generous of media.

Key motor features that enabled such flexible performance began at the Garret Air Research T03 turbocharging on mild boost, soothed by a small intercooler, and controlled by the Weber-Marelli electronic management that was favoured by Cosworth in their Formula 1 V6 turbo era.

The Cosworth Sierra turbo was mounted on the 1983–4 prototypes via a fabricated tubular steel manifold. This was changed for a two-part nickel iron exhaust manifold casting in production. There were severe NVH problems that required the assistance of Southampton University and turbo friction dampers to reduce, the iron manifold replaced for the 220 bhp 4x4 of 1990.

June 1984 witnessed the first Ford Cosworth YBB motors ready to power two prototype Sierras. Key Cosworth personnel on the project included designer Mike Hall, Mario Illien (he departed to found Illmor before the first of 10 pre-production engines was assembled), Paul Fricker (a leading figure on Escort Cosworth), and then liaison engineering executive, John Dickens.

The YBB family never became a smooth source of power, but (with suitably strengthened block engineering) it resisted over 550 bhp consistently and still had an Escort Cosworth production life ahead of it in 1994.

As for the RS1600/1800 legends, Cosworth chose belt drive for the twin overhead cams. The belts were from Uniroyal in a rubber reinforced by glassfibre, also motivating the short internal shaft that drove skew gear for oil pump and distributor. Drive belt pulleys (crankshaft and camshaft) came from the CVH Escort/Fiesta motors, which also used belt drive. Five bearings were provided for the camshafts which operated the valves (35 mm inlet; sodium-cooled 31 mm exhaust) via inverted bucket tappets 'with hydraulic lash adjustment to reduce noise and service maintenance'.

Mahle forged pistons were installed within the classic pent roof Cosworth combustion chambers, which ran an 8:1 cr and a central spark plug location. To reduce piston temperatures, the old diesel motor tweak of spraying oil from the lower end of the bores was employed. The single rail dished out 'splashing all over' when the crankshaft throws reached BDC (Bottom Dead Centre).

Enhanced engine strength came from heat-treated steel forgings for the connecting rods and a similar material for the crankshaft, although Cosworth declined to comment further on the ground-breaking process it had employed for said crankshaft, which has remained at the heart of this extraordinarily tough motor.

Yet the bore and stroke were those of a normal production Sierra or Granada 2.0, a total 1993 cc courtesy of 90.82 mm bore and 76.95 mm stroke. Boost was quoted as 0.55 bar/8 psi, but as with all turbocharged Fords it was worth ensuring this figure was actually being attained. Ford had a habit of setting boost low to defer warranty claims in favour of optimum horsepower: considerations that did not apply to press demonstrators . . .

Only the cylinder block, water pump, two pulleys and the auxiliary shaft were 'off the shelf' Ford parts. The rest were specially manufactured/

Below left Inside the Cosworth YBB-coded 16-valve, DOHC motor we can see the dished pistons and turbocharger layout. Note the belt-driven twin overhead camshaft drive and twin pulley drives from the crankshaft to the alternator and water pump.

Below The inside story as depicted in early press pack and brochure material.

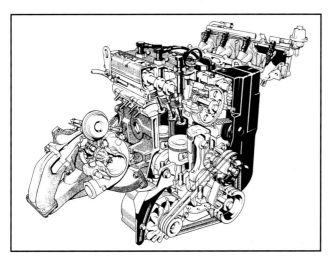

modified for this application. Similarly, Weber-Marelli multi-point fuel injection and engine management were chosen to spark and fuel the potent four-cylinder.

Why Weber-Marelli? 'Mainly because Keith Duckworth was working with them in Formula 1,' revealed Rod Mansfield. Rod continued, 'In fact we had chosen to go with Bosch, but my SVE engineers were excited by the opportunity to try the new Weber Marelli layout. I removed my original objections to Keith Duckworth's request.'

The first Cosworth production unit was rated at 204 bhp on 6,000 rpm and exuded 278 Nm, the equivalent of 203 lb/ft torque at 4,500 rpm, but you will find anything from 201 to 205 bhp quoted in Ford literature and consequent journalism. In fact my colleagues told me 230 to 235 bhp was common amongst press fleet cars. This was rebuffed by Mansfield in the late '80s: '230 horsepower talk is nonsense. The highest we have seen from a production specification RS Cosworth is 218 bhp. Press cars ran 204 to 210 bhp in our experience; good, but not extraordinary.'

In stark contrast to the rude 'On/off' turbos of the period, the Cosworth motor produced 80 per cent of its maximum torque (equivalent to 163 lb/ft) from 2,300 to 6,500 rpm. That meant driving manners that allowed refined descendants such as the 4-dr Cosworth to become credible in the BMW classes.

Statistically, Ford had a maximum of 240 km/h, equivalent to 149.1 mph, observed by the German TUV authority at the Belgian Ford test track, and this was also the figure quoted by *Autocar* at the time. However, most British magazines returned less than 146 mph, with *Performance Car* pretty typical at 142.8 mph for a lap of Millbrook, turning a best flying 1/4 mile of 144 mph.

These figures proved particularly relevant when the RS500 came along, because *Performance Car* had taken the trouble to test them both fully at the same venue, to the maximum, something missing from other contemporary sources, although side by side pictures of RS500 and the original 3-dr were frequently used to imply that was just what had occurred, all the way to 140 mph plus . . .

These pictures are separated by nearly a decade, but both show production format for the 204 bhp motor. It initially sported an under bonnet disarray of plumbing and wiring that was considerably tidied up for both the RS500 and subsequent generations of Ford Cosworth. Every early 'Cosworth' that I have looked at, even of similar models in the rear drive Sapphire generation, has minor differences in layout that betray constant development.

Ford computers predicted 0–60 mph in 6.47 sec. These figures proved very close to the independently tested truth, *Autocar* setting the standard at 6.2 sec average, a standing start result echoed by *Performance Car*. Underlining the excellent spread of pulling available, 50–70 mph in fourth took less than 5 sec in all the independent tests I saw, the spread from 4.6 to 4.9 sec, parking this Sierra firmly in the Porsche parking lot.

The fuel consumption was extraordinarily reasonable for such an obvious performer. I returned over 23 mpg over 2,000 transeuropean miles, *Performance Car* managed 23.4 mpg in their full test and *Autocar* reported 21.4 mpg, including the track session (the only activity that dropped the new

The interior caused a few arguments, too. Here we see a Cologne proposal with *brown leather* steering wheel rim and gear knob allied to blue leather (passenger seat) and cloth (driver) seat trim. This is contrasted with a higher angle shot that shows the 1985-finalized layout in grey checks. Note also the black leather rim wheel that served the Cosworth so well on road and track plus (through the separate steering wheel picture), the small XR4Ti boost gauge that was placed in the top left of the 7,000 rpm/150 mph instrument display. This detail picture also gives us a period piece recall on the rotating Ford sound balancer system for the standard radio and cassette.

fast Ford below 20 mpg). The official consumption figures were issued as 22.8 mpg urban, 38.2 mpg at a constant 56 mph, and 30.1 mpg at 75 mph.

That was all on 98 octane leaded petrols, of course, but the car can be happily converted to run on 95 octane unleaded. This ability was introduced in the 1987-manufacture of YBB motors at Cosworth, the Wellingborough facility stamping out power units even when the Ford was between models. That move matched Cosworth supply to the higher output of Ford Motor Company.

In the early '80s, the fight to get the RS into production was bloody; a struggle that proved far more difficult for Ford management under the genius of Walter Hayes (later the boss at Aston Martin) to resolve than the technical brilliance required of Cosworth and Ford Special Vehicle Engineering (SVE), which wrought such miraculously cheap speed.

Ford SVE operated under the benevolent eye of Rod Mansfield and included Mike Smith (the long suffering project leader on the original car) and Gordon Prout (aerodynamics). Ford Motorsport had a stronger input than any project up to Escort RS and that came from men such as Mike Moreton (now at TWR, Bloxham), the legendary Bill Meade (practical mechanics) who was assisted by Terry Bradley, and Ford-Cosworth engine liaison/homologation expert John Griffiths.

'We had the Sierra Cosworth on the life support machine at least twice, before it was finally born,' quipped Stuart Turner.

Others, such as former SVE manager Rod Mansfield (now retired, after doing the same job with silver tongue charm but in the USA) recalled that the Sierra's outlandish aerodynamic body kit did it no management approval favours. Rod reported, 'We started aero work and went through 92 separate layouts at the Motor Industry Research Association (MIRA) wind tunnel. [Additional research was also carried out at Cologne. *JW*] The result looked pretty horrible in card and alloy mock-ups, but it removed the high forces of lift we were getting at the rear end.

'Naturally the styling aces were horrified when they saw our pop-rivetted abortion, which then included Formula 1-style end plates for the rear wing!'

In fact, I first heard about the Cosworth aerodynamically, and accidentally. In 1984 a Canadian consultant, in a throwaway press party aside to another journalist revealed, 'You'll never believe what Ford are doing down at Dunton. They have this Sierra with the most grotesque rear wing — it's even got end plates — and a Cosworth engine; BMW and Rover haven't a prayer when that thing gets loose . . .'

The final body package was very special and included engine cooling sheet metal alterations (a rare concession from the Ford accountants), as well as the more obvious aerodynamic appendages. These were built on a 3-dr hatchback Sierra L with Phoenix-manufactured body kit. In detail that comprised wheelarch extensions, side sills, and front bumper/spoiler. The latter was a full width vertical extension with a flexible rubber 'beard' that cut front end lift and was not prone to fracturing in the inevitable pavement parking collisions of life away from the race track. The metal changed embraced twin bonnet heat extraction louvres (not strictly necessary for the road), and the air intake between headlights that contemporary Sierras eschewed. Aside from the basic steel monocoque, polyurethanes were employed, along with rubber body additions.

Dimensions outside the aerodynamic package were as for the contemporary Sierra, but it is worth noting that the basic Ford had a generous wheelbase of 2,609 mm that made it a natural for easy ride qualities with an exceptionally forgiving nature in such a powerful rear drive format.

Other statistics were not particularly notable, but the rakish Sierra RSC looked quite slim in standard or Group A competition trim, where regulations limited wheel rim widths to less than 10 in. In the showroom, a length of 4,458 mm versus an overall width of 1,727 mm, rested on a track of 1,450 mm and a rear spread of 1,470 mm. It was not particularly low slung at a height of 1,377 mm, nor light with a kerb weight of 1,240 kg.

A production drag factor of 0.336 Cd was revealed for the 1986 RS

Let's talk pre-production wheels: here we see prototype RST12 out in the open on a clean disc design. One that had also been attempted in the style studios, for our side shot, shows how the 10-slot wheel would have looked alongside the finalized aerodynamics.

Say aah . . . For fans of the first 3-dr model, the original white finish highlighted the outrageous street aerodynamics perfectly.

Cosworth (versus 0.351 for RS500 and 0.32 for the old biplane XR4i), leaving the front with a lift figure, albeit one sharply reduced even over XR4x4.

At 124 mph rear downforce in the Ford Cologne wind tunnel was measured at 164 Newtons, compared with a 513 Newtons lift figure for the production Sierra equipped with a boot lid wing. For comparison, a 200-hour Cologne wind tunnel programme for the Escort Cosworth yielded downforce front and rear in the 90s, 45 NM at the prow and 190 Nm rear, both measured at lower speed than the Sierra: 112 mph.

SVE aerodynamic specialist Gordon Prout asserted, 'That downforce figure was the reason we had such a high wing on the RS Cossie, and it had to be in that position. Any lower and its effect was nullified, any higher and the drag figure went up to an extraordinary degree. We would have loved to extend the wing rearward for even better figures, but the law prevented protrusion beyond the bodywork. Besides, the expense of an extended bumper put that approach out of the question.'

In 1984 the first pair of RS prototypes looked like XR4i biplanes, for it was a subsequent Ford management decision to opt out of the unsuccessful XR4i three door ('six lites' in Fordspeak), which had three side sections of glass. Ford opted for a plain base: the 3-dr Sierra shell of two side windows that was a rarity in Britain, marketed only briefly in RHD.

Both steering and gearbox required work between the December 1985 press debut and June 1986 commencement of production. In fact my Cosworth mole remembered an eve-of-press presentation panic: 'We did not have the latest level power steering pump to engine bracketry to hand and there was a bit of whistle-round to meet the Spanish deadline,' he recalled.

In fact it was a Borg Warner T5 gearbox problem that delayed Ford at Genk putting the car on the line by nearly half a year over the original plan. The Borg Warner five-speed had been proven, sharing its first four ratios with the 2.3 turbo Mustang built by SVE's transatlantic counterpart, SVO (Special Vehicle Operations), but top gear for the Sierra RS was an 0.80

overdrive, rather than the American 0.73 fifth .

However, opportunities for continuous high-speed running in America are rare and that aspect of the five-speeder's durability had not been tested with the same ardour as is common practice in Europe. The American-sourced Borg Warners expired, 'only when we fitted up half a dozen pre-production Sierra RS types for durability trials at Lommel at speed around 130 mph. All the gearboxes gave trouble, and there were failures within 100 km/62 miles, including seizures,' SVE engineers told me.

A change in specification of the gearbox bearings helped equip them for sustained high speeds of a nature not encountered at the lower dual carriageway speeds of America. The BW box remained part of the 1986–90 Sierra/Sapphire RS specification, but it was replaced when Ford had their own MT75 five-speed ready for the 4x4 in 1990.

Improved lubrication overcame the problem in later Cosworth derivatives, although the change was often sticky. Reverse was often virtually unobtainable after a cold start in rear drive Cosworths of all types, requiring patient negotiation with lever and clutch pedal.

The chassis and steering were widely praised, but still SVE made a number of changes between the Spanish launch and the beginning of production in June 1986 at the Belgian-based, German-controlled, Genk plant.

Prior to production steering feedback was 'de-sensitized' in Rod Mansfield's contemporary words. 'We decided to go away from the planned [press launch specification *JW*] use of solid, plastic, inner pivot bushes for the Track Control Arms in our strut front suspension. Secondly we altered three of the primary settings with our Cam Gears-TRW power steering,' reported Rod. The quick action of the rack and pinion steering remained at 2.63 turns

Clean Cosworth. Back on the right wheels and tyres, correctly badged and aerodynamically attired. But this 1985 publicity shot lacks the showroom's glass sunroof, which was cut into all but Motorsport bodies.

lock-to-lock, power steering was standard throughout the run, and the action was valved to produce more assistance as lock at the steering wheel increased.

In production form the inputs relayed to the driver were not so 'nervous', a complaint voiced by the press of the original set-up — which I thought was simply fabulous, albeit a trace lively over the deep cambers of the very rapid country roads deployed in Spain.

From the start, a new cast iron hub was installed at the bottom of the MacPherson struts, which raised the front roll centre by 92 mm to 143 mm (over 3.5 in increase). This had been demanded by Motorsport, but was ditched in the subsequent Sapphire RS because it only really made sense at slick-shod racing ride heights!

The dampers were gas-filled, twin tube units from Fichtel & Sachs, the supplier SVE preferred for all Cosworth Sierras and Escorts. The springs were linear rated all round at 19 KgNm front, 47 KgNm rear, where the action of the trailing arms distorts the rating required.

John Hitchins, an SVE stalwart with exceptional detail suspension development credits to his name along the RS line, quipped of the deliberate avoidance of then fashionable progressive rate springs (which had found Ford favour on the back of the first Escort XR3 and the XR4i), 'I don't like progressive springs. When somebody designs variable rate dampers to match them, I might change my mind.'

The layout was originally specified with negative cambers front and rear: 1° 15″ front and 1° 48″ rear. Castor was pulled back from the initial pre-production specification of 1.5 to 2° to a tighter 0.5 to 1°, the latter move occasioned by justifiable Genk production concerns that the front wheels could foul the extended arches.

Another SVE development was the switch from a 26 to a 28 mm thicker front anti-roll bar. This eased the ferocity of initial understeer, but the trait

Big impression: the first Cosworth Ford was hard to ignore on the street (here with the correct sunroof installed), and almost impossible to beat on a race circuit as well in production-based formula.

reasserted itself to a surprising degree when unmodified cars were taken to a race track.

The trailing arm rear end of the RS Sierra featured uniball joints replacing more conventional rubber bushings. Low pressure, gas-filled monotube dampers from Fichtel and Sachs utilized much of the Sierra XR4x4's layout in association with a 14 mm anti-roll bar. Some features, such as the Viscous Coupling 190 mm differential unit and the 273 mm solid back disc brakes, were also shared with the Granada Scorpio line.

The front discs were generous in dimension: 283 mm units of 24 mm thickness. The Sierra RS rendition of Alfred Teves GmbH ABS had 'pressurized hydraulics and two microprocessors', plus sensors at each wheel and Teves four-piston front callipers. It is important when reading the price comparisons later in this chapter to remember that Ford fitted electronic ABS braking as standard, an item that demanded £1,000 in many rival optional equipment lists.

An electric pump raised hydraulic pressures to provide a pleasing brake pedal action, although it could be erratic at track speeds over bumps, when the ABS 'froze' momentarily in response to multiple high-speed inputs.

Porsche specifications created the original German-developed and German-produced D40 Dunlop tyres of 205/50-VR 15. In later track and fast road use experience, I would recommend Bridgestone, Yokohama or BF Goodrich for an additional measure of grip (only Bridgestone also proved better in the wet to my satisfaction), but Dunlop was a sensible all-round choice that preserved an excellent ride quality in a then ultra-low profile 50-series sizing. This assumes you are not interested in original Concours competition, as does the tweak of slightly oversizing the rears (say 225 section) to gain vital rear end traction under boost, especially in wet conditions.

Those 'Dunnies' were installed on ATS/ Rial-manufactured 7 x 15 in alloy

The front format changed little from those original pre-production cars we showed you at the beginning of the chapter. This example of an original model was photographed in 1994 and was only externally modified with the addition of an RS Owners Club badge . . .

rims that looked like BBS products and were a swine to clean, although the following Sapphire was just as bad with a replacement design.

The Ford Sierra RS Cosworth was something of a performance bargain when it went on sale in the UK on 15 July 1986 at £15,950. The Ford's performance per pound spent was unmatched and a reminder of what the company could achieve at its best, so that the Sierra line all benefited from the warmth of its media reception.

Autocar nominated a £20,000 BMW or (ironically) the 2.3/16 Mercedes 190E of £22,000, but closer to home was the grunt of the TWR-inspired Rover Vitesse V8 (£17,029) and the contemporary SAAB 9000 was just a fiver under £16,000 in front-driven turbo format. None was really in the same performance league (it was actually best matched against a £10,000 more expensive Porsche 944 turbo), but Ford had to put as many showroom goodies into the standard price as possible to avoid outright disbelief that they could compete in this category.

Thus these Sierra Cosworth customers were cosseted with Ford cashmere cloth-trimmed Recaro front seats, an immensely strong and wieldy three-spoke, leather-rim steering wheel, extra instrumentation (the incomprehensible American XR4Ti boost gauge, 170 mph speedometer, 7,000 rpm tachometer), tinted glass, electric front side glass operation, and electrical assistance for the dual mirrors and central locking. Also on the list was the faithful Ford tilt and slide glass sunroof (wind it yourself) and a four-speaker stereo radio/cassette player. ABS was a standard feature that many contemporary cars listed only optionally.

Despite the rather low rent cabin and obvious Ford mass production handicaps against the prestige badges, 'the Cossie' (as it was almost inevitably dubbed) was warmly recommended to readers of the specialist motoring press. One of the most significant comments came from Jesse Crosse, award-

At just under £16,000 has there ever been a greater performance per pound bargain than the original Sierra Cosworth?

winning editor of *Performance Car* magazine, who dismissed Lotus Excel and Porsche 944 alternatives as lacking comparable performance, and closed the Spanish launch piece with, 'a thoroughbred, rear drive, high–performance saloon of a unique type. It will undoubtedly rank as an all time classic.' Enough said?

There were considerable running changes in specification. In 1986 production, SVE tackled brake judder by a specification change to Ferodo F3432 pads for the front discs; tighter torque tolerances on the ex-Scorpio hub bearing races and a 'significant increase in clamp torque figures'. The wheel bearings were always a weak 24-hour racing feature . . .

Head gasket failure was extensively publicized amongst the 847 LHD models recalled in Germany. A 130 mph BW gearbox durability test at Lommel discovered 'the water was getting blown out of the engine at sustained speed'. Initially the answer appeared to be in redesigning engine ancillaries including overflow water bottle and piping, plus work on turbo 'hot spots' and cylinder head water flow rates. Gaskets still failed, so Ford went back to Cosworth. Rod Mansfield told me, 'It wasn't as simple as beefing up the head gasket. We found that some cars used for shopping suffered the problem, which was traced to temperature differences and the lack of expansion/contraction ability between head and block. A new cylinder head bolt design involving tapered or more correctly yield bolts was employed, along with extra meat in the Coopers gasket to accommodate different heat expansion rates, the gasket capable of expanding to fill any gaps. Such changes were introduced in mid-1986, when more than 4,000 Cosworth RS engines had been completed.'

In fact 2,300 Sierra Cosworths manufactured between August and December 1986 were recalled. In 1987 Ford of Britain told the press about the recall in distinctly PR terms. They stated, 'it is a tidy-up operation.

Cosworth characteristics are detailed here with the finger-scraping hostility of the lattice-styled alloy wheels, flexible front spoiler extension (vertical), drooping single tail pipe and black edging to the rear wing.

There have been some problems with the engine management system caused by water getting into the sensor unit on the wing panel. This will be modified to avoid this. There are to be changes to the turbo-damper unit also.'

Whatever its service and vulnerability to theft, the Sierra RS Cosworth was a magnificently bold concept. It was certainly a commercial success in the UK, though not such a hit in Germany where the bulk of the engine-related snags occurred. Cosworth were not held to blame. It was the RS symbol that was deleted for most LHD models, until the advent of the Escort RS Cosworth.

The Cosworth Sierra was executed with remarkable finesse, considering the limited manpower and financial resources applied to such a fundamental re-engineering project. Later we will explore what Ford Motorsport and the specialists made of the car in its natural role: as a racer.

Cosworth 3-dr Sierra, the nineties ownership experience

Seen from the '90s, owning one of the original 3-dr Sierra RS Cosworths is a very different proposition to the nearly new cars I surveyed for a book first published in 1987. This Ford has definite collector status, but the hostile UK environment of constant theft, vandalism and consequently sky-high insurance premium rates held values down to the point where you could almost make an argument for buying the first Cosworth-badged Ford and preserving it like a giant model, glass box and all.

Fortunately our owners are a pluckier bunch than that. The most loyal owner/driver I could find was TV commentator Mark Cole. When I talked to him in 1994, he still had the white RS original that *Motor* magazine long-term tested, actually his personal car for more than 134,000 miles. Bought in October 1986 from Hartford Motors outside Oxford, registered D928 NJO, Mark revealed, 'It's still on the original engine. The gearbox did all but the first month and the only clutch change was 104,000 miles ago' he said with satisfaction.

I asked the *Eurosport* microphone man his opinion of the fast Ford? 'It was obviously built to last, and it's still quick. I had it showing 155 mph at Spa in 1993 and I still enjoy driving it. Besides I don't know what you could possibly buy for the same money that has anything like this performance.'

'Perhaps an Escort Cosworth?' I ventured.

'Don't be silly,' came the laughing rejoinder. 'Those are for cowboys! I mean, that 4x4. Anyone can drive one. These need a bit of steering. You need to be a bit of driver to love it.'

Working with RS Ford dealer Brooklyn at Redditch I found that their tuning and technical service personnel had seen plenty of 3-drs pass the 100,000 mile mark without major trouble, often at 250 to 285 bhp. One of their own cars had managed such a total with a variety of elevated horsepower conversions under assessment.

There are potential snags lying in wait for the high-mileage/second-hand

There are not too many Ford motoring feelings to beat the prospect of a drive in a Cosworth Sierra RS . . . *(Car courtesy of Steve Rockingham)*

Cosworth Ford owner. So I will emphasize, before telling the tale of a pristine 3-dr bought in May 1993, that body and trim condition is monstrously important when owning a decade-old Ford.

In the Sierra's case, Ford (under dealer pressure) have authorized some basic body repairs with recompense for regular customers (watch for cracking around the MacPherson strut top mounts). Ford also recognized that the body was not the strongest or most rattle-free, with a number of basic strengthening/sound deadening moves in the Sapphire 4-dr bodies. In Sierra Cosworth terms, the 4x4 is stronger still, having had some basic stitchwork improved with an eye to Group N rallying, whilst the Escort RSC was readied — in the strongest public production body to date.

This is the story of buying an original 3-dr in the '90s, as told to me by an exceptionally discerning and capable Ford enthusiast. I have seen the car and been a passenger in it. I can confirm it as one of the best non-factory examples I have ever seen. Steve Rockingham has owned a second generation RS2000 since the '80s. He also operated a rear drive Sierra Cosworth 4-dr before turning back the clock to buy D538 NOK in 1993.

Steve reported, 'Having rejected BMW M3s and Lancia Integrales, primarily for their servicing costs and similar insurance premiums to the RS Cosworths, finding a good and original RS Cosworth was very difficult. Many were accident damaged, stolen or generally abused. I wasted a good deal of time being told lies by dodgy sellers who often did not even have the basic paperwork to back up their stories.

'The RS Owners' Club magazine was the key, and I finally found a car down Southampton way with a mature owner. He had obviously pampered the car, with services every six months — in many cases with only a few hundred more miles added to the believable total of 26,000 miles. There were no stone chips, an unused spare and the trim was literally "as new".'

The purchase price was up to £2,000 more than became the norm for good examples during those difficult times, but for £8,000 Rockingham had a car that satisfied his exceptionally demanding criteria.

D538 NOK (probably personally plated by the time this is read) had a few minor problems that Steve attended to 'soon after purchase. At seven years old, it was not surprising that the exhaust was blowing. The water radiator electric fans were not working. I changed the sender, relay, fuses and thermo sensor, before a corroded wire was traced to the front of the radiator and required a 450 mm length to repair'.

The original car wandered around so much that Steve replaced both front control arms to detect 'a slight improvement'. Really a case of 'Don't worry mate, they are all like that.'

Of course, Steve Rockingham was well aware of the chances of theft. He reports 'The usual Cosworth headache of where I can leave it (if anywhere) exists in the '90s, but with immobilization, alarms and other paraphernalia it makes weekend use viable. Apart from not being able to go shopping in it and leave it in a multistorey car park for fear of theft, it is not such a nightmare. After all, what other car has this performance at this price and such cheap servicing?"

Overall, Mr Rockingham is well pleased with his weekend road warrior. 'It only dips to 23 mpg when driven hard, the looks are stunning and the performance never fails to amaze. Super responsive steering and outstanding brakes are all part of a driving experience that never fails to entertain, though it might be tiring to use one every working day.

'The Sapphire makes more sense for daily transport with its four doors, more comfortable ride and less conspicuous looks. Yet overall the hatchback *must* be the true enthusiast's Cosworth,' concluded our private buyer in 1994.

The end of our original 3-dr story, but the beginning of the Cosworth Ford production alliance for the showroom . . .

Race and rally charger

The Cosworth Ford Sierra combination steamrollered all but BMW on the race tracks, but found the lack of 4x4 a constant handicap in world class rallying.

The first Cosworth was the most honourable of the Sierra-based rally cars, winning and placing in the top three well after rear drive was obsolete in the premier league. Despite a glorious production racing record, the 3-dr was of limited international Group A racing worth. Despite its turbo horsepower it struggled to beat BMW and was succeeded in its first season by the RS500, a pre-planned homologation device that proved critical in defeating their old adversaries at Munich.

Considering that the Sierra RS Cosworth was conceived as a racing machine to eliminate the monotony of Rover wins in the UK and to snatch European Championship glories, it proved to be extraordinarily versatile.

A rear drive turbo was out of its depth in the slippier World Rally Championship roles that patchy Ford motor sport management pressed it to.

Typical Cosworth loose surface power oversteer handling, captured by the author at the debut of the Securicor Cosworth Challenge: the Citroen-backed Bournemouth Winter Rally. These Sierras were wonderful entertainment and deadly quick, once underway. However, loose surface traction was never going to be an asset of this charismatic turbo car.

FORD SIERRA RS COSWORTH WORLD RALLY CHAMPIONSHIP BEST FACTORY/FORD-BACKED PLACINGS 1987 (REAR DRIVE, 3-DR)

Event	Pos	Drivers
Sanremo, Italy	4th	Auriol (Fr)
1000 Lakes, Finland	2nd	Vatanen (F)
	3rd	Blomqvist (Sw)
RAC Rally, UK	2nd	Blomqvist
	3rd	J. McRae (Sco)
	8th	Auriol

World Championship

Drivers	7th	Blomqvist
Makes	5th	Ford Motor Co

British Open Championship

	1st	J. McRae (RED)

Best race results (pre-RS500 of August 1987)

12 April 1987

Silverstone, BTCC	1st	Rouse (Rouse-ARE)

10 May 1987

Dijon, France WTC-3	3rd	Niedzwiedz/Soper (Eggenberger)
	4th	Ludwig/Dieudonne (Eggenberger)
	5th	Rouse/Tassin (ARE)

May 1987

Thruxton BTCC	1st	Rouse (ARE preparation)
Estoril 500 (Euro round 2)	2nd	Soper/Niedzwiedz
	3rd	Ludwig/Dieudonne (Eggenberger)
Jarama, Spain (Euro round 3)	4th	Ludwig/Dieudonne
	5th	Soper/Niedzwiedz (Eggenberger)

June 1987

Nurburgring 24-hours (non Championship)	1st	Niedzwiedz/Ludwig/Soper (Eggenberger)

12 July 1987

Nurburgring, 313 miles (WTC round 4)	1st	Ludwig/Niedzwiedz (Eggenberger)
Zolder 500 (Euro round)	1st	Soper/Niedzwiedz/Dieudonne
	2nd	Ludwig/Boutsen (Eggenberger)

Yet the original 'Whale Tail' came home with a solitary World Rally Championship victory that its 4x4 Sapphire successor failed to equal.

As a racer it continued to please the crowds even after its homologation expired (the close of 1992 season), Britain's BARC allowing it to race on against Porsche and Saab opposition and saving many clubmen money in the process.

The Sierra RS Cosworth rallied regularly before homologation into Group A was granted (January 1987). Ford and Securicor allied to run the Securicor Sierra Challenge, a series which ran within British National Championship events of 1986. Overall Champion was Welsh borderer Phil Collins, driving for Brooklyn at Redditch in one of seven C-plate pre-production Sierra Cosworths on loan from Ford Motorsport.

Later best known for fielding winning UK Championship Toyota 4x4 Celicas for double champion David Llewellin, 'Fiery Phil' also recorded an outstanding third overall against the highly developed Group B and special cars that faced him on the Isle of Man for the May 1986 Marlboro/*Autosport* Championship event. Altogether Phil Collins/Roger Freeman won the Securicor category within three of five qualifying rounds. Cheshire solicitor Freeman also guided Phil to third overall on the Marlboro Lindisfarne Rally. Quite a debut year for an unhomologated competitor.

Those 1986 Securicor Sierras ran according to an agreement on maximum power from Cosworth of 300 bhp. They were still a rapid, and an accurate preview of what was to come in competition Cosworth Ford Sierras. *Autocar*'s figures in the winter of 1986/7 demonstrated that a front-running Securicor Sierra (C236 HVW, from the original Spanish press preview batch, as were all the leading contenders) was comparatively slow off the mark (0–30 mph in 2.2 sec). But when the wheelspin had abated, it took only 0.6 sec more to reach 40 mph, followed by 0–50 mph in 3.6 sec and the benchmark 0–60 mph in 5.1 sec.

C236 HVW romped on to conquer 0–90 mph in 9.9 sec and 0–100 mph in 12.6 sec, exactly four *seconds* faster than the time in which myself and John Griffiths managed to fifth-wheel one of the legendary Escort RS1800s for *Motor Sport* in 1976. Ten years later the Securicor Sierra demolished the standing quarter mile in 13.6 sec and 110 mph zoomed on to the read-out just 1.5 sec later. To pull such acceleration the final drive had been radically lowered: 125 mph demanded 6,900 rpm!

Ford had a tricky World Rally Championship preparation problem in the winter of 1986/87 winter, because in 1986 their promising RS200 Supercar had been outlawed, along with the rest of the Group B Supercars. Ford would deploy the rear drive turbo Sierra RS Cosworth against 4x4 machinery such as Lancia's Delta and Audi's big 200 Quattro.

When I visited Ford at Boreham that winter to see how the factory were progressing with the 1987 World Championship Sierras, it was obvious that Peter Ashcroft and John Wheeler (the overall and engineering bosses respectively) saw the Securicor cars as a convenient horsepower maximum along the lines agreed for 1987 World Championship rallying. Little else would be common to the 1986 non-homologated and 1987 homologated Sierras, but there were signs of schizophrenia setting in. The 1987 'game plan' called for the use of the cumbersome and slow V6-engined XR 4x4 wherever slippery conditions demanded all-wheel drive. This was to lead to big problems for the team, not only in preparation, but also in spares and legality.

Skimming through the Sierra homologation forms it was evident that Johns Wheeler and Griffiths had found the time amongst their overwhelming 1986 RS200 commitments to homologate a decent pile of suspension, braking and general chassis equipment for both XR4x4 and Sierra RS Cosworth. For racing and rallying an enormous variety of braking equipment was homologated, particularly in diameters from 315 mm to 285 mm, mostly cross drilled as well as radially ventilated.

As for the suspension and vital hub components, some of the competition wear was descended from RS200 experience. Meanwhile the front disc brake/MacPherson assemblies used in Group A, along with the larger rear discs and hubs, dated back to Ford Germany Motorsport development for the Merkur XR4Ti.

The biplane turbo 2.3 Ford was campaigned by Andy Rouse in the 1985–6 British Championship, winning the UK title with something over 350 bhp, but it was unsuited for further development as the engine was heavy and unsophisticated compared to the Cosworth concoction.

British-run works rally RS Cosworths and XR4x4s got off to a rocky start in the 1987 Monte Carlo Rally. Snow turned Kalle Grundel/Terry Harryman's efforts in D370 TAR to a slithering mockery. Stig Blomqvist's heroic run in an XR4x4 with some very competitive icy stage times netted nothing. The Ford was retrospectively disqualified for using a non-homologated electronic fuel injection and management system, and a hefty fine was also imposed on the UK Motorsport facility. The XR4x4 was run again, notably in Sweden (a sixth that year, an amazing second for Blomqvist in 1988), but had no outright winning potential for the complete world series.

In 1987 Portugal Ford Motorsport did not send a works team for safety

July 1987, BTCC
Silverstone 1st Percy (ARE)
  (GP support)

WTC challenge continued by RS500, August 1987. Makes title won. See RS500 in competition, chapter 5.

1988: Rallying only (rear drive, 3-dr)*

Portugal Rally	5th	Blomqvist
Tour de Corse, Corsica	1st	Auriol
	5th	Sainz
1000 Lakes, Finland	3rd	Auriol
	5th	Blomqvist
Sanremo, Italy	5th	Sainz
	7th	Blomqvist
RAC Rally, UK	6th	Blomqvist
	7th	Sainz

World Rally Championship
Makes   2nd overall   Ford Motor Co

British Open Championship
            1st J. McRae
            (R-E-D prep)+

* Ford factory entry from Boreham scored a second place on Swedish World Championship round via an XR4x4 for Blomqvist.
+Last British Open Rally Championship title won by Ford until 1994 Escort.

1989 (rear drive, 3-dr only)

Tour de Corse, Corsica	7th	Cunico (I)
New Zealand Rally	5th	C. McRae

British Open Championship
            2nd Brookes (Mike Little)
            3rd Lovell (Mike Little)

Start to a startling career: six Brooklyn Ford boys refurbish one of the original press fleet Sierra Cosworths (C240 HVW) for the 1986 Securicor Rally Challenge. All over the world in the late '80s workshops resounded to the noise of Cosworth Fords being encouraged to provide performance that surprised even its creators.

Below right How it worked out: Phil Collins with the completed C240 HVW in April 1986. Phil went on to win the 1986 title and provide brave and valuable feedback on how the Ford Cosworth saloon car racer would perform over rally trails. Performance figures for the car can be found in our Appendices; those with sharp eyes and inside knowledge get Brownie points for spotting present-day Toyota Team Europe co-ordinator Phil Short's elevated outline slipping away in the background . . .

Bottom Strong underbelly: chassis engineering was the key to competitive speed and here we see some of the key moves that helped drivers aim more than 300 bhp, restraining the modified Group A rally cars with replacement parts. Note the simple front end compression struts to locate the track control arms and strengthened rear trailing arms with leading front anti-roll bar and trailing rear.

reasons. Mike Little prepared a decent 295 horsepower RS for Carlos Sainz. Weighing little under 1,200 kg the Michelin-shod machine in Marlboro colours showed the pace-setting Lancias, Mazdas and Renault 11 Turbo the way around the Estoril opening stage to the tune of 6 min 17 sec versus 6 min 25 sec for the nearest rival. Sainz showed his potential and that of the car with six top six times, two fastest overall, before a turbo failure eliminated the Spaniard.

The factory and factory-backed Cosworth Sierra World Championship

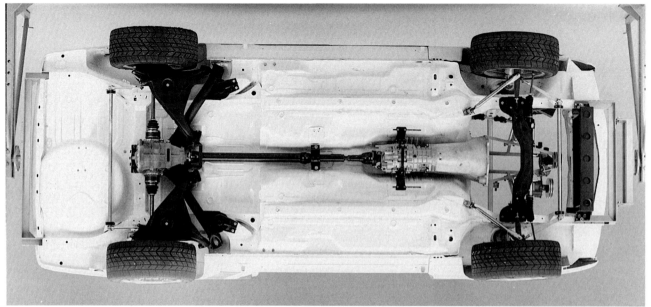

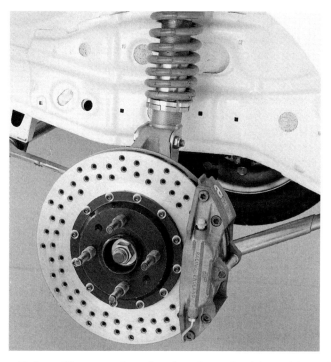 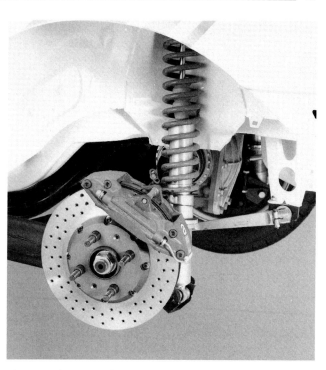

rallying efforts continued to be plagued with problems in the opening months of 1987, to the point where the complete programme was re-examined in May. Unhappy memories by then included Easter, on Safari. The Ford team were based out of touch with the start, a contributory factor to the extensive road accident damage upon Blomqvist's car versus a cow *before* the start.

On the event itself both Blomqvist and a second car for Robin Hillyar set top six times (one fastest apiece), but both were eliminated by electrical defects.

Ford's factory Corsican outing was over just two stages into the event! In Corsica the Mike Little-prepared and entered RS Cossie for Carlos Sainz/Antonio Soto and the RED-run RS for Didier Auriol/Bernard Occelli scooped up World Championship points and revived Ford respect with seventh and eighth, pointing to a tarmac World Rally Championship potential that would be fully realized in 1988. Auriol ran as high as second overall in what was a fine Ford of France/33 Export beer-funded project, to seize the French title.

In France the early season combination of smoother gravel or outright tarmac stages in national championship events also suited Sierra. Lyons Charbonnieres has always been a good event to Ford (right back to the Capri's formative sporting years) and 7/8 March 1987 produced a marvellous RS result for Sierra. First, Rigollet/Bathelot (Group A Sierra RS Cosworth); second, Monsieur Beaux's Renault. Third overall was the 'showroom formula' Group N Sierra RS of Rouget/Bounours. By the end of the year the Sierra had won not only the French title, but also those of Belgium and Spain as well.

If the works team was to get the best out of the potent Sierra at World Championship level a new plan was required. The Boreham factory rally

Front and rear end detail from the 1988 homologated Group A parts list with AP brake callipers to the fore, 'coil over' rear spring/strut units, filleted and strengthened steel trailing arms and blade-type anti-roll bar linkages.

effort was now aimed at the RS Cosworth rather than the XR4x4/RS duo; a scheduled outing on America's Olympus Championship qualifier was scrubbed.

This 1987 refocus on car type and preparation paid off with much better results in the second half of the season. Auriol's fourth overall in Sanremo went largely overlooked, but should have told any of us what speed lurked in the French newcomer to the World Championship scene. Traditional Ford strengths such as the 1,000 Lakes in Finland and the home showing on the RAC Rally put the blue oval and Cosworth back on the world class rallying podiums with the Sierra RS Cosworth. Swede Kalle Grundel was dumped for the 1,000 Lakes in favour of former Ford legend Ari Vatanen. Ari justified the decision, just beating Blomqvist around the 'Finnish GP', but the drive did not predict a long term reunion between Ford Motorsport and the driver they nurtured, but the alliance was reformed for the 1994 Escort.

Whilst Easter 1987 was a works disaster in Africa, it brought a fine first outright victory for the home team RS Cosworth on Britain's home international series. Jimmy McRae's eviction from years of trusty GM service and a brief flirtation with Lancia's Delta HF abruptly went in favour of a Ford-backed rally ride with RED.

Jimmy grasped his fifth win on the Circuit of Ireland after a magnificent event-long scrap with David Llewellin's non turbo Quattro coupe. This RS was a works registered Cosworth (D541 UVW) run by RED at Widnes in the North West of England and was far from fully sorted; the pairing also used D418 SVW during the season. They finished the Welsh home international fifth, running a *Motoring News*-reported 290 bhp in 1,250 kg with the same indomitable crew.

In fact 'Jimmy Mac' and Ian 'Grinding Rod' Grindrod then beat the works-run Mark Lovell to second on the Scottish. Lovell had his revenge on the tarmac of Ulster (McRae was third). The year ended with another superb Sierra battle, one that was resolved in McRae's favour by just 43 sec after 250 miles in 41 stages, before team orders were reportedly issued.

Jimmy went on to win the 1987 British title, finishing third on the RAC Rally after Per Eklund's privateer Audi had been disqualified, promoting both Blomqvist and McRae in works-backed Fords.

The affable McRae senior also won the 1988 title for Ford, but son Colin took his '90s UK titles outside the company. They were scooped for Prodrive Subaru after the youngster had learned much of his atomic stage craft *chez* Ford. It's worth adding that it was also Ford who first recruited both Carlos Sainz and Didier Auriol at World Championship level, but Lancia and Toyota benefited from that talent-spotting ability.

Ford Motorsport simply did not have a competitive programme to offer their newfound stars as they struggled towards the obvious combination of Cosworth power and 4x4 traction. If it had been football, the Ford sports managers in the UK (and their liaison points within the mainstream company) would have been ejected ruthlessly, for cash, commitment and equipment lagged far behind the opposition in the '80s.

The 1988 season would yield that one and only World Championship event win (see the second part of this chapter for a detailed drive and specification story), but Ford and Cosworth showed much more consistently than

The British Open Rally Champion 1987.

The Ford Sierra RS Cosworth

Ford's pan-European (except Germany) advertising agency, Ogilvy & Mather in London, produced this starkly simple celebration of the 1987 British Championship victory for Jimmy McRae/Ian Grindrod.

previously. The result was that the company finished second in the World Championship, a long way behind Lancia, but ahead of respected names such as Audi.

Aside from Auriol's airborne victory in Corsica with D372 TAR (accompanied by Baroni's Group N win, ninth *overall*), this points tally was accrued by Blomqvist's second on the Swedish. That came courtesy of XR4x4, a project Stig largely co-opted with works help to avoid the 1987 confusions.

Then there was Auriol's breathtaking 1,000 Lakes outing of 1988, when he beat Blomqvist and many other Scandinavians to finish third overall in this apparently obsolete rear drive Ford! Blomqvist totalled enough 1988

In 1988 Jimmy McRae again won the UK rally title outright in the R-E-D Sierra Cosworth, but this time his co-driver was subsequent Mitsubishi Ralliart co-ordinator, Rob Arthur.

Championship points to be fourth in the series, while Auriol was equal fifth.

The 1989 season naturally saw a sharply diminished World Championship presence from Ford, or their mercenaries, as the 3-dr RS Cosworth had passed out of production two years previously, the rear drive Sapphire 4-dr body was equally unsuitable for a full season against the 4x4 mob, and the 4x4 Sapphire 4-door would not be produced until 1990.

Colin McRae underscored his potential with a fine drive to fifth in New Zealand (the scene of his first World Championship win in 1993, the first for a Briton since Roger Clark on the 1976 RAC!). Franco Cunico got in amongst the points in 1989 Corsica with seventh overall in the rebodied D372 TAR, which had been totalled in Sanremo in 1988. As for McRae, Cunico returned to win his first World Championship qualifier in the 1993, but he was Ford mounted: Escort Cosworth, 1993.

Of course the 3-dr Sierra Cosworth went on winning for years at lower levels of club motor sport (especially on tarmac), but 1989 was effectively the end of its international rally career. One that was never intended at the planning stage, but at which it had done exceptionally well with only two wheels driven . . .

Racing record

In racing Ford finance and Texaco's rumoured £750,000 cash was directed via Lothar Pinske, Ford Germany Motorsport, to the Swiss based German-speaking team of Eggenberger. These masters of the immaculate touring car had presented winning BMWs and Volvos in previous Group A racing seasons, taking the European title for Volvo in 1985. The black Texaco Fords were often nicknamed the 'Texaco Stars' for 1987 and were the smartest of competitors.

Ruedi Eggenberger picked drivers from Britain, Steve Soper, Germans Klaus Ludwig and Niedzwiedz, plus Belgian journalist/driver Pierre Dieudonne. Their planned debut was the opening World Touring Car Championship qualifier, Monza March 1987. Unfortunately they did not even start this troubled debut, an event in which the leading six BMW M3s were disqualified!

The FIA and Eggenberger-Ford could not agree on the technical regulations, for the works Sierras were presented with Bosch Motronic engine management rather than production Weber-Marelli. Andy Rouse did get a start in his Zytek-managed Sierra, on the basis that this was a rework of the production item rather than a complete brand and type substitution. Andy grabbed pole position in the red RS he was scheduled to share with Thierry Tassin, who had brought the only money they had for this underfunded 1987 season, but it went out with a head gasket failure before a dozen laps had elapsed . . .

The Eggenberger machines were certainly thoroughly prepared for their Ford PR-predicted 320 km/h (198.7 mph!) absolute maximum performance. The Pinto wore a 91.2 mm bore in place of the production 90.8 mm but the stroke remained a production 76.95 mm; my Casio makes that 2009.7 cc.

It seems pretty certain compression was reduced from 8.:1 to 7.5:1, but

Steve Soper (*left*) and Klaus Niedzwiedz line up with the first generation Sierra Cosworth Group A racing machine from Eggenberger. This format was not enough to conquer BMW's agile normally aspirated M3, but the subsequent RS500 put the Fords beyond reach in the later '80s.

boost went up enormously over the production 9.25 psi. Eggenberger drivers were allowed to dial a maximum 1.5 bar (21.3 psi) minimum 1.3 bar (18.5 psi). This was said to provide alternative horsepower readings from 385 to 350 bhp; average peak power was fairly quoted at 365 bhp on 6.400 rpm. Peak torque had moved from the production 204 lb/ft at 4,500 rpm to 323 lb/ft on 4,800 revs.

Racing weight for the Eggenbergers was quoted at only 1,035 kg and a five-speed Getrag (again previously used on XR4Ti) was employed. Racers referred to this as the 'light' Getrag gearbox, and a heavier duty number was selected for the subsequent RS500.

Away from works glamour, the rate at which privateers purchased the Sierra RS Cosworth for production racing at national level ensured that the

The Cosworth Ford was an instant hit with the production racers, well able to cope with the Mercedes Benz 2.3 or 2.5/16 in showroom formula. (*Courtesy John Gaisford*)

As far as the production racing eye could see, it was Cosworths all the way. Mark Hales and Kieth Odor head the Castle Combe bunch in 1989.
(Courtesy John Gaisford)

results started looking good within months. In March 1987 British disc jockey/TV personality Mike Smith won the opening two rounds of the Monroe British Championship with a 260 hp Group N RS, and the model was obviously set to dominate sprint race results of 1987 UK production (Group N) races in the Monroe and Uniroyal series.

In fact the Sierra RS Cosworth showed surprising debut season reliability, winning both the Group N Willhire 24-hours and the Group A (non-Championship) Nurburgring 24-hours over the same late June weekend.

Eggenberger looked good for international race wins, just as soon as they had put Monza behind them at international level. The Texaco stars were only robbed of victory by over-zealous officials in the second round of the European series (Estoril in Portugal) finishing second and third.

In the second round of the world series (Jarama, Spain) both Eggenberger Sierras also finished, this time fourth (Klaus Ludwig/Pierre Dieudonne) and fifth (Steve Soper/Klaus Niedzwiedz) behind the BMW M3 armada.

At the 10 May third round of the World Touring Car title hunt, rain interrupted Dijon play and the works Sierras had to be content with third and fourth, Eggenberger's Sierras still durable enough to make the finish of a near three-hour event. At the finish Sierras occupied 3–4–5 positions. Andy Rouse/Thierry Tassin had followed the works-backed Eggenberger RS Cosworths home upon Dunlop rubber, rather than the factory Pirelli choice.

To pummel home the fact that they had arrived on World Championship-winning form without the eagerly awaited (by Ford) arrival of the RS500, the works team chose the fourth WTC round at the new Nurburgring as the scene of their first world class success. On the July weekend that Nigel Mansell was winning the British Grand Prix for Williams, the Eggenberger Fords started getting their winning act together, pole position snatched by the man the Germans nicknamed the Mansell of saloon car racing: Steve Soper.

Driven by the pairings Steve Soper/Klaus Niedzwiedz and Klaus Ludwig/Pierre Dieudonne, they qualified first and second fastest, 0.05 sec apart, and Ludwig set fastest race lap (1 min 48.59 sec, 94.11 mph) into the bargain.

So Eggenberger Sierras and their drivers led the world series, before the 1

August homologation of the RS500. However, the original Eggenberger Sierra Cosworths still had the rigours of the Spa 24-hours to face in the opening days of August, even though the RS500 was just homologated by then. The homologation date with destiny was not kept to rigidly, Eggenberger preferring to run the familiar 3-dr rather than RS500 for the 24-hours.

As anticipated, the cars qualified well (first and second again) and led away. *Not* anticipated was the way that Eggenberger dominated much of the event, running first and second until the Soper/Dieudonne/Phillipe Streiff had pitted after three and a half hours. The car made a magnificent recovery to twelfth, but then suffered further delays (including the need for a clutch change) before motor fatigue set in after 18 of the 24 hours.

Pole-setter Klaus Ludwig and company had a two-lap lead by dawn and was never headed — save during routine pit stops — until the motor also let go with nearly 20 hours completed. Cruel.

16 August and Brno in Czechoslovakia meant a trio of Texaco stars (two to race, one spare) were rebuilt from original Cosworth 3-drs to biplane RS500 format. They had a minimum horsepower gain around 100 bhp and aerodynamics to match. Once that had happened, the qualifying gap to BMW opened up to seconds and the Cosworth Ford Sierra became a racing certainty, barring acts of God.

It was an almost exact role reversal of what BMW and the legendary 'Batmobiles' had done to Ford with wings and things in 1973. Ah, the symmetry of it all . . .

April 1987 and Andy Rouse scores the first of three British wins for the Group A racing Cosworth Sierra at Silverstone, fittingly Cosworth's 'local' track. The Rover V8s that inspired a new breed of racing Ford were not far behind at this stage . . . *(Courtesy John Gaisford)*

Comeback Cosworth!

Here is 'one I made earlier'. This period piece is the original of the story submitted to *Motor* magazine in 1988 to celebrate what turned out to be the only World Championship victory for the Sierra RS Cosworth. The magazine also accompanied chief engineer John Wheeler whilst acceleration figures were secured with their usual timing equipment bolted on to D372 TAR. The specification and performance panel for this car will be found in Appendix 2, alongside those for other works Sierra RS Cosworths.

* * *

Ford's recent World Championship victory in Corsica marked the factory team's first win since the 1979 RAC Rally. We sent Jeremy Walton to drive the works RS Cosworth that bounced the Boreham boys back into the big time.

Corsica, early May: the mountainous Mediterranean island hosts the fifth round of the 1988 World Rally Championship. Its tarmac trails will reverberate to the sound of the latest weapons in rallying warfare from Toyota (GT-Four), Lancia (the apparently invincible Integrale having won *all* the previous 1988 qualifiers), and BMW's British-run Corsican winner in 1987, the M3.

After some disastrous outings in the first half of 1987, including Corsica, the Boreham-built and entered Sierra RS Cosworths lurk with winged menace in the 'long shot' category. They will be hurled over 387 miles in 30 special stages by 1986/87 French Champion, Didier Auriol, and 1986/87 Spanish Champion Carlos Sainz. Both their 1987 titles were won in Ford Sierra RS types.

The striped multi-national Fords turbocharged to first and fifth. A more production-orientated Group N Ford RS was ninth overall, winning its class.

The winning Ford was always on the pace, but needed only five fastest times versus 22 from Lancia's Yves Loubert, to win. Loubert suffered a gear linkage derangement on a critically long stage. Auriol picked up an instant eight-minute advantage, celebrating with an accident at the end of that vital stage! The extensive rear end damage was repaired in just 14 minutes.

Boreham Airfield, Essex, late May: instead of Southern sun to glint from its dark green and bright white panels, Auriol's factory Ford glistens wetly under gloomy Essex skies.

Ford Motorsport engineer John Wheeler is to guide and demonstrate the prowess of the machine that broke Lancia's 1988 victory monopoly. The 39-year-old former Porsche employee (he joined Ford Motorsport in 1980) generously ensures plenty of full boost time twirling the scuffed suede rim of the ironic 'Stig Blomqvist' autographed Luisi steering wheel.

It is an exhilarating morning amongst the devilish cones and ramps of Boreham's infield complex. One that was used to develop the long travel suspension speed of the RS200 Supercar and that is still rapidly subjugated by 620 bhp of Martin Schanche's rallycross Evolution RS200.

Compared with the factory Lancias and Toyotas that *Motor* has also assessed in the past six months, the Sierra has awesome presence. There is no mistaking this monoplane with the plump undercarriage for a suburban hatchback carrying fancy decals. A lightweight side exhaust adds to the potent aura of this tarmac racer.

Whilst the complex depths of the cabin await our presence, filled by the beat of an impressively even 1,100 rpm tickover, John Wheeler outlined his development philosophy.

Mindful that the rough road Sierra RS competitors were escalating beyond 1,200 kg (2,640 lb, almost exactly the standard vehicle weight), Ford Motorsport put the bulbous Cosworth on a strict diet. One that resulted in them barely exceeding the 1,100 kg class minimum on the Corsican weighbridge.

Specifically John mentioned, 'the body shell and its integral, Tig-welded T45 steel roll cage, which eliminates all the bolts and brackets normally needed to secure the cage. I reckon that has saved us 12 kg.' Unsaid, but relevant is that such a big hatchback also benefits from any extra body strength that this integral backbone (extending to front and rear top shock absorber areas where input loads are highest) provides.

Also on the Motorsport weight reduction recipe were: titanium suspension springs (abandoned after testing, they were simply manufactured to the wrong rate), 50 litre 'sprint' fuel tank; hollow anti-roll bars, saving grammes rather than lbs.

Redesigned or modified in the cause of losing 'an average 80 to 100 kg', were the one-piece magnesium wheels in association with the smallest spare needed to limp to the next service. Even the simplest nuts and bolts were examined for the weight contribution they could make, many manufactured in titanium rather than alloy. The jack and wheelbrace were also substituted by lightweight items.

There were many more items on the diet, varying from seat rails and supports, engine and gearbox mountings; front and rear hub flanges to thinwall discs, but it was the latter that caused most drama.

The night before the event, a final mountain pass check upon the rally car revealed that the discs would only operate at even temperatures with the practical step of 'heat stress relieving each disc on Mark Lovell's service support Sierra, passing the treated discs along to the service vans for installation at the next halt. When I first noted the vibration problem, after eight stops, the discs were glowing and measuring up 600° C in local hot spots and 450° C elsewhere!' reported John Wheeler.

The tarmac specification Sierra Cosworth was a mighty blend of rally and race car that stomped from 0–60 mph in less than 5 sec. *(Courtesy Mike Valente)*

Hearing the 2 litre turbo grumbling at the length of our chat, reminded us to ask which of the power figures so widely discussed for the Sierra were true? International rallying was threatened with a 300 bhp limit and Ford have never officially quoted more than that figure. John Wheeler said, 'We worked on obtaining the best torque and mid-range manners rather than racing's need for maximum high rpm horsepower.

'When we started using the engine it went to 7500+, but now it is rarely above 7,000 and you can see that maximum power is quoted at 6,000 rpm. I can tell you there is more than 300 lb/ft torque between 3,500 to 5,500 revs, so it is a very civilized engine by competition standards.

'So far as horsepower quotes go, I've heard the media and our rivals talking about 360 bhp for our car. I can tell you that is nonsense. We can get 315 bhp, but that is the limit of the standard turbo compressor and intercooler that we must use. The limiting factor is inlet air temperature, a thermal bhp bottleneck. So our genuine horsepower hovers around 300, with no more than 308 installed.'

The Terry Hoyle-built engine (former Boreham engineer Graham Dale Jones is now a partner at the Maldon concern) of this winner was not running the 1.5 to 1.2 bar we had previously been told to expect.

We have respected Ford's competitive wish not to disclose the experimental boost reliably held during our cool and damp test day. The Corsican victor was prepared for a subsequent week testing underbonnet temperatures under high boost. It could not have had that sustained boost, or power, in Corsica, but the massive mid-range torque was representative of an essential characteristic in the rally success of this transplanted racer. So was the lack of traction in comparison to the 4WD Lancia and Toyota . . .

The LHD cockpit is far from an estate agent's beloved 'Des Res'. Naked steel panels are intermittently overlaid by a massive aluminium footplate for the co-driver, complete with buttons for the horn and Terratrip rally computer. The test car also had a digital temperature gauge before the navigator, monitoring turbo inlet levels.

Vying for the crew's attention are seven dials in a quartet of fascia panels, plus auxiliary switchgear to control exotic pumps, such as a those for the rear differential oil cooler and a pair to ensure fuel supplies.

Cabin details that mark this RS as an effective all-weather competitor include the heated front screen and emery gridding across the floor, brake and clutch pedals, preventing wet soles from slipping. 'Great for the job, but they have ruined more shoes than I care to remember,' says John Wheeler amiably.

Engineering fallbacks to keep the Cosworth mobile in all foreseeable circumstances include 'two identical computer engine management boxes', mounted above each other on the navigator's side and a jack plug point for additional battery power.

Flashing lights include the traditional large orange device for low oil pressure, below 1.9 bar. A very subtle sensor analysis light blinks out nine coded sequences to identify possible electronic engine problems.

Should things take a turn for the worse there is a Lifeline extinguisher with internal, or external, activation. Plus the choice of damping out an engine bay fire, or of dousing the cabin as well.

There are 24 current Cosworths on Boreham's books at press time, but D372 TAR appears in three guises. We drove it in Corsican tarmac trim, but it then goes on for further cooling test usage, followed by a complete rebuild to gravel road specification to serve Auriol on August's 1,000 Lakes Rally. Ford Motorsport also list six XR4x4s and have all the 2 litre turbo Transit service vans to care for as well. Not all the RS types contained in that total are built by the small workforce on site, which comprises only 15 mechanics, and just five design staff, including Mr Wheeler.

Continual development and parts supply are time consuming. They have had to keep Jimmy McRae (until his departure for the British Toyota GT-Four) winning, Mark Lovell collecting Championships, Bertie Fisher tearing over tarmac and Russell Brookes in a Ford return, never mind the obvious works entries.

Sub-contractors such as RED at Widnes, Mike Little preparations in Carlisle and Gordon Spooner in Essex share the load on specific Ford programmes. Even works drivers like Stig Blomqvist may find themselves in a car that Boreham did not build, for Ford-contracted regular Carlos Sainz has had both factory machines in Corsica and Mike Taylor preparation for his Spanish outings.

The harsh motor literally starts on the button and is quick to raise the crew to oven-ready cooking temperature above its flame-spitting exhaust.

The journalist's 6,500 rpm limit and a 200 km/h (124 mph) speedo respond lazily to a preliminary warm-up around the extremely quick and mildly bumpy (in a rally car) perimeter track at Boreham. Didier Auriol's close contact driving stance had been replaced by a more conventional posture. Supportive Recaro seating and Sabelt location is additionally braced by a beefy alloy footrest.

Time to take stock: noting what it takes to win between runs alongside John Wheeler of Ford Motorsport.

All the Group A contenders we have driven at *Motor* recently have had non-synchromesh gearboxes, but none has had the swift charm and easy selections of this Getrag. It has a racing pattern, first closest to the LHD operator and is matched to a tough but progressive clutch.

There are no transmission tricks. Ratios clacked to Rose-jointed selection rods, changes accompanied by just a cursory droop in the exhaust's aural menace.

The power steering and the intimate embrace of seat and harness supply all the clues you need on a wet day to apply so much power with confidence. Yet none of us escaped spinning as the rear Michelins steamed into extinction and the rain worsened.

In such conditions the main handling impressions must be of power oversteer, which becomes such a seductively regular habit that you ponder its likely illegality. It becomes an obsession to ease the receptive steering the instant an apex is past, avoiding the jeers of onlookers that greet yet another rotating voyage into rural Essex.

Assuming the Cosworth is snarling happily above 3,000 revs in any gear, the driver does not have to queue for a giant power injection. The turbo effect arrives after no more than a raised heartbeat, the hapless boost gauge needle twitches with a ferocity that publicizes 'loads and loads' of pressure beyond atmospheric. The enormous escalation in power was prefaced by a burst of exhaust flatulence, newly pressurized mixture gatecrashing the ignited remnants of the exhausted gases.

Inside, the eased steering lock always proved a wise precaution, even this quick action rack needing prompt reactions to balance full low gear output against the limited grip. The steering is never light, but the power assistance does take the sting out of the long and strong understeer period that prefixes power in slower corners.

In fourth and fifth gear curves, this Sierra still has enough surplus power to invite a tailslide over wetter sections. Despite the 70–105 mph velocities,

The LHD wheel of the winning Ford Cosworth. Its driving manners were mostly controlled by the amount of turbo boost generated at any given moment . . .

and the need to precisely return to second or third gear speeds, the works car merely threatened unruliness, rather than punishing a stranger.

The enormous, 13 in diameter, discs provide stopping speed to match the astonishing acceleration. The 'AR/AV' French abbreviations on the brake bias control dialled up an answer to counter the car's initial front wheel locking over sodden concrete.

Perhaps the most astounding impression from the passenger side is watching John Wheeler approach a first gear hairpin (or second, using the flyoff handbrake to keep the turbo on boost) at full noise in fifth.

As the brakes bite, it is literally a job to change gears fast enough to match the sharply reduced pace. At one moment you are power boating along in a 100 mph ball of spray. Those huge discs sever speed so sharply that it is as if you had been water skiing and some smart-bottom cut the tow rope!

Stability is exceptional and I would not have assaulted the angled third to fifth gear skips over Boreham's launching ramps had I not seen John Wheeler do the same thing, twice as fast. Logic says the car must tip over. Yet it lands with such gradual shock absorption that only the pale face of the looming lens hero tells of a short flight by a 2,433 lb automobile.

Wearing its bent back crossmember and blazing a path around the tricky course, this charismatic Sierra was the sweatiest and most satisfying of driving challenges. Do not mourn the RS200s and Escorts of yesteryear, their spirit has been reborn in this winning Sierra.

Riding with Mr B

This was the heading I chose to describe the only RAC Rally co-driving I am capable of, accompanying Stig Blomqvist on a one-venue preview day. The year was 1987, at the close of a character-building debut season for the Boreham-built Sierra RS Cosworths. I am indebted to Nigel Fryatt at *Cars & Car Conversions* for permission to print the original text.

* * *

Stig Blomqvist has suffered 20 years of carting the hacks around on demos. Jeremy Walton snatched the chance to celebrate that landmark with a morning at Weston Park's pre-RAC bash, sharing the works Sierra Cosworth that finished third on the 1,000 Lakes.

The day looked fine for a little journalistic initiative. The M5 and M6 were clogged as Britain's weather practised its RAC Rally monsoon season upon lines of contraflows, roadworks and cones that bred in the night. Not many hacks would venture from their lairs, even for the promise of rides in Stig Blomqvist's works Sierra, Malcolm Wilson's ill-starred Astra, or Russell Brookes in the rented Lancia.

The sole Ford Motorsport at Boreham entry, Stig Blomqvist, co-driver Bruno Berglund, plus two Ford service Transits, and the enormous Texaco hospitality trailer, loomed large over stately parklands.

I hardly believed my luck. No officials, no lists, no queues. Just sign the

The front and back of the 1987 Lombard RAC Rally device for Stig Blomqvist. The Cosworth finished an unexpected second overall in Texaco colours. Boreham-built Sierra Cosworths were also second (and third) on that year's 1,000 Lakes for Ari Vatanen and 'Mr B'.

proffered marshal's dead persons list and wait for Stig to patiently clear the previous incumbent's brolly from the locked hatchback.

Clambering around the steel roll cage and a steamy matt black interior would not be warranted to improve the temper of most star drivers. Yet Blomqvist is quite happy to chat in the sing-song Swedish accent that persists, despite years of residence in London's Barbican.

'OK, this is not the car I will use in the rally, but it has done a lot of good work: it was third for me on 1,000 Lakes, did three days of testing with me in Finland, more in England, and was also used by Mark Lovell on Audi National [10th overall, 4th GpA *JW*]. Today, same engine, same most things!

'Before 1,000 Lakes we were really down and people said to me, why do you go? But, in this sport you never know what happens. It was the first time we (meaning Ford at Boreham) really have the time to prepare the car, because we have done so many things with outside teams this year,' Blomqvist reminded us.

Whilst the Cosworth-constructed 2 litres idled at 1,100 rpm, seatbelts snapped into full harness embrace in and around Kevlar and cloth seating. Berglund's full-face helmet clicked, and Velcro-stuck its dual straps, to protect me. I had time to summarize the Sierra RS Cosworth cabin for the seriously committed.

Compared to the old Escorts, or the Group B machines such as RS200, the overwhelming impression was of 3-dr space. Blue OMP fireproofed accommodation ensures the helmets are cosseted between stages, whilst an enormous drilled aluminium footplate supports the co-driver in this traditional Scandinavian LHD machine, carrying a small button for the horn.

The usual plethora of rally car dials and lights jiggled and blinked their messages. The rev-counter carried a 7,000 rpm taped warning band, matched by a 200 km/h speedo that was definitely operational: I don't know how accurate it is, but I do know that it displays the equivalent of 60–70 mph through gateways and twists that you might feel were daring the Gods to do their worst at 45 to 50 mph.

Minor dials include a central boost gauge, which flicked to 1.5 bar on this cool and wet day before the whistling wastegate intervened. Ford use about 1.3 to 1.4 bar to generate an official 299.99 bhp that feels like 399.99 whenever, that is, those poor Pirellis get the remotest hint of traction from this classic front engine rear drive concoction.

There are minor monitors sprawled across from the driving dept to the centre console (two), along with seven switches. Dials cover fluid temperatures, fuel pressure, plus fuel tank contents, the latter displayed in front of the temporary co-driver, who also has Halda's navigational aids and two Weber-Marelli control boxes for electronic company. The crew share Bosch radio equipment onboard, diplomatically accessible between the seats, along with the handbrake and its ball-jointed linkage.

As ever Boreham use a bright orange lamp to signify really low oil pressure, and that occasionally blinks to alertness during frequent parking speed manoeuvres forced on Stig to fit BBC TV interviews between runs.

There's a miniature lake of Premier-encased Texaco in the back and generous firefighting appliances. I still have the lingering memory of the marked petrol tank stick Boreham's best used to wield in distrust of fuel gauges at the height of the Escort era!

The Getrag competition five-speed does not emit the old Escort ZF clatter on idle, but does select an isolated first in the usual competition saloon manner:

$$
\begin{array}{ccc}
R & 2 & 4 \\
1 & 3 & 5
\end{array}
$$

Yes, reverse is opposite first, and yes, we do need it on a wet day to back away from the BBC encounter. Traction on the mild grassy bank is insufficient even for Blomqvist's clutch cleverness (dip, dip, and mild blip, blip) to shift the black and red Ford forward!

Wheelspinning away from the soggy line is totally different to the Quattros and Lancias I've been lucky enough to experience, where grip and acceleration are the immediate response to a lifted clutch. First and second are almost redundant for the Ford, 7,000 revs blaring into the cabin at each whistle of the wastegate and subsequent quickfire change.

I recall Stig has always had traction on his side through the SAAB, Audi and RS200 eras, wondering aloud how he coped with obviously phenomenal torque and horsepower, seeking grip?

'For the first 10 metres, OK, is not too much you can do . . . but when it takes, oh it really takes off,' Stig says animatedly. Too true! As the Sierra slewed straight, we got the message.

That gruff power unit pulls from 3,000 to 7,000 like nothing else in World Championship Rallying. In seconds fifth gear is well engaged and the Sierra romped over 140 km/h (87 mph), hungering for 160 km/h (100 mph) before *that* hairpin left swum into the clear heated front screen's frame.

The brakes are as impressive as you'd expect from their massively ventilated dimensions: the speedo appears to have broken, so fast is the loss of velocity. A light touch of handbrake in second gear and the Sierra literally whistles toward the finish line marshall. End of tarmac session, and its worth noting that the fabled left foot technique was not employed.

STIG BLOMQVIST: THE STATISTICS

Born: 29 July 1946, Orebro, Sweden.

Rally debut: 1964 in SAAB 96.

First International success: 1970 Swedish, 2nd in SAAB V4.

First International wins: 1971 Swedish, 1,000 Lakes and RAC in works SAAB 96 V4.

1972–80: Most significant results in factory SAABs except 1978 Swedish, 4th in Lancia Stratos. Results in the period included wins on the Swedish (72/73/77/79), that 1979 win the first for a turbo car in the World series.

Other 1972–80 wins on: Cyprus (73); Polar (75); Boucles de Spa (76); Hankiralli (77).

1981: Started carving a career as a freelance driver with SAAB on Swedish, also helping Talbot Sunbeam-Lotus World Championship win with an 8th in Finland, 3rd on RAC.

1982–84: Most significant results in Audi Quattro Group B (but top 10 on RAC with Talbot, 1982). Won: Swedish (82); RAC (1983); Sweden (84); Acropolis (84); New Zealand (84); Argentina (84); Ivory Coast, the latter 1st win for Sport Quattro.

1984: FIA World Champion Rally Driver.

1985–87: Contracted Ford driver during RS200 development, no outright wins but a third on Swedish RS200 debut.

1987: Group A Sierra RS Cosworth placings: 3rd on 1,000 Lakes; 2nd on RAC.

The original 3-dr and the RS500 had plenty to celebrate by the closing stages of 1988, 24 international wins and assorted podium finishes. *(Poster courtesy of Ogilvy & Mather, London)*

SOME 1988 RACE AND RALLY RESULTS.

JAN 23	Mazda Winter Rally	Pete Doughty	Sierra	1st
FEB 19/21	Cartel Rally	Gwyndaf Evans	Sierra	3rd
MAR 12	Skip Brown Rally	Trevor Smith	Sierra	1st
27	Silverstone	Jerry Mahony	Sierra	1st
27	Monza	Soper/Dieudonne	Sierra	1st
APR 1	Oulton Park	Andy Rouse	Sierra	1st
1/3	Circuit of Ireland	Jimmy McRae	Sierra	1st
17	Donington	Whoops! Did not finish.		
23	Cordiners Granite	Trevor Smith	Sierra	1st
29/01	Fram Welsh Rally	Jimmy McRae	Sierra	2nd
MAY 8	Estoril	Soper/Niedzwiedz	Sierra	1st
15	Jarama	Soper/Ludwig	Sierra	1st
15	Donington	Andy Rouse	Sierra	1st
21	Oulton Park	Hales/Mahony	Sierra	1st
29	Dijon	Soper/Niedzwiedz	Sierra	1st
30	Thruxton	Andy Rouse	Sierra	1st
JUN 5	Vallelunga	Niedzwiedz/Dieudonne	Sierra	1st
5	Silverstone	Andy Rouse	Sierra	1st
11/13	BM Scottish Rally	Jimmy McRae	Sierra	1st
18/19	Willhire 24 Hours	Abbott/Scarborough	Sierra	1st
JUL 2	Kayel Graphics Rally	George Donaldson	Sierra	1st
10	Nurburgring	Soper/Ludwig	Sierra	1st
10	Silverstone	Andy Rouse	Sierra	1st
23	Manx National Rally	Trevor Smith	Sierra	6th
24	Brands Hatch	Andy Rouse	Sierra	1st
29/30	BM Ulster Rally	Jimmy McRae	Sierra	1st
31	Snetterton	Andy Rouse	Sierra	1st
31	Spa Francorchamps	Ludwig/Boutsen/Dieudonne	Sierra	2nd
AUG 14	Silverstone	Sean Brown	Sierra	1st

This is where we are.
Here's where we're going.

SEP 11	Nogaro	
14/16	Tudor Webasto Manx	
18	Donington	
24	Quip Forest Rally	
25	Brands Hatch	
OCT 2	Silverstone	
22	Audi Sport Rally	

Ford Sierra.

What did Blomqvist feel had been the technical story of the 1987 season?

Stig said, 'It was a good engine in the first place, but now it is even better with torque everywhere. You don't get full boost at 3,000, but it's enough for the traction . . .

'The brakes, OK, you would expect these to be good because Ford has plenty of racing knowledge with these cars. Also we use the gearbox ratios of the racing Getrag. I think the traction is pretty good for this kind of car; we have played with some other differentials, but we knew quite a lot about this Viscous unit from RS200 days.'

I commented that the car looked pretty heavy, what with the steel cage and sturdy panels, and found it weighed 1,220 kg on the 1,000 Lakes. Stig felt, 'It's not *that* heavy really. Anyway, in 1988 there is a minimum of 1,100 kg, so there is no point to try and reduce too much now.'

Asked about the Bilstein-damped suspension, Stig replied, 'The suspension has been much better since our work on 1,000 Lakes. I keep these settings for the RAC, tarmac or not, because there is so little service time. OK, so maybe you lose 10 sec on the Sunday, but that is better than going into the forest with racing suspension! Anyway, it is good enough for me . . .' he says with a dismissive and typically self-mocking shrug of the shoulders.

I looked out for his times on the 1987 RAC, and observe he's fastest on the first Oulton Park stage, as well as some of the faster and longer North Eastern forest tests.

Now it was time to tackle a very short and muddy loop around the Weston water bath. You would not dignify it with the special stage status (just a sector of RAC's Sunday fare) and I didn't see Stig in anything higher than third on this section, pushed to exceed 65 mph. Yet three assaults on that Mini Mouse of a Mickey Mouse test were an exciting education.

For Blomqvist never stops trying, or learning. Our first ride featured lots of off-boost inertia. The second saw the water splash cleaved with real vigour, a sharp right unrolling through the clearing screen with startling speed and the reappearance of stones peppering the underside.

By the time we reached the exit gateway, third was firmly rammed home and the Sierra rocked between stout wooden uprights with 6,000 rpm menace.

The third exhilarating blast saw even more attention paid to balancing power against traction at every corner's exit, where so many drivers would simply have pressed harder on the loud pedal and admired the subsequent sideways travel. Without timing equipment I would have judged that more than 1.5 sec was saved between first and second runs with a couple of tenths shaved away for our final rush in the company of this deeply impressive car and driver.

The rides were all comfortably damped on the comparatively long wheelbase. I could see Stig was enjoying similar luxury with the Personal wheel's suede rim responding to the power assistance that rally drivers have come to appreciate since the Group B era.

For sheer excitement and education this informal encounter with the works Ford will rank in my mind as strongly as the 'out-of-the-blue' chance to drive Lancia's Delta. They are as different as can be, but the Ford was much better than my expectation.

Biplane rarity

The winged racer. Born to beat the best on the racetrack, the RS500 road car was the basis on which to create more performance per pound spent than was decent.

The Ford Sierra RS500 ('500' referred to the production number needed for its evolution homologation into 1987 Group A) was a consistent competitor, but an erratic road car. Extended aerodynamics, a modest 10 per cent power boost, and alternative rear suspension mounting points were the primary public features behind triple RS500 decals and two side stripes. All the modifications were applied to a 500-strong batch of cars from the first production run, which had been stored at Frog Island, Essex, in the Ford company compound. The Belgian-built leftovers were transferred to Tickford at Bedworth for mass modification ceremonies to be enacted.

These changes, wrought for racing, did not offer practical street benefits (with the exception of additional aerodynamic stability), but each RS500 came with the potential to be one of the finest rear drive performance Fords in the company's charismatic history.

What appeal does the RS500 hold for road car buyers in the '90s? It is best approached as the basis for a fantastic road car, one that can have Italian supercar power for a fraction of the usual cost. Or leave it as original as is practical to keep as a true collector's classic.

For the public road customer with £19,950 to spend in July 1987, almost exactly a year after the original 3-dr materialized at £4,000 less, the RS500 meant little more than limited production kudos. All were sold in the UK, and of the 496-strong production run 392 were black. Four prototypes were used to reach the homologation minimum. Yet this comparatively rare Cosworth prompted an immediate collector's market for the black majority, or 52 examples made of each in Moonstone or White. The limited market did not stabilize until beyond the £20,000 barrier. In 1989/90 you would have been asked to pay over £25,000 for a good example.

By the '90s, prices were settling at £10,000 to £15,000. Or £15,000 secured a top class 9,000 mile example, one preserved to register in 1988. Those 1993 low figures account for the ravages of recession, the 'Top of the Steals' chart image and insurance quotes that add noughts faster than creative chip tuners.

I still say the RS500 has the most collectible pedigree and investment potential offered since the RS200, and RS500 has a much better world class winners record.

Although the RS500 was part of the Sierra RS Cosworth plan, little managerial time was allotted 200 staff, plus Ford Motorsport personnel loaned to Tickford at Bedworth and Newport Pagnell, to make the RS500 into an emission-certified production car. They completed the manufacturing task in *very* short order, stored Cosworths arriving at Tickford in June 1987 and announced for sale in RS500 form on 22 July that year!

However, that quartet of prototypes completed many of the contemporary Ford engineering tests, plus some that Tickford and Motorsport engineers devised in the heat of the moment. We should remember that the last of the homologation run RS500s was completed less than 48 hours before official Motorsport homologation commenced . . . It was *that* much of a close-run call.

At a cost of little over £500,000 Ford executed all durability testing and the manufacture of four prototypes, as well as the 496 homologation run through five assembly stations. Three pre-production RS500s went through 100,000 miles of endurance tests, including 6,200 miles each at 140 mph, plus 1,000 miles of Belgian *pave* tortures.

Heart of Tickford and Cosworth work was the engine bay, for such tempting targets as the suspension, brakes, wheels and tyres were all ignored; even the interior stayed the same. That meant those wonderful LS Recaros, a sturdy three-spoke, Ford, leather-rimmed steering wheel and period ex-XR4Ti boost gauge, very accurate but working an American scale! It flickered

Spring 1987: Awaiting rebirth. The original Cosworth Sierras in Ford of Britain storage compound in Essex, ready for the call to become RS500s.

Above It may look as though it's been in a major accident, but this Cosworth is in the middle of the Tickford transformation to becoming an RS500 in the summer of '87.

Above right Aside from illustrating the overall underbonnet layout, this shot also recalls how the RS500 was produced by parallel teams of workmen in a multiple stage conversion process that — including significant development and repair costs — was sub-contracted by Ford to Tickford at more than £500,000.

its red needle amongst the usual dials for water temperature, fuel content and 7,000 rpm rev-counter, accompanied by 170 mph speedometer.

Where the customer did get value was in the provision of a specially cast 'thickwall' iron block, the delivery of four auxiliary injectors (two per cylinder) and a replacement plenum chamber. This plus a larger intercooler and turbocharger (the hybrid T31/T04 from usual suppliers, Garrett AiResearch), running the usual 0.8 bar. The intercooler now ran across the back of an increased cooling area for the water radiator, whereas the original had a smaller unit, simply mounted on top of the engine water radiator. Inlet and exhaust valve sizes remained as before, but the inlet tracts themselves were opened up 9 mm to handle incoming mixtures at a racing 2 bar/28 psi boost from double the number of injectors. It was this factor, plus the enlarged intercooler and the higher rpm working band of the bigger turbo,

Motor magic: the 204 bhp original engine was removed to be replaced by 224 bhp and the potential to surpass 550 bhp.

that raised racing horsepower from 350–360 bhp of the original YBB four injector engines to 480–560 bhp (depending on the year) for a fit example of the Group A, eight injector, YBD.

The standard RS500 motor wore a dropped alternator mounting and many internal changes that had been bought about by earlier durability work on the YBB, particularly in the pistons, water circulation and head gasket, all externally signalled by the adoption of a three-bolt thermostat housing.

For road use the RS500 was built around the standard dimensions of 1993 cc (bore x stroke: 90.82 mm x 76.95 mm) and a compression ratio of 8:1. Both power and torque were slightly elevated, officially 20 bhp more than the original 3-dr and 3 lb/ft torque bonus, both at unaltered rpm points.

The official RS500 road output totals were maximum power 224 bhp at 6,000 rpm and peak torque of 206 lb/ft 4,5000 rpm. The specific output per litre was up to 112.39 bhp per litre and was coupled to a brisk power to weight ratio of 180.65 bhp/tonne. Dimensionally, the RS500 was as its parents, save an increase in weight, quoted at up to 35 kg.

Those power figures were the absolute minimum output realized. I was told by a leading engine assembly specialist that sleeves were used in the RS500 exhaust manifolding to hold down the power, which could otherwise have threatened an assortment of ancillary component warranty claims.

Tickford also attached the body kit additions. Now we had a reworked Sierra L with Phoenix manufactured body kit plus specific RS500 modifications: rear wing to Ford design with 30 mm 'Gurney' lip plus lower RS parts secondary spoiler with cutout for upper wing pylon. The usual Cosworth wheelarch extensions, side sills and front bumper/spoiler were joined by extra RS500 air intakes (five in total, including official deletion of auxiliary lamps inside flashers) and hard plastic lip/extension spoiler blade, which coiled up the leading edges of the front wheel arches. The double twin bonnet louvres and air intake between headlights were those of the original Cosworth.

Available only in the 1986 colours of Diamond white, Moonstone blue/grey metallic and black, I was unofficially told that the aerodynamic drag factor included a Cd of 0.351. That meant it was up an infinitesimal 0.015 on the first edition, but the gains in downforce — particularly at the rear — were almost as desirable as the extra power for the racers.

The body parts raised rear downforce dramatically. An extra 105 kg was quoted at the back, 20 kg at the front. If you think that was unbalanced aerodynamically, you are absolutely right. The Sierra RS500 had a tendency to understeer at high speed circuits 'out of the box', and Ford took a lot of wind tunnel time on the Escort Cosworth RS to ensure that the mistake was not repeated.

Incidentally the original wind tunnel work on the first Sierra Cosworth featured significant input from Ford Cologne Motorsport employee Eberhard Braun, as well as the more obvious input of subsequent Lotus engineer John Miles. The German oversaw much of the John Miles work referred to in other books, as I understand it from Ford sources. It was Eberhard who saw that the twin wing layout would be the answer for sports needs at 170 mph and more.

Whilst wind tunnel tests for both editions of the Sierra Cosworth were

Job complete: the RS500s in the back yard at Bedworth have been counted towards 1 August 1987 homologation and are now ready for distribution to the dealer network.

The finished job, before the public got their hands on Ford's fastest production Sierra.

executed in Britain (at MIRA) and Merkenich (the Cologne based Ford of Germany R&D centre), some British insiders remember the secondary German check tests on the Cosworth as 'meaningless', objecting to the use of XR4i or model bodies in late 1983.

And yet it was the Cologne-based Ford Motorsport department which had the job of racing against BMW through their sub-contract with Eggenberger. It was Cologne's Braun who made up the pieces of sheet aluminium and card that were so practically helpful in finding a working format for this Ford biplane. The XR4i/Merkur 'double decker' had been a styling feature, rather than functional.

These revised RS500 body kits were made by Phoenix in Germany, as were the originals, but (as with everything else in this programme) there were last-minute panics that included air-lifting the extra panels from Germany to Britain. Time ran out on the December 1986-July 1987 Tickford schedule, just meeting inspection deadlines for Paris-based FISA (*Federation Internationale du Sport Automobile*) officials. They did ratify the car for its racing role by 1 August 1987, but only after a marvellous June to July six-week extra effort from the regular work force and hastily recruited 'subbies' (many with factory Ford competitions connections) during the preceding month. They managed to hit output of nearly 30 cars per shift, about the same as the Ford Advanced Vehicles Operation (FAVO) managed in the '70s.

Ironically that FISA inspection team included one man who probably knows more about road and race performance saloons in action, whether from Ford, Audi or BMW, than anyone. Thomas Ammerschlager had engineered the Cologne Capris, and conspired on the wild aerodynamics of the wild

Zakspeed Capris before a spell at Audi on the chassis engineering of the fabled Quattro. He departed Ingolstadt in the late '80s, masterminding the BMW Motorsport M3 road car programme, from which Munich employment he took time off to make his visit to Bedworth with the British FISA delegate!

The RS500 racing evolution — not applicable to international rallying, or Group N, but used very successfully in rallycross — was desperately needed, because the 2.3 litre BMW M3 had proved capable of beating the original Cosworth in Group A racing, rather than just racking up class wins as had been expected from its normally aspirated specification.

Ford were fortunate that loyal British showroom customers of the period would cheerfully pay four grand extra for something that gave them no obvious performance or public road advantages, save that perceptible bonus in aerodynamic stability. Unless, that was, RS500 punters further modified the hardware supplied.

Then the RS500 was the first supercar clothed mass production suit that could (if the modifications were extensive) humble allcomers, regardless of price. Thus modified there was the 170 mph potential for a 500 bhp road car with 0–100 mph in less than 8 sec and 50–70 mph, in third or fourth, a blink under 2.2 sec.

I know, because the RS500 I raced in 1991 was road registered (G819 JWN), had road legal Bridgestones and retained power steering. It was used on the road regularly in 1990 and developed 520–550 bhp (adjustable boost; 2 to 2.5 bar), courtesy of Collins Engineering in Congleton, Cheshire. But the point was that it was no rarity: Collins alone reckoned to have done 50 such engines.

Additionally, Andy Rouse confirmed at the February 1993 racing Mondeo launch that his company had 'sold 30 complete RS500 race cars and more than 100 engines'. Now add in all the other specialists around the world, racing or road conversion centres. The potential in RS500 was more accessible to a broader public than the primarily Asia-Pacific works activities of Nissan with the even more powerful, and complex, Skyline GTR.

Back on the street, Ford RS500 Cosworth customers would have found crude U-bolt brackets and four bolts under the rear floor. These were all that FISA had required of Ford to homologate an alternative rear trailing arm mounting point, one almost 2 in forward of the original Sierra layout.

Other street changes comprised three extra decals with RS500 embellishment and a single side stripe per side. At the rear it read, '*Sierra RS500 Cosworth*'.

No options were offered, but all the equipment of the first Sierra Cosworth was carried over (literally, since it was a batch of original 3-drs that were converted), including only one cloth interior finish: the original Roma and Cashmere cloth. There was the minor detail that the radio aerial had to be power assisted to retract whenever the hatch was opened. Otherwise, it would foul the additional (lower) wing.

What was the finished result like to drive?

As a road car, a mild disappointment. Take these contemporary quotes: 'The evolution model is no quicker than the previous drooping snouted winged wonder, slightly tardier in fact, even if it has got the biggest turbo you have ever seen shoehorned in under the bonnet.' *Fast Lane*, October 1987.

'Fun as it might be, the RS500 isn't really meant for you and me. Ford will be pleased if we buy it, but only to put the icing on a very rich cake. It's a thinly disguised racer: the aerodynamics don't come into their own until you're well past three-figure speeds and that roadgoing engine is only hinting tantalizingly at its ultimate potential.' *Performance Car*, October 1987.

Finally here is a more recent view of the RS500 for the car buyer of the '90s: 'But it's best not to get too excited about RS500s; they're really for collectors or saloon car racers. In road form it's a disappointment; actually harder to drive and slower in acceleration than the stock item because the big capacity turbo suffers more from lag.' So said *Buying Cars* in August 1991.

What was the showroom performance truth?

Mixed, in a word. A mild top speed advantage could usually be recorded, but in-gear flexibility was measurably worse, as was fuel consumption. Not all the magazines bothered to measure that aspect, so I will comment that there was generally a 2 mpg loss as the demand for extra rpm extracted a penalty. I measured 18.9 to 20 mpg overall, rather than 21–23 mpg in the original rear drive Cosworth.

On the drag strip, standing start acceleration runs were so closely matched in back-to-back trials of 1987 that there was rarely more than a couple of tenths between the two 3-dr hatchbacks on the benchmark 0–60 mph dash.

We use the usual industry norm, *Autocar & Motor*, for all our statistics, but on this occasion it is also worth looking at *Fast Lane* and *Performance Car* results, particularly as those of *Performance Car* directly compared the 204 bhp Sierra Cosworth with its RS500 sibling.

I will let you judge their worth with a six-column table that should fuel many bar room arguments though the '90s. The chart and rereading the copy also confirms that motoring journalism has yet to reach the uniform standards of consistency that it demands of the motor manufacturing business!

One magazine went on about the ease of driving the RS500 compared to the original, how its manners had been sanitized and so on. I repeat, the production suspension was unchanged over the previous specification, right down to the tyres.

	0–60 mph	0–100 mph	50–70 mph (4th)	Max Mph	Mpg
	(sec)	*(sec)*	*(sec)*		
Autocar & Motor					
204 bhp	6.2	16.1	4.9	149	21.4
224 bhp	6.1	16.2	N/A	154	N/A
Performance Car					
204 bhp	6.2	16.6	4.6	142.8	23.35
224 bhp	6.2	16.3	6.8	144.5	21.1
Fast Lane					
204 bhp	6.5	16.0	4.8	143.0	N/A
224 bhp	5.9	15.5	5.9	146.8	N/A

For myself, I felt the bigger turbocharger and sleeved exhaust manifolds ensured that the power delivery was pretty quirky. You needed 3,500 to 4,000 rpm to wake up this performer. Sod's Law dictated that was exactly the point at which the Cosworth four pot reverberated through that tall, thickened, iron block — and the turbocharger hung alongside.

With the 4,000 rpm fire alight, the subjective performance felt tremendous, but that was really the contrast between off and on boost performance. This characteristic was much more marked in the RS500 (lasting approximately 1,000 rpm longer) than the original.

A long weekend, including a dash to a Ford RSOC function in Leicestershire in the autumn of 1987, provided the bulk of my standard RS500 road car experience in E201 APU. I had been driving the pre-production version of the Sapphire (rear drive) 204 bhp 'small' turbo and the initial impressions of the black Cossie were not favourable.

It really was a 'count to four' job, before the turbo did anything but loll against the exhaust gases. The extra lip to the wing meant you could not even see the bared teeth of the police behind.

Also annoying were the wayward manners of the original whale tail suspension — especially twitchy over bumps — and the limited grip of 205 section Dunlops in a rear drive turbo application. Clearly, some perceptible public improvements should have been provided for the extra £4,000.

If I owned an RS500 today, I would be very tempted to install some of the later Sapphire rear drive handling manners, including the revised front geometry. Plus a modest oversize on rear tyres (225 to 245 section) and a Viscous Coupling tweak that I learned in Proddy racing to balance out some of the initial understeer.

Replacement brake pads and constant monitoring of disc condition would lead me to Tarox/AP replacements in retardation too. I cannot see much

This shot was meant to promote Cellnet phones, but then Benetton Formula 1 team manager Peter Collins (at Team Lotus in 1994) is actually showing us that his loan car has the proper cooling ducts fitted alongside the flashers, instead of the auxiliary lights that many members of press and public found on other examples.

point in having the RS500 unless you explore some of its power potential in the knowledge that you can stop . . . time and time again, without the usual judders.

I would start off running around 285 bhp. Provided the rest of the chassis proved capable enough in that very modest programme outlined above I would slightly modify that tough motor, perhaps to 320 of the 350 bhp I experienced on the road through Mountune's eight injection cockpit-adjustable boost, development road car of the late '80s. On a wet day the full 350 bhp led to some epic power slides, but I was surprised how fast you adapt to such grunt.

A genuine RS500 is hard to come by these days, but there are plenty of fakes around; that is why I have held off some of the identification details in the engine bay and the VIN plate; fakers are professionals too.

If you are able to satisfy yourself that any prospective example is the real thing, or you can authenticate one built from scratch around a Motorsport (no sunroof) shell, the RS500 is to be prized above all previous rear drive production Fords in Europe. It was bred of an immaculate sporting pedigree.

It not only achieved a lot in the sports arena for others, but can satisfy any demand you are ever likely to make of an affordable rear drive sports saloon.

Double dose

The above heading was used for a winter 1987 story I wrote in *Cars & Car Conversions*. I would like to acknowledge the cooperation of the editor Nigel Fryatt in allowing me to reproduce much of the material, which was published in the opening months of 1988.

* * *

When the man who motivated Robb Gravett's winning Sierra RS turns to road runners, we pay attention. Jeremy Walton drives RS 500s from Mountune, including the cockpit-adjustable boost of a development Sierra that sensationally delivers 200–400 bhp . . .

Maldon is an Essex port town that is threatening to drown in the welter of competition-bred preparation specialists. Normally we would see former Ford competitions engine ace Terry Hoyle, but it could just as well be Graham Hathaway or today's target: David Mountain.

Based at Causeway Industrial units, Mountune operates with eight employees on a comparatively spacious 3,500 sq ft. They came to CCC's attention by providing reliable and competitive production racing turbo power in Sierras and Escorts.

Mountune's 1987 Sierra RS Cosworth 2.0 packed over 265 bhp and durability that Robb Gravett demonstrated all season long. Robb won the Monro and Uniroyal class titles in 1987, and far more races than his rivals.

We had been slow on the uptake, for a massive 'Champions choose Mountune Race Engines' board celebrates success back to 1979 in categories from Braintree Hot Rod Championship to the 1986 Toyota Trophy of

July 1987, and the tails have it: RS500 signature was the double wing layout, which was a lot more effective than the front end in providing aerodynamic downforce.

Portugal. Racing, rallying, rallycross (Barry Hathaway was a 1985 Mountune Shell Oils champ) and drag racing have all seen the 'Maldonese' motors out there, winning.

Created in 1979 after a mechanical apprenticeship and employment at Swiftune for the boss, Mountune presently offer to modify plenty of cars outside the Ford range, but we stuck to the blue oval on this occasion.

I felt the RS Cosworth was a more important subject than the price tag of an RS500 indicates because there are an increasing number on the second-hand market in the £13,000–£15,000 range. There are a lot of concerns offering instant horsepower bonus through electronic manipulation, and I wanted to be sure that the company CCC highlighted had a proven track record with the RS Ford.

Dave Mountain was disarmingly open about some of the basic changes/measurement checks made within his most expensive conversions. Too much detail could sabotage his expensively gathered knowledge, but it is worth recording that the under-piston oil cooling sprays have to be realigned in most cases to hit their targets!

Mountune also discovered the hard way that some iron standard Sierra (as opposed to RS500) blocks must be scrapped for being outside manufacturing measurement tolerances in the bores, and that RS500 owners will find that their exhaust manifolds have been artificially 'strangled' with sleeve inserts that are absent on 204 bhp Cosworths.

Brake test results on the dynamometers within Mountune have shown that the earlier 204 bhp unit tended to give more power than advertised, closer to 210 bhp than 204. In contrast the RS500 gave less than advertised, just below 220 bhp. Mountune operate two dynos, a 'modified Go-Power' and, recent arrival, one Heenan & Froude from Cosworth capable of absorbing 1000 bhp.

Mountune list three power stages for Sierra RS types. Stage 1: plus 40 bhp for five hours labour and £454.25 (all prices including VAT); Stage 2: plus 80 bhp, including eight hours' work and minor parts, such as cockpit adjustable boost, at £1,144.25. Finally, aimed at the RS500 owner, an eight-day Stage 3 which activates both injection rails of an RS500 (eight in total) to co-operate with a completely rebuilt engine that has LC (7.2:1 cr) forged Mahle pistons.

To energize and manage both sets of injectors, Mountune had opted for the standard RS500 Electronic Control Unit (ECU) which appears to be the usual 204 bhp Cosworth ECU, minus rpm limiter. Plus a secondary injection/ignition management box that was developed in association with Microdynamics.

A by-product of the eight-injector conversion, and any Mountune work in which the electronics are re-mapped against the 256 point grid, is better part throttle fuel economy. This is because the standard Weber-Marelli-managed Cosworths are mapped in the mid-range to run around 8 per cent rich.

If a customer wants very high horsepower from the four-injector layout Dave Mountain warns, 'bottom end fuel economy will be poor because we have to use such large injectors in comparison to the fine spray of an eight injector RS500, on which we'd expect 18 mpg'.

That secondary system is activated beyond 10 psi and customers for both higher stages of tune are given an adjustable boost control adjacent to the steering column. Incidentally Ford production boost figures for the 204 and 224 bhp RS Cosworths centre on 9.25 psi.

Normally 6–18 psi is the scale of Mountune adjustment allowed customers, but the development car could be twizzled to 20 psi. Then 'pull the adjuster out completely, if you don't care any more and want to try 30 psi', laughed Dave Mountain. Dismal rain pinged off his Maldon lair and standard Dunlop 205 D40s glistened above the floodtide . . .

We experienced both the higher stages of tune on RS500s and ran them through the sodden Essex terrain for back-to-back comparison.

Our initial acquaintance with the 304 bhp RS500 told us a lot more about

It was obvious that the Sierra Cosworth RS500 was strangled in street form, so many were sharply uprated. This car was owned from new by Roger Mayers and had over 400 bhp by the time Dennis Foy, the editor of *Performance Ford* magazine, photographed it in April 1990. The businessman owner now has a Porsche . . .

what it lacked. For D. Mountain was wrapped within the wall of water ahead and the 'twin rail' development Sierra was disappearing from our (tamer) white RS500 at astounding speed.

As our customer RS500 reached 4,000 rpm in each gear it seemed to set the engine bay ablaze with energy, whipping its BF Goodriches in pursuit of the development biplane. Between 4,000 and 7,000 rpm, it could live in the same league as the eight-injector RS500, but it was much harder work to stay on that sodden road pace.

As for the twin rail car ahead, the +80 bhp RS was perfectly docile at traffic speeds. Yet there was a missing ingredient, and that was the eight-injector 500's low rpm boost. For Mr Mountain had come up with the logical road-going conclusion to the RS500's normal lack of low speed *oomph*: he had swapped the big T04 for the 204 bhp car's T03.

'The T03 is a gnat's too small to do the higher rpm you occasionally use on a road car, so we do enlarge its internal airflow capacity,' said Dave Mountain, adding, 'We think this gives the best of both worlds with low end power and top end boost. Incidentally most people don't seem to realize that the standard boost gauge is extremely accurate (we cross-check against the competition VDO 2 in gauges) to within + or - 1 psi.'

As a 12 month development project, the RS500 we drove did not have the lightened and balanced engine that customers receive, but it did have the £500 option of the smaller turbocharger. Expect to pay £4,600 for the complete twin rail motor and turbo swap, if you are intent on the ultimate Mountune.

Instead of the rare RS500's standard 224 bhp at 6,000 rpm and 206 lb/ft of torque at 4,500 revs, the Mountune Stage 3 RS gives '350 to 360 bhp at 5,600 to 5,700 rpm with the capability of producing 400 bhp. 'It's amazing, but the head needs no further flow work to achieve the 400 horsepower,' reported Dave Mountain, 'just more boost!

'The peak torque is obviously up, but we haven't measured a quotable figure. What we can tell you is that the maximum is moved a couple of hundred rpm down from an RS500, about 4,200 to 4,300. On the subject of revs we aimed to make the roadgoing RS500 more flexible, but for Group A we'll be looking at a peak bhp figure centred on 6,500.'

Back to the byways of Essex and I quickly realized that this was the most civilized, as well as most powerful, converted car I have driven on the road.

Whether dialled for 6 psi or 20, tickover was an evenly maintained 750 rpm. Progress from a chuffing 1,500 rpm arrival of boost beyond atmospheric pressure, on to 3,500 rpm full boost in third, fourth or fifth, was surge free. Beyond 18 psi I sensed, rather than felt, some pulsing under full throttle. Since the black RS500 had then dispensed with a main road 'queue' of three cars rather than the usual single possible on lorry-laden Essex routes, I was exhilarated rather than critical.

The development car was not equipped with the £230 replacement road springs (plus 25 per cent stiffer, lowered ride height by 1 in at the rear only), or the Mintex 171 pads for the standard four-wheel discs.

So I had an energetic but impressive session over deep puddles and bumpy cambers and would recommend the chassis changes listed above. Especially for a Ford so obviously capable of exceeding 150 mph; my guess, based on a

OWNING THE LEGEND

Les Beerling is a London-based builder by trade, a Cosworth RS500 owner by inclination, and a successful sprinter by the weekend. So far as the Sierra 3-dr Cosworth is concerned — from a 350 bhp original to having the garage door wrenched off to steal his pride and joy — Beerling's been there, done that.

So it is not a surprise to find that he now runs a 480–502 bhp road registered RS500 with cockpit adjustable boost. 'I did have the RS500 as standard for a couple of months after I bought it 2¹/2 years ago,' he says. There was a pause and chuckle, 'but it seemed slow after the 350 horsepower I had before, so I started to work toward having a Group A car that could be used on the road, or to sprint in the six or so different sprint (against the clock competition) and hillclimb championships I enter every year.'

Motor modifications were all credited to Mountune, including the 450 lb/ft torque eight-injector motor, after Les had 'toured round all the companies and got the most sensible answers from Mountune'.

Modifications do extend outside the engine bay and include a roll cage, Group A bushes for the uprated suspension and replacement rear cross beam. You may have seen the car in the 1993 Cosworth edition of *Heritage*, published by the *Fast Ford* people. If so, then you will know it is a radically modified road runner, one protected pretty effectively by 'four alarm and immobilizer systems' says Les. He reports one attempted break-in to date, for which repairs cost £250.

Les Beerling paid £18,000 for this immaculate black RS500 through the Gerard Sauer-owned Greenlite performance specialists in London. Back in 1991 it had 16,600 miles to its credit: by early 1994 that was 30,400. There is also an XR4x4 2.9i to take the road strain, when required.

Since there are no plans to sell the car, Les is perfectly happy at the price paid and loves the performance delivered. 'It really is a classic and a great car to drive,' he concluded.

Above This road-registered RS500, driven by the author in the 1991 Vecta Fast Ford Championship, came complete with power steering and more than 500 bhp. It was far from the only RS500 to deliver such accessible mega-performance levels.

Above right The best picture I have seen of the showroom underbonnet layout, one dominated by the big T04 turbocharger. It was the best because Ford photographic nicked the bonnet!

V8 Porsche of more than 300 bhp would be an honest 160–165 mph maximum on 18 psi boost. Acceleration from rest to 60 mph is unlikely to occupy more than 5.5 sec, if the driver can connect power to dry tarmac. It was fun learning to live with so much power that the wheels would slither in third and fourth. That is the trouble with the eight-injector RS500. It is completely addictive!

You start off in a downpour thinking that some social responsibility is in order. You get used to 10 psi; twiddle rapidly to 15 psi. Then get withdrawal symptoms at anything less than the 18–20 psi setting. On a wet day its attendant 350 plus bhp and armfuls of steering correction have become the norm.

A brief flit on to a local motorway's assortment of long curves and undulating straights, put the illicit zone of the boost gauge on display and flung the rev counter needle around the dial so fast that it'll go in my hall of memories alongside the Ferraris and Porsches.

Sustained speed also showed that the twin wing spoilers of RS500 do offer a stability advantage that this Mountune motor can exploit: sensational!

At the finish of a day in which I drove the most powerful car we've tried in this series, which outperformed some of the V8 legends with casual ease, I was delighted we'd picked this 'new' name.

Biplane blitz

The RS500 grasped all the track honours expected of it . . . and more. So much more that it was effectively throttled or banned throughout Europe. But not before the fastest Ford Cosworth to date had scooped race wins and national titles across the globe.

Mention the RS500 to a Ford follower and the mental pictures of track prowess automatically flow. Above all, these were tremendously fast saloon cars. At Bathurst the Eggenberger examples were timed at 167.7 mph in 1987. Andy Rouse agreed that suitably geared his 1989 cars could reach over 180 mph. Andy estimated the performance of the all-conquering, Kaliber-sponsored cars to include a 0–60 mph time of 3 sec, and 0–100 mph in some 7 sec (almost half the time of a contemporary supercar). These were machines that could *average* 110 mph around a full lap of the Silverstone GP track. Fuel consumption could slump

Supreme World Championship chargers: Klaus Ludwig leads an Eggenberger Sierra RS500 Cosworth 1–2 formation at Zolder, Belgium. The fleet Fords took the first and last World Manufacturers' title that controversial season, leaving arch-rivals BMW with the Driver's award.

to 3 mpg in continuous full boost warfare. Return 5 mpg, and you were doing well . . .

Aside from the first and last saloon car World Championship win in 1987, who could forget the flame-spitting feats of the 560 horsepower plus RS500s? Masters of the 1989 Spa 24-hours and multiple editions of the equally important Bathurst 1,000 km in Australia, there was practically no major European or Asia-Pacific circuit that did not witness the double decker Ford flying on the ground to another victory. Unlikely as it sounds, the RS500 could also be found flying higher still in European Championship rallycross, a regular winner for a variety of Scandinavian drivers contesting the Group A class, including 1991 Champion Kenneth Hansen.

No national saloon car racing title was safe from Ford in the RS500's August 1987–1990 homologation heyday, and it went on winning into the early '90s, its official homologation expiring at the close of 1992.

This stunning Sierra was always superbly raced by saloon car craftsmen such as Klaus Ludwig, Klaus Niedzwiedz, Dick Johnson, Alain Ferte, Bernd Schneider, Gianfranco Brancatelli and Win Percy overseas. The last three finally broke BMW's stranglehold on the Spa 24-hour race.

Robb Gravett, Steve Soper and Andy Rouse were a stirring sight in British battles, while Soper was even more effective outside Britain. The racing RS500 was also was the machine the Germans effectively throttled with constrictors. Yet it still blasted the BMW and Mercedes horde to win their national Championship in 1988 and was second in the 1989 title hunt, before Ford withdrew from a series in which they had a record to compare with the most prestigious German national companies.

The racing RS500s, particularly those from Eggenberger in Switzerland, Andy Rouse Engineering and Trakstar in England, or the fabulous Australian Dick Johnson examples, were never outgunned in unrestricted competition. They were not quick off the mark; they were designed for rolling starts, but once moving they could paralyse anything of their era in a straight line,

Hindquarters: the Frank Biela/Gianfranco Brancatelli Eggenberger RS500 at Zolder during the works-backed 1988 assault on the European Touring Car Championship. In the '90s German Biela switched to a touring car career with Audi and has won both the French and German national titles.

No doubt about it: the 1988 Eggenberger Ford RS500s were unmatched in the last European Touring Car Championship. Again Ford had to settle for the Makes title whilst BMW put one of their drivers on the Championship podium for individuals. You could say such success was the kiss of death to prestige saloon car racing, for neither World nor European titles were held after the acrimonious Ford versus BMW years of 1987/8.

whooshing along the straights and spitting their way disdainfully into the lower speed corners that would allow agile BMW M3s and the like to romp all over their hindquarters.

For sheer power, it took 'Godzilla' to crush the ultimate 3-dr production Sierra. The apt 1990 Australian term referred to the monstrous twin turbo Nissan Skyline six-cylinder that brought 4x4 and 600 horsepower to saloon car racing, redefining the parameters of technical sophistication at 700 to 800 bhp as Japan Inc took revenge for the '80s drubbing the fast Ford had handed out, winning the Japanese title in 1988.

Even the 30 examples of the racing RS500 assembled and sold all over the world by Andy Rouse Engineering differed in their individual specification, but it is worth recalling some generalities of the fastest Ford racing saloon to date. Much of its success was owed to the integrity of the Cosworth competition engine components that so many utilized and so few credited as being anything other than their own work.

Power output varied according to the skill of individual engineers. Cosworth did no more than a 1987 dyno test to prove the 400+ bhp efficiency of the replacement racing parts they would supply for the competition coded YBF version of the thickwall block RS500 YBD unit. Outsiders then developed these rapidly from an immediate, but initially cautious 1.6 to 1.9 bar boost, realizing 450–485 bhp on the contemporary electronics.

Courtesy of ever more sophisticated competition electronic supervision from Bosch and Zytek, plus higher boost levels (in association with trick fuel mixtures), a regular 560 bhp, and upward, was possible for 1990 on 2.2 bar.

Competitors outside the front-running Eggenberger-Rouse-Johnson enclave were dependent on the assembly abilities of suppliers such as Essex-based Terry Hoyle (a former factory engine builder at Boreham), or the young Dave Mountain (Mountune). Mountune provided the punch that took Robb Gravett and Trakstar to the last British title for the RS500, that of 1990. Robb Gravett originally bought two Johnson Sierras for the 1989 season, the team then switching over to UK-built RS500s and engines, but Japanese Yokohama tyres.

Racing RS500 motors of 1989/90 would remain at the stock 1993 cc, but run lower (*circa* 6.2:1 up to 7:1) compression in association with massively increased (more than doubled) turbocharger boost. With all eight injectors hooked up, plus a side exhaust with oversize bores to feed the turbo on its way out, expect to go from the strangled road car figure of 224 bhp to more than 540 bhp (112 bhp a litre to 271 bhp a litre).

Since the RS500s were also stripped down to the class minimum weight of 1,100 kg (140 kg lighter than the road car, despite girder-like roll cages and extensive safety and body reinforcement work), power to weight ratio also escalated sharply. On the street you could expect 181 bhp a ton, on track it more than tripled, to 602 bhp per ton, at a racing weight just under an imperial ton. Thus the spectacular performance.

Beyond the motor from Mr Universe Inc, the front engine, rear drive, transmission sounded conventional. Yet the independent rear end differential (a 9 in unit) featured the Ford love affair with the Viscous Coupling in its most powerful expression since the RS200 Group B supercars. Although Getrag five-speed gearboxes were well proven at BMW and Jaguar, as well as Ford, the blue oval tried more Getrag derivatives than their rivals. Ford deployed both race and rally versions in the Cosworths to replace the BW T5, plus a replacement heavy duty racing Getrag for the RS500.

The rest of the transmission was less satisfactory. Throughout their international racing careers against the BMW M3, the Sierras were slow off the mark. This was the rolling start philosophy gone mad, emphasizing a light clutch and flywheel against a tall first gear (good for 65 mph on Silverstone gearing!).

The works-backed Eggenberger team spent a lot of time nagging their drivers to take it easy away from the rolling starts in Europe, worried about the differential under the impact of the RS500 steroids. When they had to contest the standing start Australian Bathurst 1,000 km in 1987 with an unchanged drive line, even the factory drivers limped away slowly, hoping to prolong active clutch racing life.

Heeling into Copse at Silverstone in 1988, the spare Eggenberger RS500 and its fishtail side exhaust prepare for the battle of the '80s versus Andy Rouse and Dick Johnson opposition.

Once moving, the Getrag sliced through ratios with the ease of an outstanding road box, returning the following mph gear speeds at 7,500 rpm on Silverstone GP gearing (4.4:1 final drive): first, 65 mph; second, 90; third, 112 mph; fourth, 132; fifth, 152 mph.

As for the transmission, the suspension of the front-running RS500 did not sound particularly clever, but was actually full of tricks. You divide it up into those who had racing layouts and those who adapted Ford Motorsport tarmac rally parts, then take a further premier league step with the Eggenberger interpretation of the rear end trailing arm (triangulated trailing links) versus the more conventional (but vastly strengthened) tubular arms from an outfit like Rouse Engineering, which had some discernible production link.

On a modified trailing arm layout there could be the use of 'coil overs' (coaxial) coil springs wrapped around shock absorbing telescopics that would typically come from Bilstein for Eggenberger. The only visible common ground was in the placement of the telescopic rear shocks behind the back axle line. That damper could equally well be Koni or other leading brands outside those with Ford Motorsport supply links/contracts, Rouse developing the Spax very successfully.

As at the rear, the front suspension owed a substantial amount of its basic strength and low unsprung weights to the 1984/86 work carried out by Ford Motorsport and Eggenberger, racing the earlier XR4Ti in mainland Europe and Britain. It was based on independent MacPherson strut principles, but all road car components were replaced, including wheel hubs and bearings, front uprights and top mounts, lower track control arms (TCAs), coaxial coil springs, competition struts and inserts.

The Ford Motorsport front anti-roll bar layout, aft of the front axle, was a popular UK choice. You could also adapt a drop-link Group A rallying rear anti-roll bar from Ford Motorsport, but Eggenberger had such a radical rethink from their days with XR4ti as a racing test bed that they went their own way in virtually every chassis item.

The beautifully direct power-assisted steering was usually sourced from Ford Motorsport. Lock to lock was set around 2.5 turns. On all the race RS500s I drove (three teams) it was the driver's best friend, accurately and sensitively countering the naturally wayward habits of a turbocharged, 500 bhp, rear drive racer, one based on a body not noted for setting an industry torsional strength benchmark.

Slowing it all down was not a major problem in the longer races, but then it was customary to employ brakes of *very* generous dimensions. In fact disc diameters were bigger than the wheels of some economy cars! At the front you would find 330 mm vented and cross-drilled discs. Behind, the discs might well be radially slotted, conventionally ventilated and the same 330 mm. The system would usually feature hydraulically assisted, cockpit adjustable brake bias, front to rear and twin circuits.

In Group A form, tyre and wheel rim widths were sharply curtailed, so the drivers had a careful hand and a superb sense of balance to coax these 500 horsepower monsters along on comparatively small rubber contact patches; by racing standards for 500 bhp, the tyres carried up to twice the weight a top line driver would expect to find in the equivalent sports and formula car.

Most of the top Sierras, from Australia to Britain and back via Japan, used

ly..

Unique Eggenberger homologated rear suspension with triangulated trailing arm is shown alongside two cockpit studies. The rear one reflects how fast roll cage design has been asked to provide the primary body strength rather than subsidiary protection. If the author remembered, you can see a similar shot of the 1994 Rouse Mondeo for comparison in our last chapter. Finally we show brake size and engine compartment layout, including triangulated strengthening bars.

a BBS split rim, settling on 8.5 x 17 in (Germany allowed a 10 x 17 in rim) to accommodate slicks, 225/430–17 and 240/650 R 17 at the back. With so much power and so little tarmac contact area, tyre supply became even more critical than usual. The big money Eggenberger-Texaco Sierras ran and won on Pirelli.

Rouse was a Dunlop loyalist for 1987 in his Cosworth Sierra/RS500 career and used that company's radial for the first time at the Bathurst 1,000 km. Although its practice performance and early showing was promising, Rouse had suffered a performance deficit on this front through most of 1987 (plus the smallest Sierra budget in Europe).

Andy's dominant British Championship years in the Guinness Brewing Kaliber RS500s (they won 10 of 13 British Championship rounds in 1988!) saw Andy Rouse Engineering on Pirelli, which meant an awful lot of customer cars (15 serviced in 1988, five in Australia, two in Japan) also used Pirellis, where supplies were available.

When Robb Gravett and business/driving partner Mike Smith assembled the RS500-equipped Trakstar equipe for 1989, a new tyre force finally arrived on the British scene. Having astounded Australians and converted conservative BMW to their rubbery merits, Yokohama were overdue for UK recognition.

Gravett won the 1990 UK title, the last BTCC award for Sierra RS500. Robb nearly equalled Rouse's dominance of 1988 as he amassed one less win, securing the RS500's last UK victory (Silverstone, 7 October 1990). It would be three years before Ford won again in Britain's premier league, but Yokohama swept the UK title up with BMWs from 1991–3.

The 3-dr hatchback Sierras were usually built from a Ford Motorsport shell, which came without the standard showroom sun roof. Rouse Engineering estimated it took over 1,000 hours to build a racing RS500, and much of that time went into the basic construction and fabrication. That did not mean just the obvious roll cage installation, but laboriously seam-welding every stress-bearing stitch in the Sierra L steel shell to take the shock of life away from a shopping trolley.

Common to all racing Sierras were the provision of fireproofing/onboard extinguisher plumbing, plus a safety fuel tank (the 120 litre Premier was popular in the UK) and the team's personal preference in instrumentation. Some were excessive — one rally team fielded 10-dial instrumentation and a plethora of switchgear. The important thing to remember was a nice big boost gauge, the best with white faces and quivering needles that reminded us of a bygone era in steam railway locomotives.

The roll cages themselves became ever more specialized. Eggenberger ensured that the front and rear suspension loads were fed into the cage, but it was really a very simple affair compared to the multi-point tubing seen in the '90s. The German Wolf preparation concern had their cage most thoroughly proved in 1989 when Klaus Ludwig hit Armin Hahne at 112 mph! At the new Nurburgring. Head on.

Both drivers walked away, the Sierra 'bent like a banana' according to German reports. The Mercedes had lost its front end, too. Hardly surprising, since one horrifying TV shot captures them in a deadly airborne embrace, nose to nose at more than 100 mph.

So the racing Sierra was a time-consuming exercise in body-building, every man-hour worthwhile in the life-saving and competitive qualities conferred. What went outside?

All the usual RS500 Phoenix manufactured body kit had to be in place for FIA international Group A competition. That meant the usual RS500 additional aerodynamic package built on the existing Cosworth panels, especially that 30 mm rear 'Gurney' lip. In fact it was not the aerodynamics that upset the Australians when the visiting Eggenberger Sierras steamrollered Bathurst with a 1987 1–2, but the wheelarch extensions.

Former BTCC Ford touring car star Frank Gardner, then settled back in Australia and running the JPS BMWs, stuck with a protest that the Sierras were running illegally modified arches to accommodate larger rubber. The point was proved, but not until after the black Sierras had made a lot of Australian enemies and had secured the first and last world touring car title for makes at the Japanese final.

Back inside the cabin of typical RS500 racer, doors were trimmed internally, but you would find no floor covering, just a single racing seat (the best funded had Kevlar construction). Eggenberger would always go with Recaro, but plenty of other suppliers surfaced, especially Corbeau in Britain. A four or more often full six-point harness (that's with the crotch straps) could come from Sabelt, Willans or Luke.

How much would all this weigh? Target was 1,100 kg (down 140 kg on road RS500), and British sprint cars easily achieved this. In Germany they reported a bare race weight of 1,080 kg was also achievable, but by 1989 they were carrying all sorts of penalties (dependent on driver success) plus 100 kg from the organizers, racing at 1,180 kg. This had a drastic effect on the power to weight ratio of course. German Championship Fords of 1989 had to win on 418.6 bhp a ton, rather than the 602 bhp/ton quoted for the unrestricted Sierra RS500 in 1989/90 UK trim, brimming with 560 bhp.

What did it all cost? Aside from the fuel consumption of 3 to 5 mpg and mounds of racing tyres, the British specialists reckoned in 1988 to build a race RS500 for £63,000 in the Rouse mould. I came across one beautifully preserved example in 1993 (the Brooklyn Cossie for Chris Hodgetts in 1989) that was quoted at '£70,000 build' by MD Tim Hill. This reflected the use of their own SpecFab roll cage installation and a great deal of intensive labour in-house.

Overseas prices could skyrocket. Again in 1989, the Eggenberger mount for Klaus Niedzwiedz was quoted just beyond £100,000 and the Swiss concern also advertised in the UK press at the close of their 1988 European campaign with purchase prices beyond £100,000.

Racing record

The FIA permitted a World Touring Car Championship only in 1987, reverting to European status again in 1988 and axing any pretence at trying to cope with the constant technical hassles of policing touring cars internationally in 1989. It was 1993 before the FIA permitted a multi-nation saloon car clash once more (Ford and Cosworth were winners: see chapter 14), but the story of the racing RS500 is truly worldwide. It contains one head to head between the Eggenberger, Rouse and Johnson elite equipes that I think was worthy of true World Championship billing, despite the fact that it occurred in 1988. But first, let's see how the RS500 performed in the role it was designed for: world class saloon car racing.

From its late summer debut of 1 August 1987 to the early '90s, the RS500 was *the* overwhelming track winner amongst Group A racing saloons. 'Perhaps it was too effective,' ruminated Stuart Turner in March 1990. 'It almost killed off the World Championship for saloons on its own, it was *so* quick,' said the former European Motorsport supremo.

Outlawed in rallying, successful in Class 1/Group A rallycross, the evolutionary Eggenberger RS500s secured that 1987 World Marque title for Ford, BMW rewarded with the driver's title for Roberto Ravaglia.

The RS500 started setting the pace from its August 1987 Brno Czechoslovakian debut, Eggenberger rebuilding their trio of existing original Sierra Cosworths into RS500 specification. It was also the first time that the Brno street circuit had been employed for this traditional touring car date, but the Eggenberger Fords did not need the old downhill straight to pulverize the BMW and Alfa Romeo opposition.

The works-backed Sierras qualified in a class of their own and led throughout. However the leading Steve Soper/Pierre Dieudonne pairing were told to slow up for the point-leading German pairing of Klauses Niedzwiedz and Ludwig. Just two laps from the finish Klaus Ludwig strolled by Dieudonne and the RS500's World Championship winning ways had begun.

From thence the last of the seven European qualifying rounds to the WTC, and one of the oldest motor races (established 1905), the British Silverstone Tourist Trophy. Again the Texaco Fords were at the head of the field. Soper drove away from his team-mates, and the rest of the pursuing pack to lead by a minute when the differential failed. Then came a torrential downpour and in the ensuing chaos the BMWs splashed home, surprised winners.

Down to Australia and the most spectacular track of the lot. Bathurst had been carved about in the name of safety. Standardized pits and fresh earth all over the Caltex Chase (they put up the cash) left scars at the close of the fearsome Conrod Straight.

The Australians were not in their usual hospitable mood after a lot of interference from Europe on the way they should run their race. The sporting instinct was submerged as the black Texaco stars (part of the same multinational as Caltex) proceeded to win not only every possible track advantage (first third and fourth on the grid, a race 1–2 headed by Soper and Dieudonne), but also the Re-Po 'Best Presented Car' award of A$1,000.

That Eggenberger had won by so much, thanks to a quite superb wet weather stint from Soper, added to the insult felt by the home teams. For Steven was *three* laps in hand over the German-crewed team-mate. The nearest Holden was a further lap in arrears for local hero Peter Brock.

'Brockie' got all the cheers at the prize-giving and the Europeans were given the boos, jeers and extended digits of a disgruntled Australian audience. In the history books it says Peter Brock won in his Holden Commodore V8. In fact he finished third on the road after an amazing wet weather display,

Silverstone 1987 and the 'Texaco Star' sits atop its air jacks whilst Klaus Ludwig has his back to us talking to Rudi Eggenberger, Klaus Niedzwiedz and Steve Soper.

but was promoted by the Australian protests.

First the rival Aussie teams protested the fuel used by Eggenberger-Ford (which was found to be legal). Then, as noted earlier, there was also a bodywork protest, one that simmered on and was adjudged proven on three points out of seven against Eggenberger. All related to the wheelarch extensions. This judgement was delivered on the eve of the final Japanese round, held at Mount Fuji circuit and resulting in another Eggenberger win.

That JPS-BMW Australian protest was upheld and Ford lost the driver's title they had tried to manipulate for 'King' Klaus Ludwig and Niedzwiedz, although the company did win the Makes title.

The German pairing finally finished second in the political battle, but moral winners with four races won outright to the two of team-mates Soper/Dieudonne, who were disqualified from that Bathurst victory anyway. The losers were all who love touring car racing, for FISA swiftly killed the Championship as a result of the year-long technical hassles.

However, Bathurst was just the eighth round in an 11-round global war. The durably prepared Eggenberger Sierras went on to win at Calder raceway (complete with NASCAR style banking), thence from Australia to New Zealand for the Wellington street races for another victory, before the final Japanese appearance.

Second time Australian winners at Calder were Soper and Dieudonne, but in Wellington any further Championship aspirations were dashed when the Klauses, Ludwig and Niedzwiedz, won around one of the tightest and slowest circuits of the season. Soper/Dieudonne finished third in vain pursuit of the sandwiched works BMW M3.

Below In case my Silverstone picture gave you no clues as to what 'King' Klaus Ludwig looks like, here is how Germany's top-rated touring car driver looked in 1988. At the time he had just won his third national title in a Sierra Cosworth-Grab. *(Courtesy Bilstein Photographic)*

Below right Consistently quick and the most experienced of German Sierra drivers, Klaus Niedzwiedz had also driven the Eggenberger XR4Ti besides his European, German and World Championship front-running seasons.

The Japanese event saw the Klauses back in winning order to ensure Ford won the Manufacturer's title, Schnitzer-BMW's winning Italian, Roberto Ravaglia, added the driver's crown to his unmatched touring car title spoils.

Ludwig/Niedzwiedz were backed up at this quick track (second only to Monza in its near-100 mph pace for 500 km) not by the second Eggenberger Sierra, but by Rouse and Nagasaka. That cheered up Andy's tough season with the promise of lucrative export sales to come . . .

However, there was scattered global opposition to the winning Ford that looked most serious in Japan and Australia. The Fords (including the spectacle of former GM Holden star Peter Brock in 'a four-letter car!') did not have too much trouble with the opposition from TWR Special Vehicle Operation/Holden V8s, but Nissan did have the right elements to win in place.

First with the comparatively square-rigged Skyline GTR-S (a force in Britain and Europe, out of Milton Keynes and the Howard Marsden operation, until the Japanese axed it at the close of 1988), and then with an aerodynamic GTR that had 'the business'. Nissan 1990 technology included four-wheel drive and four-wheel steer, plus a turbocharged twin cam six. This only became a reality in the 1990 season, and was not offered for sale in England.

Away from the regulation makers. Britain enjoyed some good racing amongst the RS500 men in those final UK seasons. The leading protagonists in 1989 were the perennial Andy Rouse and Robb (1988 Production Saloon Car Champion) Gravett. There was no love lost between the two and the title went into legal dispute over the winter (Rouse was declared a class winner

Above left Straight from the Belgian school of world class motoring journalist/drivers that also produced Le Mans winner Paul Frère, Pierre Dieudonne was a proven European Touring Car Championship driver back in the '70s heyday of Luigi BMW CSLs.

Above Steve Soper, aged 12³/₄? No, this is the official Eggenberger Ford handout picture of Steven that was issued in March 1987! Today 'Soperman' is best known for his BMW seasons in Germany, Britain and Japan.

Wow! The Sierra RS500 —
even with an air restrictor for
the turbocharger — was a front
row choice in German
championship racing. Here
Eggenberger and Grab team
Cosworths get the jump on the
BMW boys in 1989. The
'Cossies' and Ford left the
German series at the close of
the season, despite a winning
record over the years that only
one other manufacturer could
approach. It would be four
seasons and 1994 before Ford
and Cosworth reappeared in a
German Championship, the
second division 2 litre series.

once more), but the racing was good and we should not ignore the front running speed of 1987 Class A Champion (Rover V8) Tim Harvey in the Labbatts Rouse Sierra either.

German Championship organizers progressively clipped the RS500's turbo bonus over its normally aspirated rivals. The Germans did this by progressive restrictions on air admission to the T04 Garrett, in addition to their usual weight handicaps. Even when it was pegged down to 360 bhp the RS500 was a formidable adversary for the Mercedes 2.3–2.5/16s and BMW M3s of 315–320 bhp that Germany wanted to see with a chance of winning the *Deutsche Tourenwagen Meisterschaft* (DTM).

In their eagerness to slash Ford horsepower, the DTM organizers overlooked torque. The 1989 Eggenberger version of Bosch Motronic management for Cosworth components yielded around 480 Nm pulling power by a leisurely 4,700 rpm. This compared to a screaming 7,500 rpm torque peak for the 2.3 and 2.5 litre Bimmers and Mercs, which had almost half the torque at 275 and 285 Nm respectively.

In 1988 Klaus Ludwig confounded all adversaries by putting a Wolf-Grab-prepared and entered Ford RS500 into outright Championship honours. Klaus then quit for a miserable 1989 with Mercedes in Germany's hothouse home international series, but team-mate Niedzwiedz continued with Eggenberger Ford for 1989.

Using Pirelli rubber, Niedzwiedz — who gave the XR4Ti its first European win — took a fine second in the 1989 German Championship series with four outright victories; these despite the turbo restrictor and an effective rival team of Fords fielded by Wolf for Armin Hahne and Alain Ferte on Michelin rubber.

In 1988, the final year of European Championship racing, BMW grasped the honours with Roberto Ravaglia (again), but the headline battles were mainly fought amongst RS500s. There was considerable upset of form when

the Eggenberger car came to Britain for Steve Soper to challenge Andy Rouse (Andy on his way to another British class title), for Rouse beat Soper in some of the closest and most exciting Brands Hatch laps I have ever witnessed.

Rouse went on to beat not only the Eggenberger *équipe*, but also the fastest lap combination at the 1988 Tourist Trophy — the visiting Australian Dick Johnson/John Bowe RS500. To me this was the World Championship prize fight of the '80s, not the back-biting '87 season.

There was a fantastic entry for the '88 TT, and 20 of those competitors were Sierra RS500-mounted. Seventeen of those survived the rigours of scrutineering and qualification, making this the largest mass gathering racing RS500s to date. (Eleven gathered for Bathurst that year.)

Just how well the dry Silverstone circuit suited the fastest Ford Sierras, racing just down the road from the Cosworth creators of their mighty power plants, can be seen from the fact that *13* of the top *15* grid places were monopolized by these fleet Fords. The quickest BMW, that of 1988 BTCC Champion Frank Sytner, was *twelfth* quickest, over 3 sec adrift of the fastest Ford.

The surprise was that pole was not the property of an Eggenberger or home team Rouse Engineering car. No, Dick Johnson and John Bowe from Australia had taken their revenge for the Eggenberger '87 home turf walkover and used the year to develop their RS500 from its initial Rouse-based beginnings to an in-house trick machine: one that owed a lot of its pace to Kiwi Neal Lowe's electronic programming capabilities, enhancing the Bosch 1.2 Motronic system with many more advanced features than Eggenberger enjoyed with the later Bosch 1.7 management. It was far from the total reason, for the Johnson machine was beautifully assembled (and driven) on the best Dunlops Japan could supply.

Rugged Queenslander Johnson — master of the inflight TV quip, whatever in-house disasters occurred within his Bathurst mounts — set a 1 min 35.49

Privateers tried for their share of Sierra Cosworth glory too. Here is the perennially underfunded Karl Jones at the wheel of the Richard Asquith Motorsport example for the British Group A Championship of 1988.

sec lap in practice. I watched the red Shell-backed Ford quiver with its stunning acceleration on that remarkable lap, some 0.4 sec quicker than Steve Soper could manage on his home track with all that Eggenberger would allow him (which was generally a lot more conservative on boost than the opposition) in the menacing black and red star car.

At this stage it looked a straight grudge match between the Aussies and three Eggenberger/Texaco factory Fords, but Andy Rouse with hot French runner Alain Ferte was fourth quickest, his 1 min 36.09 sec beating one Eggenberger mount. Even then Andy had only fractions over the Armin Hahne Wolf racing RS500 from the German Championship (1 min 36.17 sec), so it would obviously be a cracker of a race.

In fact, Johnson paralysed the opposition initially. Dick had 1.6 sec on Ludwig, Soper, Hahne and Rouse at the completion of the first lap. Johnson was 4 sec ahead of Rouse — who had battled by both Soper and Ludwig — when the first fuel pit stops beckoned.

By then the Australian Sierra had blitzed the official lap record (practice does not count in this respect), leaving it at 1 min 36.57 sec/110.68 mph. A mid-race stint by Tasmanian Bowe saw 'Team Downunder' biff back into contention, Bowe leading Ludwig (just, *only* just) in an orgy of kerb-crawling and grass-cutting before their second fuel stop. Unfortunately, that's effectively where their challenge ended, the motor wounded in the leaking water pump department and unable to do more than finish 21st.

Up front, Eggenberger versus Rouse war resumed with vigour. Andy was some 7 sec in deficit to Pierre Dieudonne (in his stint with the Soper Sierra) after the final (second) pit stop. Pursued by Niedzwiedz, Andy put in the drive of his life and the Belgian gentleman/journalist racer stood no chance. By lap 81 Rouse had dusted off the German driver and plucked the Belgian, leading to the finish.

However, there was only 10 sec to cover the first three home after 105 laps/311.75 miles, the Eggenberger pack finishing in 2–3–4 formation to make Rouse's finest hour. Between them, the Fords also handed BMW Motorsport/M Team Schnitzer's Roberto Ravaglia another European title in the M3.

'I don't believe I have won the Championship like this,' said the most

I know it's a rotten picture, but it's all I could get to pay respect to the third world class force in Sierra RS500 preparation (and driving): Dick Johnson of Australia. This is the 1988 car at a time when Johnson arguably prepared the fastest sprint Sierras in the world.

efficient title-gatherer since Winston Churchill. 'When the race ended I asked Pierre Dieudonne in *parc ferme* if he had won and he said no, I couldn't believe it. Incredible . . .'

Ford would have compensation from Eggenberger in the German Championship, but it was the most electric RS500 confrontation I can recall. A fitting win for the modest Brit who has won the most home ground BTCC races (60 at the close of his 1992 Toyota season: Paul Radisich took all the 1993 goodies in the Mondeo).

With no 1989 European title to fight for, the RS500 works cars of Eggenberger were surplus to requirements, yet the German-speaking Swiss-team came up with a most significant victory for the fastest Ford saloon.

In late July the heavyweights of saloon car racing assembled in Belgium for the annual 24-hours. Ford scored their first win since the days of the Capri and robbed BMW of their apparent right to reign in saloon car racing's toughest event, also beating a GT class Porsche 944 and sundry 911s into the bargain.

Eggenberger cars, now dressed in Bastos livery, finished first and third. Former TWR ace Win Percy joined Gianfranco Brancatelli and German F1 hope Bernd Schneider in a crushing eight *lap* victory at an average 86.96 mph.

In practice the Sierras had broken the speed traps at the highest speeds (160.2 and 158.3 mph respectively) into the braking area at Les Combes, having swooshed along the Kemmel straight. By comparison the quickest turbo six-cylinder Toyota Supra coupes managed 150.9 mph and the best of the BMW M3s had a problem surmounting 142.8 mph. Do not forget that these turbo cars ran higher boost to qualify than in the race.

The Eggenberger *équipe* also set pole position (Gianfranco Brancatelli), but did not regularly lead until the last two hours. Then both Bigazzi-BMW and the traditional leading Schnitzer-BMW alliance were delayed, the Schnitzer car failing to restart promptly after a routine pit stop for wet tyres during the usual onslaught of a sudden Ardennes downpour. It was a terrific personal triumph for Ruedi Eggenberger himself, for he had previously never won Europe's most prestigious saloon car event with either Ford, Volvo or BMW tackle.

For reasons that I still do not fully understand, Ford competition manager Lothar Pinske and European Motorsport director Stuart Turner agreed on withdrawing the Sierra from Europe's then most prestigious saloon car racing series at the close of 1989. Ford submitted to the hostility of their rivals, and the organizers (it was the only turbo car in the series and difficult to equate with the opposition). I also believe that British prejudice towards a priority for the rallying budget tilted the balance against continuing in Germany.

Ford had a pretty good winning record in Germany — whether with Zakspeed Escort and Capri, or their own Capris and Eggenberger Sierras. Hard to believe today, but Ford had won more German Championship races between 1984–9 than BMW (30 to 25).

In Britain the situation for the premier Championship was confused by the introduction of a 2 litre, normally aspirated, class. Fed up with Ford domination, RACSMA and its consultants had imposed a new category, despite the fact that it was BMW and Vauxhall who won the 1988/89 national titles.

However, nothing had won outright but a Ford for as long as TV could

Top dog in Britain in 1988/9 was the Andy Rouse Engineering car of the boss himself. Here are two studies from 1988 that show the wealth of Sierras fielded at Donington and the best action portrait I have seen, Rouse balancing 500 bhp boost against minimal grip at Silverstone. He won the class in 1988 and was third overall in the BTCC with Kaliber low alcohol beer backing.

remember in the late '80s, so the RS500 was served with notice that it would be outlawed in 1991, but allowed to run alongside the 2 litres of 1990. Then Gravett duly won the title for Trakstar after a dominant seven-victory year versus three wins for defending double class champion, Rouse.

For outright lap pace, the RS500 was never matched when unfettered in the 1987–9 period. In Britain especially the RS500 was omnipresent in the outright and class results between 1987–90. In fact the RS500 made motor sport history.

Ford established the longest winning streak for a single model in the BTCC with a string of 40 wins for the RS500 between September 1987 and October 1990. Add in the original April-July 1987 Cosworth trio of wins by Rouse Sierras: two for Rouse himself, one GP supporting event to Win Percy, 'despite stalling off the start'. Plus 14 outright wins for the April 1985 September 86 XR4Ti of Rouse. Now you have 57 BTCC wins for the Sierra.

Want to play the BTCC numbers game? Anyway you look at it, the Ford oval is a dominant force. Of 202 BTCC race wins scored by the close of 1993, Sierra's 57 was complimented by 59 wins amassed by the Capri (Cologne Group 2 racing V6s of 2.9 to 3 litres; plus uprated British Essex 3 litre V6s) over a far longer period: October 1971 to August 1982.

Other key Ford winners were the 4.7 litre Falcon V8 of 1966–9 with 24 outright wins, the legendary Mustang racked up 18 victories (1965–70, a 4.7 litre originally, reborn as the 5 litre Boss for 1970).

The Escort took 14 outright wins with the widest variety of power plants (pushrod 1.3 to DOHC 1.6 litre FVA, 'fan charged'). Galaxie 7 litre V8s rumbled to one win less (13) in a comparatively short 1963/64 Ford-backed period, their 13th win an isolated 1965 victory for the late Brian Muir.

The car most Ford freaks remember as a legend in association with driving of Jim Clark or Sir John Whitmore, was the first Lotus Cortina. Like the Escort, the Cortina TC was hobbled with class duties for most of its winning life, so the Cortina was credited with just seven outright wins. Making up the balance were three outright wins each for the Superspeed/Broadspeed Anglia renditions and the 1993 Mondeo-Cosworth V6.

Both Sierra and Capri, accounting more than half the Ford success between 1960–93, were better than Chevrolet with those grumbling V8 Camaros.

It all goes to show there now is 'a substitute for cubic inches, boy'. They call it a turbocharger . . .

Ford Sierra RS500 Cosworth Group A competition highlights 1987–92

Date	Event	Crew	Preparation	Results
16.8.87	Brno 501.6 km	Ludwig/Niedzwiedz	Eggenberger	Pole, 1st, 143.2 km/h
		Soper/Dieudonne	Eggenberger	2nd
6.9.87	Silverstone TT	Soper	Eggenberger	Pole, diff failed
4.10.87	Bathurst 1,000 km	Soper/Dieudonne	Eggenberger	1st, DSQ
		Ludwig/Niedzwiedz	Eggenberger	Pole, 2nd, DSQ
11.10.87	Calder Park 506.8 km	Soper/Dieudonne	Eggenberger	1st @ 137.1 km/h
26.10.87	Wellington 484.2 km	Ludwig/Niedzwiedz	Eggenberger	1st @ 125.6 km/h
		Soper/Dieudonne	Eggenberger	3rd overall
16.11.87	Fuji 500.6 km	Ludwig/Niedzwiedz	Eggenberger	1st @ 156.3 km/h
		Rouse/Nagasaka	Rouse Engineering	3rd overall

1987 Championship
Drivers		Ludwig/Niedzwiedz		2nd overall
Makes		Ford Motor Company/Eggenberger		1st overall

1988	Monza 500 km	Soper/Dieudonne	Eggenberger	1st overall
	Estoril 500 km	Soper/Niedzwiedz	Eggenberger	1st overall
	Jarama 500 km	Soper/Ludwig	Eggenberger	1st overall
	Dijon 500 km	Soper/Niedzwiedz	Eggenberger	1st overall
	Nurburgring	Soper/Ludwig	Eggenberger	1st overall
	Nogaro 500 km	Soper/Ludwig	Eggenberger	1st overall
4.9.88	Silverstone TT	Rouse/Ferte	Rouse Engineering	1st @ 166.3 km/h
10/88	Bathurst 1000	Longhurst/Mezera	Freeport	1st overall; RS500s 1–2–3 & F/lap

1988 European Championship
Drivers		Soper	Ford/ Eggenberger	2nd overall

1988 European Championship
Makes		Ford		Outright Champions

1988 German Championship
Drivers		Ludwig	Grab	1st overall

1988 UK Championship
Drivers		Rouse	Rouse Engineering	Class Champion

1989				
22/23.7	Spa 24-hrs 3,381 km	Brancatelli/ Schneider/Percy	Eggenberger	Pole: 157.168 km/h, 1st @ 139.13 km/h

1989 German Championship
Drivers		Niedzwiedz	Eggenberger	2nd overall

1989 UK Championship
Drivers		Rouse	Rouse Engineering	Class & overall

1990 UK Championship
Drivers		Gravett	Trakstar	1st overall

1991 European Championship
Drivers: Group A division		Hansen	Privateer	1st overall

British Champion in 1990, the last BTCC Ford Champion to date, Robb Gravett builds up Brands Hatch boost in the Trakstar Sierra RS500 Cosworth.

A driver's impressions of the race RS500

Racing the RS500 was generally the lot of the established touring car stars, but occasionally a formula car man would get in. I thought the impressions of one such guest, Jonathan Palmer, might make interesting reading before we recall how factory driver Steve Soper felt about his regular rides in the Ford. For that final bit of sparkle, popular West Countryman Winston 'Win' Percy recalls one of his rare Sierra Ford forays, that historic 1989 win at Spa.

Speaking to *Autosport*'s Bruce Jones after qualifying eighth, finishing sixth, at the 1988 TT in the Kaliber Cossie shared by another formula car contender, Guy Edwards, Palmer appreciated the difficulties of touring car racing vividly.

Asked what the difference was between the racing Ford and his then usual Tyrrell-Cosworth the articulate doctor replied, 'Well, the overwhelming difference is how crude the Sierra feels. This isn't slagging Andy Rouse's team, which is extremely professional, but merely equating how little feel you have from the brakes, how low geared the steering is, and so on.

'These touring cars are difficult to drive fast, everything feels so heavy. The main problem is that you feel as though the car is never properly set up, whereas a Formula 1 car can frequently feel as close to perfection as dammit. With touring cars, it always feels as though it is not properly balanced . . . The temptation [is] to arrive at a corner too fast, and this causes you to abuse the tyres. You must have the discipline to back off a little.'

The RS500 had more tricks to a quick lap than flooring the accelerator. It simply would not absorb full power in the lower gears without rubber meltdown.

I grabbed five minutes with Steve Soper at Silverstone Tourist Trophy in early September 1987. Then newish, the RS500 was more than fulfilling its promise. It had returned an astonishing 1 min 35.78 sec lap for Soper's pole position, versus times beyond 1 min 40 sec for the BMW M3s, which had previously managed to equal the time of the original Cosworth.

I asked Steve to explain just how the RS500 felt in comparison to the earlier version for circuit use. He grinned and quipped, 'Any idiot can feel the extra horsepower (initially around 480 bhp), but the feeling for the driver is also of a proper racing car.'

Looking back from the '90s through a mist of BMWs that had occupied his professional attention since the late '80s, Soper summarized his driving memories: 'It was always a bit point and squirt. You had to get it more or less straight and then feed in the power. I remember testing an RS500 at Silverstone and it was as quick on the straights as an F3000 car!'

Looking back at the debut of the RS500 as a racer, Steve recalled, 'When we got the RS500s, towards the end of '87, the cars were like night and day [compared to the original Cosworth 3-dr *JW*]. It went from being a good racing car, to unbelievable. At Brno we had adjustable boost and we just could not believe the power we had.'

Unfortunately such power left the engines with a legacy of cracks and unusable parts, so Eggenberger started to build for RS500 durability. This he succeeded in brilliantly — witness the 1989 Spa 24-hours result — but that was actually bad news for Steven Soper in the longer term. For Steve was charged with the job of defending Eggenberger honour in 1988 Britain, making irregular, regular, visits if you follow my Irish.

Arch rival Andy Rouse told me that the Eggenberger cars 'just did not have the power' of the British sprint-biased RS500s. Soper simply said, 'We were getting blown off! But in the European series (where he won *six* of 11 rounds, paired with Klaus Niedzwiedz) and in the World Touring car series we won more or less everything.' They did not win Spa during Steve's contract (he left for BMW at the end of 1988) but he remembered winning

The things RS500 drivers had to do for sponsorship money! The men at Chelsea Crescent on London's Thames riverbanks are Tim Harvey (*left*) and Laurence Bristow from the Rouse-built Labatt's *équipe*. Man with a Listerine Dragon companion at his home track of Mallory Park is Leicester speed business supremo, Graham Goode. By the way, the Dragon was called Clifford. Just thought you'd like to know . . .

'the annual 24-hour race at the Nurburgring, on the old circuit. To be honest I thought that was a greater achievement than winning Spa.

'The Nurburgring is a real car punisher. Maybe for a driver it was more satisfying to win at Spa, but the Nurburgring was much harder on the car.'

Incidentally Steve also drove the road-going RS500 regularly, and had them (English or German-registered) stolen with monotonous repetition. 'I lost two or three altogether,' he said with the indifference of a works driver, 'but they always felt like you could drive them flat out, all day. I don't think I ever had one let me down. They were amazing vehicles.' Amen to that . . .

I asked Win Percy for his memories of that winning 1989 Spa 24-hour drive. There were four laughter-laden anecdotes.

1 I was honoured to be asked to do the start by Ruedi Eggenberger. I was leading by about 100 yards going into the Bus Stop complex on the first lap. Not being used to Pirellis, I locked up a left front and flat-spotted it. Had to restart last, red face and all.

2 In the middle of the night, I was slowly caught and overtaken, by Eddy Joosen in our second team car [a former BMW winner at this event *JW*]. I couldn't really see why that was happening so I went for it and clashed with a BMW. Later, I discovered he had taken advantage of the cold night to run qualifiers for his stint!

3 The throttle cable broke during the night. When I got out to fix it, I could not believe what was going on under the bonnet. The turbo was glowing, glowing so much it was like daylight under there. I swear I could see right through the engine! I wedged the throttle open enough to get me back to the pits.

4 Standing on the podium after all that drama. And it was a dramatic race that year. Quite incredible, said the chuckling 50-year-old with teenage enthusiasm.

Chapter 6

A civilized suit

The Sierra Sapphire RS Cosworth was the first 4-dr RS Cosworth, selling strongly to spread the alliance's appeal to new customers.

If you have a favourite Cosworth for road use and it comes in the 4-dr body, you are in good company. For the initial rear drive (1988–90 UK sales) and its 4x4 successor of 1990–92 ilk are frequently mentioned by the connoisseurs at Cosworth Engineering as the best product for the public in their YB Ford liaison.

Remarks such as 'a proper family car, with a real turn of speed and looks that you can take anywhere' came from hardened engineers and administrators who deal with the world's most ambitious motor industries; men, and women, who acknowledged the worth of the 4-dr Sierra RS

Nearly there: in 1987 company marketeers were still debating whether to have the RS trademark of bonnet vents for the rear drive 4-dr Cosworth Ford. These crescents were laid on (proud of the bonnet) to assess their visual worth; they were discarded.

Cosworth — particularly the safe speed displayed by the 4x4 second edition of 1990–92.

One such endorsement came from a man with a 100,000 mile BMW M5. It was probably the most valuable of all, since he is one of the world's leading authorities on leading edge race and — *very* unusually — current road engine development.

Commercially, the new breed of Cossies in civilized suits was an equally dramatic success, one that has not been equalled to date, although it all ended in insurance term tears later in the 4x4 run.

The rear drive Sierra Cosworth 4-dr — which lost its RS badge in markets such as Germany and never formally received the Sapphire appellation that was often used by Ford of Britain and its customers — was the best seller. Cosworth supplied 13,390 YBB motors in the usual 204 bhp trim and some sources report sales of close to 14,000. Over 12,000 of the 4x4 successor were sold. More of that in the second half of this chapter. Now let's see how the civilized Sierra Cosworth evolved.

April 1987 saw me back at Ford's Dunton R&D headquarters in Essex to hear the development tale of the Sapphire RS Cosworth derivative from SVE Engineers, then Ford's most ambitious sally at the West German Audi-BMW-Mercedes set.

The RS version of the 4-dr body Britons knew as Sapphire drew primarily on the 1985–86 hatchback Sierra RS Cosworth for mechanical life. Yet it was a totally different car, one appealing to a new breed of Ford and Cosworth customer. One that emphasized '80s equipment and speed, rather than the 'rubber mats of the Mexico in the '70s' recalled by a slightly embarrassed and extremely senior Ford marketing man in a later interview. (He got fired, not long after he said that to me . . .)

Mechanically, the 1988 Sierra Cosworth 4-dr was largely a carry over from its predecessors, but the suspension amounted to a complete redevelopment around the basic MacPherson strut/trailing arm principles.

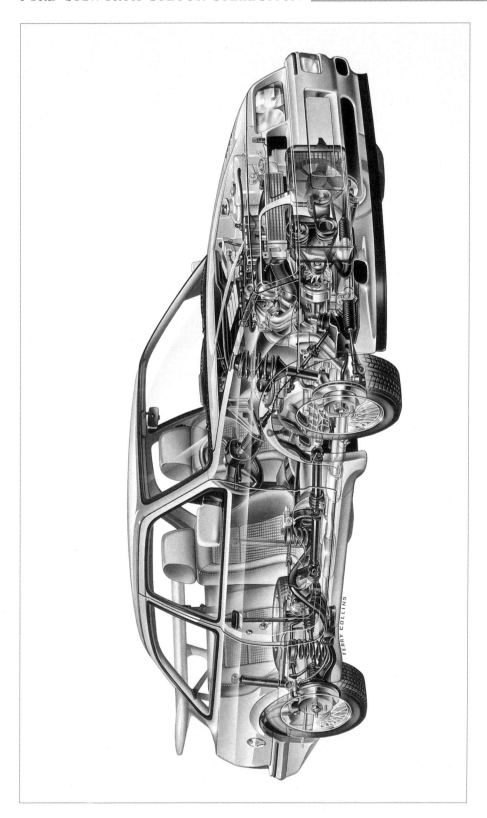

Ford Cosworth colour collection

Turbocharged, 16-valve, DOHC, advanced aerodynamics, 4-wheel disc brakes with standard ABS anti-lock action. All this 140 mph action from the first Sierra Cosworth — for less than £16,000 — put a new perspective on Porsche prices. Note the small intercooler and turbo of the original model, a point amended with vengeance in the RS500 for a competition success.

Then and now: the white Ford launch 3–door Sierra Cosworth of 1986, and a 1994 survivor from the original brood in Moonstone metallic, courtesy of Steve Rockingham.

Biplane blitzer: the RS500 Sierra Cosworth arrived in 1987, cost almost £20,000, and sold out within weeks.

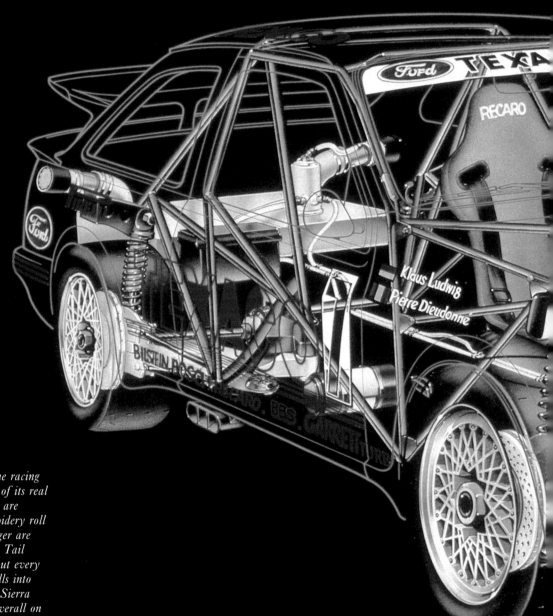

Main picture *Inside the racing Eggenberger RS500 few of its real world competition secrets are revealed, although the spidery roll cage and T04 turbocharger are prominent.* **Inset** *Whale Tail (tale): Stig Blomqvist put every ounce of his Swedish skills into flattering the rear drive Sierra Cosworth with a third overall on the 1987 RAC Rally, subsequently amended to second when an Audi was disqualified. British Champion Jimmy McRae's similar Cosworth was then third.*

Right *This silver 4x4 Sierra Cosworth replaced my* Motor Sport *road test car when the latter was stolen in the notorious Newcastle twilight zone of the RAC Rally. Many insiders think the 4x4 was the best all-round performer of all the Ford Cosworth cars; a worthy 4-door alternative to far more prestigious names.*

Far right *Not only Ferraris look good in red . . . The 1992 Escort Cosworth road car takes a break on the Luxembourg press launch.*

Far right *The winning Escort Cosworth and driver on that historic Portuguese Ford 1–2 of 1993, François Delecour and works Ford. By the end of the year François had won three of five World Championship victories scored by the Escort Cosworth in its maiden season.*

Right *New generation at Boreham: The 4x4 Sierra Cosworth nearly won the 1991 Monte Carlo Rally on François Delecour's debut with the team. By 1992 its unreliable speed was no match for Lancia and Toyota, and Delecour fought hard for fourth. Those 'personal' FMC-registrations were abandoned for the following Escort season.*

Above *The Escort was terrific on tarmac too, winning here in Corsica for Delecour/Daniel Grataloup. Our picture shows the 7th placed Biasion works Escort Cosworth on a Corsican charge.*

Right *This magnificent Ralph Hardwick 1994 action shot on the Greek World Championship event (Acropolis) captures a rare public alliance: Malcolm Wilson in the works rally Escort Cosworth. Malcolm was more usually hard at work in the background, developing a car of awesome ability on both tarmac and dirt surfaces. Wilson finished sixth in Greece, a place behind a rejuvenated Ari Vatanen's Schmidt Motorsport Escort Cosworth. Vatanen subsequently replaced Wilson as the injured François Delecour's stand-in with the factory Ford on selected 1994 forays.*

Both 1987 Sierras and Sapphires benefited from the computer-aided finite analysis of body strength. 'The body side rails and seat crossmember have been redesigned to provide improved vertical and torsional bending modes,' reported Ford at the February 1987 launch of the revised Sierra and debutante Sapphire. The company added, 'This has resulted in increased levels of body stiffness and strength, which improves the body integrity and forms a torsionally more rigid platform for the all independent suspension.' Less body flex under pressure was the welcome sporting by-product.

Those 1987 moves meant polystyrene acoustic filling of the front screen pillars and subtle styling changes, such as the extended bonnet and 15 mm taller side glass, all shared between Sierra and Sapphire. Aside from the boot, the Sapphire also had a unique hidden drip rail in its notchback outline. Aerodynamic strakes were incorporated in the back pillars, equivalent to those installed as a crosswind stability modification on the Sierra hatchback.

Ford SVE engineers started from a basic body that was a genuine advance over the October 1982–February 1987 Sierras. In April 1987 Rod Mansfield recalled, 'We always had the Sapphire in mind for the RS treatment, but it was progressed from the start as a car free from any need to carry Motorsport features. Motorsport had their Escort and Sierra RS types with an evolution of the 1986 Sierra (then RS500) to take care of their needs.'

Now SVE had the credibility within Ford — and there were some vociferous mainstream company engineers in opposition before the original Sierra Cosworth — to make a unique performer. One that would exploit the affordable performance market Ford had unexpectedly tapped. There was another unexpected factor in the Cosworth Ford alliance, and that was the provision of so much performance with absolute town tractability and enormous low speed pulling power. The unlikely source for those qualities

On the way. At first SVE tried a simple 4-dr Cosworth look with no rear wing, original 3-dr wheels and a full width air intake between the headlights. Note that the bonnet has non-production air vents . . .

PROGRAM DESCRIPTION

The 1988 Model Year Sierra Cosworth 4 door is based on the Sierra Ghia 4 door and is for all EAO Markets except Sweden, Switzerland and Austria — a restriction caused by ECE 15.04 emission level.

The following lists the major features that are different from Sierra Ghia 4 door and not basically carryover from 1986 and a half Sierra Cosworth.

- Unique body colour polyurethane front bumper/air dam, rear deck lid spoiler and rocker panel extensions
- Unique body colour front grille
- Unique badging, nomenclature 'Sierra RS Cosworth'*
- Three body colours — white, Mercury and Crystal blue
- Unique 7J x 15 alloy wheel with 205/50 VR 15 tyre

*A late 1987 decision retained RS badging in Britain, but deleted it for LHD Europe, leaving just the Cosworth connection to denote extra performance. RS-badged Fords did not have a good reputation in Germany for durability *JW*.

The document continued . . .

The following lists major features that are basically carryover from 1986 and a half Sierra Cosworth, but modified where required to improve durability, performance, to accommodate package changes, or pick up mainstream modifications

- Cosworth Engineering YBB engine with 16 valve DOHC head, Garrett AiResearch T3 turbocharger and based on the Ford T88 block
- Weber Marelli multipoint fuel injection and electronic management system
- Radiator with twin electric fans and air-to-air turbo intercooler
- Borg Warner T5 transmission

continued opposite

was not technically explained to me until I interviewed Chief Cosworth Engineering Designer, Geoff Goddard in 1994.

In an aside Geoff chuckled, 'The YA forerunner to the YB started off in the racing department because we were basically looking for a replacement to the BD series (the last blocks from Brazil sounded its death knell). We all put in little chunks of ourselves to the development and the bit I remember doing most clearly were the camshafts. When I started doing my sums, it seemed that the motors would go first to TVR.

'Simple, I thought, little bitty sports car. No weight, I can put a really square cam profile in there. Really make the thing *go*.' In transferring some of the DFV Grand Prix racing V8 cam technology to what became YBB profiles, sensational mid-range torque was conferred.

Those Goddard Cosworth cam profiles stayed on when the Ford order for a turbocharged variant came through. They proved a key factor in overturning the public and press perception of turbocharged motors as 'on/off' devils, besieged by the beloved press cliché of 'turbo lag', which simply means the delay in turbo boost response when the throttle is opened fully.

Only when faced with a motor sport need for enlarged turbochargers did the public face genuine turbo lag from the Cosworth-Fords (particularly Sierra RS500 and original Escort RS).

Detail Ford Specification of the 4-dr Ford with a Cosworth heart and a civilized suit, can be dated as at 8 April 1986. That marked the issue of a formal document ('Mission Statement' in '90s 'marketspeak'), much of it the result of Product Committee Meeting (PCM) with SVE's contacts channelled through Nigel Bunter.

Primary points were outlined as in our panel (left). I have retained the original 'Program' spelling and grammar so that you can see why I get miffed, whenever Dunton residents correct my English!

SVE development approval was received in that April 1986. They created eight LHD and RHD prototypes prior to the September 1987 pilot run of 70 production specification 4P Sapphire Cosworths. The first Sapphire prototype was running by August 1986 and lacked a rear spoiler, development of which item commanded some additional wind tunnel time at the Ford facility in Merkenich.

Initial consummation of the 204 bhp power train and Sapphire body marriage was postponed. A 2.0i trim level rather than the planned Ghia was the first such 4-dr Cosworth. A spring 1986 prototype was also built around the hatchback to give management an idea of what was to come and so they could conduct some trials unrelated to body type. It was September 1987 before I drove the car, months ahead of the 29 November 1987 scheduled start in Belgian production.

A 'rather tatty Sierra Cosworth hack' went to the Belgian Lommel test track to fight a comparison test versus the Audi 90, Mercedes 190E and 3-series BMW competition. 'It is actually quite hard to find direct comparisons with the Sapphire Cosworth,' commented one SVE engineer. 'If you do it on a price basis, then they haven't got the performance of our car. If you base a comparison on back-to-back on performance, then the competition is way beyond our price bracket.'

All RS Sapphires *should* share an identical engine specification, one that incorporated all the reliability modifications alluded to in our section on the original car. I understand that may not be the case, for Cosworth's capacity to build such engines (all around the Ford Pinto T88 iron block) was initially limited to some 2,000 units annually; by 1990 Cosworth capacity exceeded 7,500 units per annum delivered to Ford.

Personal observation also taught me the difference between two apparent brother Sierra 4-drs (both on F plates). Opening the bonnets showed a mass of detail differences, particularly to the turbo damper, an item that was uprated on my 40,000 mile car within months.

The Ford Cosworth contracts called for continuous production. That meant the continued output of engines after the cessation of 1986 Sierra RS production, a process that continued even whilst the RS500 was being assembled, storing motors prior to RS Sapphire production. Returned motors from RS500s went back to Cosworth for the purpose of eventually supplying Sapphire.

A replacement piston design was introduced for 1987 engines intended for the Sapphire. An offset gudgeon pin allowed much closer tolerances and an end to the 'dieseling' note of a cold start. Another civilization was the switch from spacer washers on the turbo damper to a more durable single coil spring that retained its grip on the damping of turbo vibrations.

All Sapphire RS units should include the engine durability modifications made to the later 1986 Sierras (yield head bolts, new Cooper gasket, revised sensor position), as mentioned in Chapter 2.

No official changes in power rating were made, but my understanding was that 204 bhp was commendably conservative. Most substantial engineering effort was devoted to the 4-dr suspension, work that continued even when I drove a September pre-production Sierra 4-dr RS, although they were then only fine tuning low-speed ride.

The fundamental change was to drop the raised roll centre and associated steering knuckle of the Cosworth Sierra that had been influenced by the thought of a slick shod car on racing ride heights. SVE chose a roll centre 'close to the standard figure'.

Program continued from previous page

with uprated 240mm diameter clutch and uprated 2-piece propshaft
• Rear axle assembly with 3.65:1 final drive ratio, 190mm diameter Viscous Coupling differential and uprated axle shafts with VL107 CV joints
• Brakes, 283mm diam front vented discs with four piston Teves callipers; 273mm solid rear discs with DE1 [ex-Scorpio *JW*] callipers, system operated by Teves ABS
• Suspension basically carryover 1986 and a half Cosworth Sierra, with revised rear roll bar and mountings and revised setting springs, roll bars and shock absorbers.
• Instrument cluster with 270 km/h/170 mph speedometer, tachometer without red sector and engine management warning light.

The 1988 launch stock was from Cologne and the press played in Sicily. Note the badge, 'Sierra Cosworth', dropping the RS label for the German market. It only returned on the Escort RS2000/Cosworth lines of the '90s.

Star of the show: standard equipment included the faithful glass tilt and slide sunroof and 204 bhp thrust.

There was also a reversion to the original castor intentions, via the first stabilizer bar design. The 1986 production Sierra Cosworth had the front wheels 'too far back in the arches; Sod's Law dictating they came out at the bottom end of production tolerances' in the words of one SVE engineer.

As to the damper, spring and anti-roll bar choices selected for the 4-dr to suit a new clientele, I am indebted to Harry Worrall at SVE for the following data table:

	1988 Sapphire RS	*1986 Sierra RS*
Front spring rate (kgNm)	21	19
Rear spring rate	51	47
Front anti-roll bar (diameter, mm)	28	28
Rear anti-roll bar	16	14

SVE achieved their objective of combining firm control with minimal sacrifices to the RS tradition of vivacious handling. The key factors were increased spring rates in alliance with softer damper settings, which remained of Fichtel and Sachs twin tube design and manufacture, as for all the road Sierra and Escort variants of 1986–93.

The 4-dr had roll bars that were different to those of the original production 3-dr. At the front, this was because of the castor/braking weave traits of the original. At the back a new anti-roll bar attachment was needed because of the 1987 model year changes to Sierra and Sapphire back trailing arms. It was mounted on a replacement tubular subframe, one that was rubber-mounted.

Final aerodynamic studies of the 1986 Sierra RS 3-dr had taken place between 18 and 20 December 1985 and revealed a 0.34 Cd. Once the Sapphire had received an enlarged back blade over the original skimpy spoiler, the RS Sapphire descendant was researched at the Ford's German Merkenich wind tunnel between 28–30 April 1986.

Using comparable body loads and suspension attitudes, the 4-dr Sierra Cosworth returned a 0.33 Cd. At the time Ford aerodynamicists reported that they had managed virtually the same drag factor and rear end lift as the Mercedes 2.3/16. Versus the Mercedes with Cosworth connection, Ford recorded a drop in front end lift and an improvement in yaw figures.

Such aerodynamic values were obtained with the replacement body kit of the 4-dr, plus the twin hood vents that were deleted late in the 1987 development schedule. Quite why this recognizable RS feature (from earlier Sierra and 'Mk 2' Escort Turbo) was deleted, after all the tooling was expensively completed, is still not known to me. Certainly SVE had found they were not necessary on the Sapphire for road use and that marketing were not exerting pressure to retain this feature, although it did reappear on the 4x4.

The second edition of Sierra RS Cosworth had developed its own low key, but still strong, visual identity. UK-based Marley body panels, sharing the same frontal identity as the 1986 car, contributed heavily. However, SVE confirmed that they had tried fitting 1986 Sierra body kit panels on the Sapphire, 'but the Sapphire had just changed the sheet metal too much for that to be practical' as a cost-cutting exercise.

Ford redesigned alloy wheels that were a bitch to clean. They wore the same 7 x 15 in dimensions, D40 Dunlop 205/50 VR 15s as had always been fitted to the 1986 Cosworth.

Incidentally, there had been a recall to check wheel bearing clamp loads on the 3-dr. This was the result of the assembly plant treating the car as a Sierra, whereas its heavier components demanded the same settings as the Scorpio Granada source from which its wheel bearing and hub assemblies were drawn. However, in higher mileages or arduous sporting use the bearings could be overloaded.

Some Ford mainstream engineers were not over-impressed by the application of wider wheels, uprated callipers and bigger brakes to this production hardware. However, it was possible to fix the original brake judder complaints by swapping to Ferodo 3432 front pad materials. Today, you will probably have to ask for the asbestos-free equivalent friction materials.

Predicted performance was little different to that of the 1986 Sierra RS, just 0.01 reduction in drag factor and another 10 kg kerb weight (the

Front, back and sides, the Cosworth Ford combination was lower profile than the original, but every bit as fast. Note that the bonnet vents were absent only on the rear drive 4-dr Cosworth.

The steering wheel and much of the dash looked the same as before, but the 'RS' symbol had disappeared from the original cover to the ECU microprocessor (on top of glove box), and the complete cabin was a quieter place to be as the Sierra had been substantially strengthened in the change to a 3 *and* 4-dr body. In the UK, the 4-dr was called Sapphire, but the Cosworth derivative was never officially badged with that label on the rear: you had to search the matte black surround of the rear window to find a 'SAPPHIRE' legend, as used on all UK 4-drs of that period. Many insiders referred to both rear and 4x4s as 'the Sapphire Cossies'. Other details displayed here include the original clear lamp cluster and UK badge, plus stock black-edged spoiler, knuckle-grazing alloys (the worst wheel cleaning job in the world) and front spoiler/auxiliary lighting; note that the flexible spoiler extension was retained at the front.

Sapphire more realistically recorded at 1,250 kg from the beginning) not having major effect.

An August 1987 Ford prediction claimed 0–60 mph in 6.1 sec, 0–100 km/h (62 mph) in 6.5 sec, and went for an homologated maximum of 150 mph (242 km/h), the figure Ford then loved to advertise, or see promulgated by the press. It was anticipated that 30–50 mph in fourth and fifth gears would take 6.5 and 11 sec respectively, this versus *Autocar*'s quicker 1986 test RS Sierra result of 6.2 and 10 sec for the same routine.

In February 1988 an *Autocar & Motor* road test reported a sub 6 sec time for the 0–60 mph dash (5.8 sec) but (as ever) the Ford 150 mph dropped to nearer 140 mph (actually 142) in independent assessment. However, the rear drive 4-dr generally outperformed its more powerful 4x4 successor on paper. Only 0–30 mph, the standing 1/4 mile and maximum speed were exceptions.

For some reason (presumably the official presence of an extra 16 bhp), the first edition recorded 4 mph less than *Autocar & Motor* managed for the 4x4.

Fuel consumption was reported as being less than the 4x4 (20.3 versus 21.6 mpg), but experience tells me the usual 21–23 mpg was more likely, albeit of leaded 4-star fuel for most of the production run. The 4x4 could always run unleaded — and *had* to in some markets where it was equipped with the 'green head' catalytic converter motor under YBG Cosworth coding.

The 4-dr Sierra RS Cosworth (they never used the UK name of Sapphire for the badging, just in some UK brochures and press packs) was put on sale on 8 February 1988 at £19,500. Standard equipment remained at the top end of the Ford spectrum and included Teves anti-lock braking, Recaro front seats, six-speaker stereo radio/cassette player, heated front and rear screens (the back incorporating the radio aerial antennae), a quartet of electrically operated side windows, central locking, 60–40 folding rear seats, leather trim to both steering wheel rim and gear knob, inadequate headlamps served by washers and supported by the lower auxiliary lights.

Those lower lamps are illegal to use in the UK in anything but bad visibility, but proved vital with the original 1.6L level lighting. The 4-dr was better, but not much, a remark that applies with equal force to Ford's much-vaunted 'high security' door and boot locks. Both boot and plastic petrol cap lock were wackily prone to failure, leading to inelegant forecourt struggles.

The cockpit looked much the same as before and was the usual efficient Ford ergonomic display, but 'petrol-heads' mourned the passing of the turbo boost gauge, a feature that engineers disparaged. Boost gauges were absent on

In leather or cloth you got the supportive outlines of front Recaros and full four/five-seater accommodation. Leather was always an extra cost option.

Today you can share in this 140 plus mph exhilaration for less than a quarter of the original £19,500 UK price.

all but RS500 and the original 3-dr, largely unmourned until the Escort Cosworth appeared in 1992. I found a boost gauge useful, if only to balance speed against economy on the motorway and to check that at least the advertised boost was being delivered.

That 1988 launch price was a healthy increase over the original, but left Ford under the psychologically important £20,000 British barrier. The company comfortably undercut anything remotely as quick, saving over £10,000 when compared with then bullishly priced Porsche 944 turbo.

The 4-dr Sierra RS Cosworth was built at the rate of more than 800 cars a month throughout 1988, but sales did slow as it escalated to £20,250, then £21,300 by the close of play on a 1990 UK G plate. As ever the model suffered from the well-known presence of a follow up fast Ford (the 4x4) and some were sold at discount. Dealers could well have pointed out that this really did look like the last of the high performance rear drive European Fords for public consumption, and that the 4x4 was going to cost over £5,000 *more*. Wonderful thing, is hindsight . . .

Overall the RS Cosworth Sapphire bore the benefits of experience with the earlier car, and was a much better product for those lessons. Sales were pretty brisk in the format Ford entitled 'Executive Express'. Around 14,000 had been built at the usual Belgian plant of Genk before the 1990 4x4 succeeded it, exactly two years after the rear drive model went on sale in Britain.

Sierra RS Cosworth 4x4

When Ford decided to commit millions to facing Lancia and the Japanese in World Championship rallying during the '90s, a by-product was the fourth generation Cosworth road car, which became a benchmark for affordable, safe, performance.

At a UK price five pounds shy of £25,000 when it was listed in February 1990, the Sierra RS Cosworth 4x4 initially achieved higher sales rates than its rear drive predecessor. A combination of British social conditions and the well publicized presence of an Escort Cosworth slowed sales dramatically in 1991.

By November 1991, Cosworth had ceased producing the two levels of emission-conscious 220 bhp engines, which could run 95 or 98 octane unleaded without adjustment.

The 4-dr 4x4 was unable to cling to commercial life for long after the advent of the Escort that took over its competitive and commercial life for 1992/3. Production officially ceased in December 1992, making way for the 1993 Mondeo. By then over 12,000 examples had been made at the usual Sierra haunt of Genk in Belgium.

UK buyers had already absorbed more than a million of ordinary Sierra 3-dr or Sapphire 4-dr models by 1990, when the fourth Cosworth Ford was announced. Amongst that million were just under 19,000 rear drive RS Cosworths of all types. There was a distinct 1990 feeling that the Ford Sierra Sapphire RS Cosworth (to give it the full UK press pack title) had to be the best yet.

That was not just my opinion. *Car* dubbed it, 'the best road car Ford has yet built'. *Autocar & Motor* reported it as 'the best four-wheel drive saloon car you can buy'. *Performance Car* stuck to their tried and tested roots: 'The revisions to the engine really work. On the Millbrook test circuit, a 0–60 mph time of 5.6 seconds was recorded several times, and one of 5.5 seconds.'

For the record *Autocar & Motor* recorded a faster 0–30 mph time than the RS200 Group B road car and went on to clip 0–60 mph in 6.6 sec, 0–100 mph in 17.1 sec, a couple of seconds slower than the rear drive model managed (15.1 sec). Kerb weight was the villain here, the test car proving 214 lb heavier than its RWD predecessor. Fuel consumption was excellent at 21.6 mpg overall and the top speed reflected extra horsepower at 146 mph, 4 mph up on its forerunner.

The *Sunday Express* quipped, 'the most exciting road car Ford had produced since the GT40'. Mmm, look who gets the credit in all this. Whatever Cosworth charge, however much those SVE engineers earned, Ford reaped a reward for *all* Sierras.

That RS 'best' was expressed in terms of civilized noise levels, and enhanced durability, as well as the obvious power and torque bonus; plus XR4x4 and Scorpio 4x4 proven unequal power split (circa 34 per cent front, 66 per cent rear), true 4x4 grip from Ferguson patents. All this to take Ford back into the World Rally Championship arena with the sporting chance of winning. One that simple rear drive had been denied on all but one occasion. More about that in Chapter 7.

The RS Cosworth 4x4 triumphantly replaced its £21,300 rear drive predecessor with stable speed (Ford claimed up to 150 mph again; 0–60 mph in a stated 6.6 sec), plus extra body and engine durability, all at lower noise levels. This RS Ford was also engineered to produce the same 220 bhp/214 lb/ft of torque with or without the twin catalytic converters specification that I assessed initially.

Such 'greenness' was cynically celebrated with that verdant shade applied to the 'DOHC 16–V TURBO Ford COSWORTH' cast alloy rocker cover, known within Cosworth as the YBG derivative of the original YB family and conforming to US '83 emission standards. Otherwise it remained in the

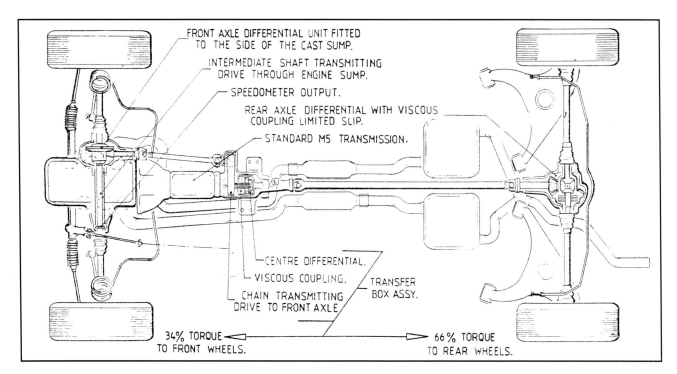

FRONT AXLE DIFFERENTIAL UNIT FITTED
TO THE SIDE OF THE CAST SUMP.

INTERMEDIATE SHAFT TRANSMITTING
DRIVE THROUGH ENGINE SUMP.

SPEEDOMETER OUTPUT.

REAR AXLE DIFFERENTIAL WITH VISCOUS
COUPLING LIMITED SLIP.

STANDARD M5 TRANSMISSION.

CENTRE DIFFERENTIAL.
VISCOUS COUPLING.
CHAIN TRANSMITTING
DRIVE TO FRONT AXLE.

TRANSFER
BOX ASSY.

34% TORQUE
TO FRONT WHEELS.

66% TORQUE
TO REAR WHEELS.

The November 1983 drawing of the FFD-patented 4x4 system, as applied to front engine Fords by Special Vehicle Engineering, was to provide the basic Viscous Coupling-monitored system for the Sierra Cosworth 4x4, including the 66 per cent rear drive power bias.

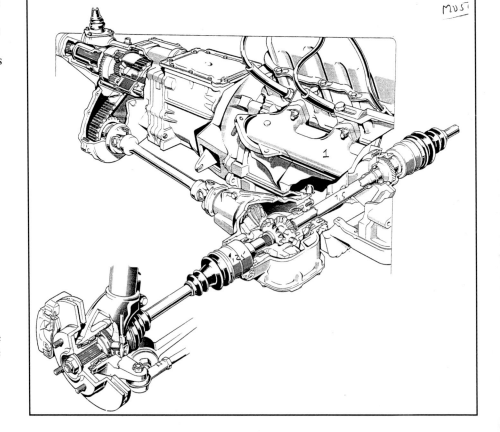

This drawing shows us how power was transferred forward on the 4x4 Fords, including the Morse multiple row chain drive and the offset differential; the NSF drive shaft travelled through the wet sump and its new alloy casting.

original red under the YBJ specification, but both were rated at 220 bhp; only 250 rpm on the peak power point indicated in the glossiest brochure that there was any difference between the pair.

After a tough two days press testing in the foothills of the appropriately named Spanish Sierra de Montseny, the latest in the Cosworth breed exhibited such astonishing road capabilities that it invited favourable and frequent comparison with the major players from Toyota, Audi and Lancia.

In other words Ford of Europe and their SVE department had a world class car on offer. Even the basic price of £24,995 for the UK did nothing to dim the press reaction.

Following the charismatic 3-dr Sierra RS/RS500 types, the later 4-dr Sapphire struggled for the kind of premium price public recognition that the hatchback motor sport winners enjoyed in the UK. Yet the 2,700 examples sold in 1989 — many at discounts over the last UK listing of £21,300 — left no urgent commercial or competitive reason for continuing the 2WD Sapphire RS. So the last rear drive RS passed into history without sentiment.

SVE was then 10 years old and had tackled 16 special projects for the mainstream company from Capri 2.8i to air-conditioned Escorts, their 17th being the 1990 Fiesta RS Turbo. They were assigned to the task of developing an RS, the 4x4 in road trim, utilizing specialist 4x4 knowledge that Ray Diggins and his group had garnered since they created the Sierra V6 2.8 and subsequent 2.9/2.0 litre XR4x4s and Scorpio counterparts. All around Ferguson patents and Viscous Coupling limited slip differentials. Ford Motorsport kept a watching brief on any competition modifications that could be incorporated at modest extra dollar cost.

The British-based SVE engineers — a maximum of 12 and a minimum of six — started work in 1988. All but two pre-production cars were built on the production line in order to simulate manufacturing problems from the start.

Radically revised engines ('80–90 per cent of all components are modified or new,' said Rod Mansfield, Manager SVE of his last major project) had to meet the normal Ford 300 hour dyno cycles of testing. 'Real world' test sessions in 30° C+ Nardo Southern Italian speed bowl heat and Finnish ice were also completed.

Although the engine looked much the same DOHC turbo Cosworth conversion of the old Pinto 2 litre as before, little was unchanged. As I understand it, all that was left were: 35 mm inlet and 31 mm sodium-filled exhaust valves and their springs; heat-treated steel connecting rods and caps; gudgeon pins; timing pulley and belt; front oil seal housing and main bearings.

Capacity and compression remained as before at 1993 cc (90.82 mm x 76.95 mm) despite the installation of so many new parts, including the revised iron block.

The biggest engine changes were to the cylinder head and block castings, more rigid to meet a noise reduction and durability programme. Ford reported, that the block represented, 'RS500 knowledge but our usual production process, and the head is strengthened whilst also enhancing its resistance to thermal distortion'.

The block was also summarized as of RS500 casting thickness but utilizing the original core plug sizing. A new head gasket was specified and knock

Underbonnet layout for the 4x4 featured either green or red rocker covers (this is the catalytic convertor model for Germany and other LHD markets); note the more conscientious heat shield-cum-air collector above the Garrett turbocharger.

sensing incorporated on the rearward (fourth) cylinder.

Complementing those basic changes came a new cast aluminium sump pan to run with 4WD, replacement oil and water pumps served revised water and oil distribution systems, new camshaft profiles and 8:1 cr Mahle pistons with replacement rings 'to improve oil consumption'.

The water pump was driven by twin vee belts from the crankshaft nose and was equipped with an improved impeller design to increase flow throughout a new bypass system, which also improved heater output. All this was fundamental evidence that durability had been a development priority, one that Ford allowed some serious cashflow to support . . . And about time too!

There was some RS500 lore within the fuelling rail of the stiffened alloy inlet manifold, plus fine changes that made a T3 turbo a TO3B in official brochures. T03B turbocharger modifications encompassed a lead seal to protect the wastegate against unwarranted intrusions, plus turbo case profile changes to ease low rpm boost arrival. Water cooling of the casing remained, but the intercooler (a pretty puny item on 204 bhp engines) was enlarged at this point. The larger intercooler was credited with 'greatly improved efficiency (78 per cent)'. Maximum boost was set at a reported 0.55 bar/7.81 psi.

Motorcraft's first platinum tip plugs were deployed ('We have to find more spark than they need in F1,' reported one engineer). Synthetic oils only were specified, Mobil 1 the favourite.

Subsequent research showed that Cosworth have had to work with spark plug companies through the basics of their business, from F1 downward. I learned that the Motorcraft branding had been applied to NGK plugs during the later development of the YB family.

There were myriad other motor moves. They included 'revised profile' for the flywheel 'to permit easier fitting of Motorsport clutches and to improve cooling', the latter accompanied by the return of the bonnet vents. There was

also another Motorsport programme to speed turbocharger changes in WRC events via the number of bolts employed and their location. The exhaust manifold no longer needed a turbo damper as 'outputs beyond 500 bhp are not expected', said one insider with a straight face. A revised turbo casing and replacement exhaust manifolding all provided improved driving manners in the mid-range.

The main objective was durable, quieter power. It was not the escalation from 204 to 220 bhp at an unchanged 6,000 rpm peak (6,250 rpm with cat), or the gain from 203 lb/ft to 214 lb/ft, 1,000 rpm earlier, that mattered most to Ford and Cosworth.

Their concerns were an improved warranty record and continued potential for competition, this time with the accent on accessible rallying power in the 350 bhp zone, rather than any racing 500 bhp ambitions. My competition sources told me that Ford expected 'no less than 400 Nm torque', in Group A World Championship trim, a massive 290 lb/ft that demanded new transmission components for competition.

On public roads, SVE knew 4x4 transmission and an official weight gain of 70 kg (45 kg of that 4x4) would absorb much of the 7.9 per cent power and 5.5 per cent torque gains.

Ford SVE project leader Ray Diggins explained the contradictory objectives met to me at the Spanish launch: 'We had to incorporate 4WD. Make a worthwhile car for motorsport purposes, and remember this was still a family car, one that had to sell alongside the rest of the revised Sierra range. The engine had to meet 83 US emissions standards with catalytic converters, yet offer increased power and torque. Finally it had to do all this and be a more civilized, quieter and more durable, car to drive and own.'

Mass production practicalities eliminated the most radical body modifications that Ford Motorsport had in mind, but a tremendous amount of detailing went into the 4-dr body.

Ironically, the Northumbrian police had to buy Cosworths to catch the large number of similar cars that were stolen in their car crime-ridden area . . .

Diggins reported, 'There is a stronger mounting point for the rear dampers and bracketry to tie between rear cross member and the turrets. The inner wings are thicker than a standard Sierra and the complete body takes slightly longer to build than usual, so the modifications are restricted only to Cosworth Sierra 4x4.

'The benefits from a stronger C-pillar are associated with use of composite glues to stitch things together, whilst the front bulkhead and inner wings have detail strengthening that you cannot see at a casual glance. It all helps complete the integrity of the body in road and special stage use, when it will be equipped with an integrated roll cage of course,' said the articulate Diggins.

Having controlled the action of the body upon the suspension — particularly at the back where competitors will know the older 3-dr RS types displayed extensive flexing — the road car suspension was overhauled. Positive wheel cambers were visible evidence that 4x4 characteristics had arrived, but the Sapphire RS front and rear spring rates were retained.

These were reported as 21 kgNm front, 51 kgNm rear, a lot stiffer at the back than all but the hardest progression offered in the back of the variable rate XR4x4, along with gas damping from Fichtel & Sachs for the RS Cosworth. Roll bars were stiffened up 2 mm front and rear. This brought front roll bar thickness to a sturdy 30 mm and the rear to 18 mm.

Much of the credit for this Cosworth's uncanny adhesion was attributed to effective 4WD, revised suspension and the replacement of Dunlop D40 tyres by an ER90 branded Bridgestone. We were told this was uniquely developed for SVE; other sources whispered that the Japanese started from the fabled RE71. Either way it was an ace tyre for 1990, offering minimal squeal and eye-rolling grip.

This ER 90 cover was not further developed, Bridgestone opting for the Expedia S-01 route in the '90s. In my experience — and that of other users on the same small fleet of Cosworths — the wear characteristics were uneven and I went for another brand in less than 20,000 miles.

The BF Goodrich was not a better all round tyre, it had too much bump and thump for that nomination — but it did wear better and grip was at least the same, possibly more in the dry on the standard dimensions of wheel and tyre.

The 4x4 aspect, manufactured by the GKN-ZF partnership at Viscodrive under agreement with Ferguson and Ford, remained fundamentally the same as for previous SVE applications mentioned earlier. That meant a power split almost in thirds: 34 per cent front and 66 per cent rear. Achieved by epicyclic gears, further modified on slippery surface demand by a central and rear axle Viscous Coupling. Unlike the Group A works rally car, no front limited slip differential was used for the public offering, or Group N.

The Viscous Couplings were set up quite loose in the road car. The aim was not to interfere with the standard fitment of electronic Teves ABS braking. Rival manufacturers say the VCs are too slack to contribute more than showroom presence, and the Escort featured tighter settings.

The centre differential was housed in an aluminium transfer box, which replaced the standard MT75 gearbox extension housing. Other SVE developed components abounded, most from the first XR4x4 programme of

1983–85. It is worth noting that the front drive came via a multiple row chain from the central differential.

Then a short propeller shaft ran to the front differential, one that served the specially cast aluminium sump pan. The right hand drive shaft was conventional with CV (Constant Velocity) joints at either end, but the left hand drive derived power via a shaft within a short tubed sector, one that passed through the oil sump to a support bearing. The result was an equal length driveshaft system that effectively resisted torque steer.

Accommodating the front drive facilities was a very important cast aluminium subframe, one replacing the usual Sierra pressed steel structure. Ford commented, 'New nodular cast iron front wheel knuckles support large preset bearings for forged steel wheel spindles fitted with 94 tooth rotors for the ABS sensors.'

The rear drive system was via the old propshaft and differential system of a Sierra, sharing the Cosworth preference for a rear limited slip differential. This using the second VC unit within a 4x4. Total extra weight was put at 50 kg, 45 of that added to the front in a total 1,280 kg.

Braking was upgraded to a quartet of vented discs of fractionally under 11 in diameter. However, it remained a weak point in the Group N rally car, so serious road travellers may need to look at friction materials and fluids for harsh use. I did not find that a necessity in 26,000 miles that included RAC Rally coverage.

The electronic ABS from Alfred Teves (since taken over by a larger group) remained in constant touch with varying road surfaces. The system kept the pedal toward the top of its travel; none of the disconcerting increases in pedal movement that the original hatches exhibited over bumps at speed.

The official factory cutaway by the unmatched Terry Collins shows the chain transfer for front drive is set well back in the transmission layout and that the front end was now becoming pretty complex.

The 4x4 badge was discreetly placed on the side panel, not on the back.

Rear end badges on the UK model remained as before, but the 'blackout' look was applied to the rear lamp cluster.

It is easy to overlook just how well equipped that 1990 road performer was in showroom format. Electronic anti-lock braking, central locking, electric power windows and mirrors, plus extensive stereo equipment were taken for granted. Ford had to provide yet more equipment as part of the most expensive Sierra showroom deal.

As ever, LHD models did not crave exactly the same standards, but there was little material difference: in LHD you lacked the power rear glass; there was no lumbar adjustment of the passenger front seat; and halogen headlamps lacked the mandatory UK 'dim/dip' sidelight setting. The only early options in either market were metallic paint, air conditioning (not previously offered with a Cosworth engine), CD player and leather upholstery.

The air conditioning option did not become a reality until Cosworth had incorporated the appropriate pulley on the water pump and extra belt drive, remounting the power steering pump to rejig the front end power take-off points. That work was complete in time for the 1991 Ford Model Year (September 1990).

Taking a look at the exterior first, the most obvious sports identity lay with those knuckle-skinning 7J x 15 in alloys of previous Sapphire usage. Test cars were all shod with the ER90 Bridgestone of 205/50 ZR 15.

The body was little changed externally over the previous 4-dr Sapphire RS, but note the blacked out back lamps lenses of the 1990 Sierra, plus a 'white out' effect to the front flasher lenses. The extra body kit panels and mirrors continued to be colour keyed: the 1990/91 no extra cost colour choices were: Diamond White, Magenta Metallic, Ebony Black and Moondust Silver.

For its final year in production, a smoother alloy wheel and stiffened dashboard design were incorporated from mainstream models, along with a replacement steering wheel that lacked inspiration.

Other RS body details that spanned its production life included the colour-coded body kit (auxiliary lamps in the polyurethane front spoiler/bumper assembly and raised rear spoiler), and a return of the hood vents that had been deleted from its rear drive predecessor. Check to see that the slight spoiler extension lip is still in place up front and that tinted glass is installed all round, as per standard specification.

The door locks of these later models should provide a slight security bonus over the original 'Please steal me' units. An anti-theft alarm that simply activated the horns was standard. I had two 1990/91 specification cars with these locks: one went to Newcastle and never came back, the other survived a cinema car park onslaught.

Sound equipment was based on the Premium 2007 Ford radio/cassette unit with 4x14W amplified and speakers; the aerial was incorporated in the heated back screen. A 2008 coded CD player was a common option, such cars lacking the usual seven-band graphic equalizer.

The filler cap was specified as a locking item beneath a tacky plastic (colour-coded) flap. Expect a tilt and slide manual glass sunroof with slatted and mobile blind unless the potential purchase is demonstrably a car built using a Ford Motorsport competition bodyshell.

Internally the level of trim echoed the Ghia line with that dated graphic display to warn of door open, boot ajar, frost (very sensitive and useful), or

The grilles are back! Front end of an early 1991 Sierra Cosworth 4x4 displays bonnet vents and white-look for turn indicators.

bulb failures. Recaro seats remained, plus a 60/40 split for the back seats to remind us of its hatchback origins, and which are useful for removing larger household white goods.

The handy three-spoke Cosworth wheel continued in black for the 1990–91 output. New for 1990 was the provision of steering column adjustment. The MT75 gearbox change pattern had one quirk: a gear lever collar that lifted before you could shift into reverse, opposite fifth.

The Japanese taught Ford to provide internal boot and fuel filler flap releases. There was both lumbar and height adjustment for the driver's Recaro. Another Oriental touch was the overhead map reading lamps and the multifunction LCD digital clock. The German prestige industry had taught Ford to provide a torch key; its battery expired faster than a politician's promise.

Initially, the 4x4 sold well. Cosworth reached their peak production of 7,570 YBG/YBJ units in one year (1990). But the bubble had burst on ambitious pricing and the UK public would no longer stand a list price that had escalated from the launch promise of under £25,000 to sell at £25,960 on a G plate. That was £27,060 by the later 1990 H plate and £27,648 during the 1991 J plate period.

Over 12,500 of the two emissions-conscious motor types were delivered by Cosworth to Ford, but by 12 November 1991 Ford knew they were in trouble with the Cosworth-Ford Sierra showroom alliance.

Ford requested a halt in engine production at Cosworth, and it was four months before the line restarted to service the Escort Cosworth YBT successor. Since Ford have to pay stiff penalties if the Cosworth output drops below an agreed number daily, never mind ceases, Ford did not take this decision lightly. Output of the YB engine family varies; at the time of writing, January 1994, just nine a day each of the YBT and the FB-coded Scorpio 24v V6 were being made.

Missing: the black and leather 4x4 I borrowed for the 1990 RAC with the intention of subsequent purchase managed four of the five days before it was stolen outside Newcastle, the night after this Whitby port shot was taken. It had been dozing with another 'Cossie', and a Toyota Celica GT4, under an arc light and the equally torpid eyes of a hotel security guard. I found some of the Cossie's trim remnants in a tunnel under the A1, including a disembowelled CD player and most of my clothes. I never found my wife's kit, so I am still looking for a team of Geordies dressed in black lace and frilly frocks . . .

It took even longer for the UK public to be told about the sales slow down of the '155 mph' (newspaper sub-editors exaggerate the size/speed/frequency of *everything*) Sierra Cosworth. *The Daily Telegraph* wrote in April 1992 about the Cosworth Ford sales being 'hit by insurance premiums after a spate of thefts by joy riders and other criminals'. They quoted £2,000 yearly premiums, or a simple refusal to quote for younger drivers, and commented that sales were down from 1,426 in 1991 to 250 for the first quarter of 1992 (corresponding to less than 1,000 a year).

Just four months later (27 August 1992) the *Telegraph*'s Motoring Correspondent, John Langley, was back on the case. 'End of the road for Sierra Cosworth' was the headline, and the story opened 'Ford is to stop making the Sierra Cosworth, a favourite target for joy riders and other criminals.'

Now the top speed had dropped back to 145 mph, but only 486 had been sold in the first half of 1992 and insurance quotes of 'more than £14,000 for dubious risks' were reported. A sad end to one of most versatile performance Fords ever made; any remaining market would be mopped up by the June 1992 Escort RS Cosworth anyway.

The Sierra RS Cosworth prompted even the *Telegraph* to admit that it was 'potentially one of the safest cars on the road, with four-wheel drive, superb handling and acceleration and powerful anti-lock brakes . . . Those that survive are likely to be regarded as classics in a few years' time,' was the more upbeat conclusion.

Period piece

Here is how I viewed the progress offered by the '90s Sierra RS Cosworth 4x4 over the legendary RS Fords of the '70s. I am grateful to the editor of *Motor Sport* for permission to reproduce this feature, which originally appeared in March 1991. I actually drove two 4x4 Cosworths for the roadgoing material as the first car (black, leather interior, CD player, the lot)

By 1992 a number of minor cosmetic changes saw out the Cosworth 4x4. These included replacement alloy wheels, new safety-orientated steering wheel and slight fascia mods.

was stolen on the 1990 RAC Rally! In the light of my comments, it is interesting to note that Ford lopped £6,000 from the list price in 1992 and that under £10,000 bought a good example of less than two years old when this was written.

* * *

RS Ford motoring

In the mid-'70s I wrote a *Motor Sport* feature about a selection of three RS-branded Ford Escorts. All of them — RS1800 (2.0, DOHC, 16V, 120 bhp); RS2000 (2.0 SOHC, 110 bhp) RS Mexico (1.6 litres, SOHC, 95 bhp) — were timed against our then current fifth wheel equipment. The results were unique in that the second generation Mexico was not so tested elsewhere, and all the cars were tested on the same day.

Judging by the widely reprinted use (official and unofficial) of these figures, this group has stood the test of time and fuelled a few saloon bar arguments. For the record, the slowest of that 1976 trio (Mexico) reached 106

Voted the finest driving experience provided with a Ford badge since the GT40, the Sierra Cosworth 4x4 commanded prices over £25,000 in the early '90s. By 1994 you could buy a Cosworth 4x4 for less than half their new cost, although it has to be said that many were initially discounted, particularly when the Escort Cosworth arrived in 1992.

mph, the fastest (RS1800) managed 111 mph, and their 0–60 mph times ranged from 11.1 to 8.6 sec, the fuller torque curve of the 'beak nose' RS2000 allowing that quickest 0–60 mph time of the day.

Fuel consumption figures of the old leaded four star were 27.2 mpg (Mexico), 26.5 mpg (RS1800), and 24.7 mpg (RS2000). A glance at the data panel (page 127) shows that the current Cosworth 4x4 can nearly equal such fuel economy, but on cheaper unleaded grades. Furthermore 15 years of progress delivers an average of 6.5 sec to 60 mph and almost 142 (rather than the claimed 150) mph.

Naturally costs have climbed through the roof. An RS1800 Escort was listed at £2,990.12 in Custom Pack form. Now items such as standard power steering, sunroof, central locking and electrical assistance of side glass and mirrors boost purchase price to roughly 10 times more. The official list price of the RS 4x4 tested was £27,060 plus optional leather at £500 and 'Premium Sound' system, which included a CD player in one car (the first was stolen before figures could be taken).

Recently I had the opportunity of measuring just how far we have come since 1976, spending successive time with a 41,000 mile rear drive Sapphire RS (2.0, DOHC, 16v, 204 bhp), stepping straight into a factory seven-speed rally car (circa 300 bhp, as used to finish seventh on the Monte Carlo rally in the hands of Malcolm Wilson).

A current 4x4 version of the RS 4-dr with the usual 220 bhp was then allotted to me as transport for an Oulton Park racing weekend. A break in which I would conduct a Collins Performance Engineering RS500 3-dr (the biplane homologation version of the Ford Cosworth 2 litre), this particular example was credited as delivering over 500 horsepower to its Bridgestone road tyre-shod rear wheels.

I did not performance test all the vehicles mentioned, but even in wet conditions the RS500 I drove ascended from rest to 100 mph in less than 11 sec. We also attached our electronic Correvit equipment to the standard 4x4 RS in order to establish a benchmark for future work. The results and a specification for that car are appended as guidance to the now accepted norm in performance motoring.

Today the converted RS Cosworth seems just as common in the '90s as the Escort RS did in the '70s, so many may wonder why it is worth increasing the performance of an already seriously rapid motor car.

The factory rally example posed no questions as to the whys and wherefores of its existence. From its Ford design and initial Ferguson manufacture of a seven-speed gearbox, to suspension and braking that share only principles with the production car, it proved an uncompromising and captivating competition car.

Rapid beyond expectation, the factory rally car was demonstrated at the snowy Boreham HQ of Ford Motorsport by the man who had led the Monte Carlo rally in a sister example, François Delecour. The unexpected speed comes from a man determined to upset the established World Championship rallying order (he had not won an event of any status as at this March writing), plus a beautifully modulated horsepower and torque curve, one that seems to spread from 2,000 to 6,500 with equally appealing vigour.

Further escalation in rpm toward the 7,600 rpm electronic limiter is rendered almost pointless by the official power peak at 6,500 rpm and the gentleman's agreement figure of 300 bhp. Maximum torque is reported as 322 lb/ft at 4,250 rpm. Ford sources indicated that 0–60 mph should be covered in 'less than four seconds' and that the Monte Carlo maximum speed was around 135 mph at 7,500 in seventh. A velocity the grinning Northern French *pilote* described as 'happening very often', which gave me pause for thought as a routine task over icy Alpine terrain, in total darkness . . .

We were allowed to drive in what passed for daylight on an exceptionally cold and icy day and then repaid the compliment by allowing Mr Delecour his first RHD miles at the wheel of the rear drive RS Cosworth that *Motor Sport* has operated for several years. Monsieur Delecour spun our vehicle twice — once in fourth gear — and we repaid the compliment at much slower speeds in the factory example.

One did not expect much in common between a works rally car and the showroom brethren in the days of the World Championship-winning (1979) Escort, but the international groupings used today (A and N) only mean that old non-standard attitude exists in Group A. Even then there is a restrictor on turbocharged cars in an effort to ensure some general compliance with a 300 horsepower ceiling.

In Group N far more standard features have to be retained, but the five-speed Ford factory examples that are used for World Championship reconnaissance duties, or in their successful forays within the category for Welshman Gwyndaf Evans, develop some 285 bhp. As such they are not a lot slower in a straight line than the full house Group A machinery: the difference lies in the cornering speeds where the liberal allowance for replacement braking and suspension components allows the Group A vehicle truly gripping cornering abilities.

The seven-speed gearbox of the factory Group A Ford was originally homologated as a six-speed unit plus a 'crawler' L-for-Low initial ratio. Thus the main change pattern of all non-synchromesh ratios two to seven lies in H-pattern swaps, first protected by a collar and closest to the LHD suede wheel rim.

Change quality is outstanding for the rapidity of swaps, but the gate is not quite so neatly defined as that of the six-speed units I have driven from Peugeot (Pikes peak 405), BMW (Prodrive racing M3 saloon) and Toyota (Xtrac of Woking equip the World Championship Celica GT4). There is plenty of transmission whine accompanied by some awesome flamethrowing from the imposing side exhaust, but the Q8-backed factory Ford remained recognizably a Sierra RS Cosworth: rapid, rough, tough and effective.

It was something of a shock to climb out from the security of the 4x4 powerhouse to our old rear drive 4-dr RS. It feels comparatively unstable over snow and had amused all and sundry with its Boreham test track antics over slippery surfaces, apparently with no rear traction at all. Yet it remains a faithful friend that has survived a very tough life with three determined drivers at the helm.

As a contract hire vehicle F332 ODX does not get a lot of favours, but a recent 41,000 mile/£401 service at Hartford Motors in Oxford left it still faster in acceleration than the press fleet 4x4 demonstrator. It is a notable proposition as a second-hand performance per pound buy at current

KEY FEATURES — FORD SIERRA COSWORTH 4X4 RS 4- DOOR

Tax-inclusive price: £27,060 (£27,560 with leather, as tested); two types of in-car entertainment tested were £475 and £710 optional extras.

Body: Steel; 4-dr+ ancillary spoilers and body extensions in plastics and rubber. *Drag factor:* 0.32 Cd.

Engine: Inline Ford Cosworth 4-cyl; 1993 cc (90.8 x 76.95 mm); DOHC; 16-valve alloy cylinder head; 8:1 cr Garrett AiResearch T03B turbocharger and intercooling; Weber-Marelli electronic fuel injection and ignition management. *Power outputs:* 220 bhp @ 6,000 rpm; 214 lb/ft @ 3,500 rpm.

Transmission: Inline engine drives all wheels; permanent 4WD by Ferguson features Ferguson patented Viscous Couplings and central differential with epicyclic gears to split power 34 per cent forward, 66 per cent rear; Ford MT 75 five-speed gearbox. *Ratios:* First, 3.61; second, 2.081; third, 1.36; fourth, 1:00;

Fifth, 0.83; gives 22.24 mph per 1,000 rpm; final drives, 3.62:1.

Running gear: *Suspension* MacPherson strut front suspension with gas damping, coil springs and 30 mm anti-roll bar; independent semi-trailing arm rear suspension, gas filled dampers, separate coil springs; 18 mm anti-roll bar. *Steering:* Power assisted rack and pinion, variable effort, 2.5 turns lock-to-lock. *Brakes:* Ventilated 278 mm/10.94 in front discs; 273 mm/10.75 in solid disc rears. *Wheels and tyres:* Alloy 7 x 15 in and 205/50 VR Bridgestone ER90 test tyres.

£10,000–12,000 prices for F plated examples such as ours.

The H plated Ford demonstrator was similar in all major presentation respects to the rear drive model, but there are some useful details that have changed as Ford have tried to keep the Sierra/Sapphire range in touch with GM Cavalier success. The 1991 boot is now released via an internal pull lever that releases the plastic fuel filler flap when depressed, or the boot when pulled upward; the exhaust has changed from unashamed drainpipe to chromed orifice; and the steering column is adjustable in a vertical plane. The character of the 4x4 version is a lot more restrained than the original hatchback RS Sierra. The heavy but effective 4x4 element ensures that its road manners are a lot tidier even than the comparatively tamed Sapphire rear drive predecessor. Wheelspin becomes almost a memory and power sliding is unlikely to occur, save on the greasiest of roundabouts with the most provocative of drivers.

The MT75 gearbox is the Ford unit that replaced the Borg Warner unit of the rear drive RS types and there are those who like its slick changing habits better than the notchy precision of the American original (which was also found in North American Mustang and Bronco products). I am not a fan of the later MT75 unit, but I would be if they tightened up the long throw shift quality and the 'floppy' nature of the gear lever. The ratios are logically set and allow just about 60 mph in second gear at the harshly attained 6,500 rpm limit.

Driven back to back, the 4x4 model is a lot quieter and smoother than its rear drive forerunner, which can be regarded as a considerable achievement in view of the extra gear sets involved. However, I must stress that these comments do not imply that the Ford has become a naturally smooth performer that belongs automatically in the £25,000 to £30,000 sector of the market.

What the RS Ford Cosworth does in terms of performance and handling/adhesion abilities to provide driver pleasure is unmatched outside the LHD-only Lancia Delta Integrale (or BMW M3, for rear drive fanatics). Yet Ford fit and finish remains too uneven to be credible in the £25,000 plus sector.

For example, the plastics are of markedly varied quality, the sound system looks garish (the radio particularly prone to interference and loss of selected station) and the instrumentation is sparse, ugly and becoming cluttered amongst the speedometer digits.

A simple run up and down our timing strip, using a 4,000 rpm clutch start point, created our performance figures effortlessly. We then left the car on idle for more than a minute and drove away, calculations complete. An enormous cloud of oil smoke apparently announced the mortality of turbocharger or a piston at this point. Our imperturbable companion (the appropriately initialled MPH of sister paper *Motoring News*) said assuredly, 'I had one do that not long ago, it'll be OK in a minute.' So it was, but a litre of oil was required to restore the oil level and we had cause to bless the sturdier and more accessible 1991 dipstick.

Summary

As a long distance companion, one full of entertainment and capable of sustained high speeds, the Ford Sierra 4x4 RS derivative is unmatched at the price. Not only was it proved around our test track, but another example also managed all but one day of the Lombard RAC Rally in our hands, underlining its all-weather capabilities.

The Ford is painfully priced almost adjacent to the (just) sub £30,000 Audi S2 that we tested last month, and that is its only serious flaw: it should be a lot cheaper. Then the obvious mass production flaws (plus rather a lot of panel/paint defects on the second test example) would not be *so* unacceptable.

In other words, it is about time that Ford, whilst waiting for a new generation of bodies and engines for the Sierra, started to price a lot more aggressively. Those RS Escorts (and their Capri 3 litre stablemates) of our introductory paragraphs gave the customer the sort of value for money that made the blue and white oval a worldwide symbol for value for money. The product has advanced by an enormous margin; but the tenfold plus UK pricing policy is too pricey by far. It has taken Ford from its traditional pastures into the executive classes, a category that houses too many conscientious competitors for comfort.

Owner comments

I have kept both types of 4-dr Sierra Cosworth. I also asked for rear drive comment from former colleagues at *Motoring News* and *Motor Sport* to add a little depth, alongside those of company car 4-dr (rear drive) operator, Steve Rockingham. Rockingham kept the best records, so he starts.

'The new price was then slightly beyond my company budget. So I bought a May 1989 registered (F514 SNO) example for £16,500. That was in April 1990, when it had less than 10,000 miles recorded and a healthy dose of Ford Extracover, which was to prove invaluable in two and a half years and nearly 50,000 miles' ownership.

'In addition to the routine servicing, we had the following work completed, usually under that extended warranty:

Claimed performance:
Maximum speed, 150 mph; 0–60 mph, 6.6 sec.

PERFORMANCE HIGHLIGHTS — FORD SAPPHIRE RS

Millbrook Proving Ground test site, *Motor Sport* staff using Correvit electronic measuring gear.

Acceleration (average of two-way best runs):
0–30 mph, 2.2 sec; 0–60 mph, 6.5 sec; 0–100 mph, 16.9 sec; 0–120 mph, 26.8 sec; standing 1/4 mile, 94.4 mph.

Flexibility: 30–50 mph; *Fifth gear*, 6.7 sec.

Maximum speeds: @ 6,500 rpm first, 34 mph; second, 60 mph; third, 91 mph; fourth, 122.5 mph; @ 6,228 rpm over a 2.189 mile bowl, fifth, 139.5 mph; at 6,321 rpm, 141.6 mph peak sustained speed.

Test fuel consumption: Overall, 22.5 mpg; track, 8.7 mpg.

Government mpg figures: Urban, 22.1 mpg; 75 mph, 30.4 mpg; 56 mph, 37.2 mpg.

H335 GRT ('Gertie') was wonderful when she was going. Here 28 years and the Atlantic Ocean separate her from the Falcon V8 I raced in 1992 courtesy of Miller author Mark L. Dees.

23,000 Gears hard to select: new clutch.
30,000 Reverse/1st gear hard to select: box rebuilt.
36,000 Electric fans failed to activate: rectify wiring fault and new head gasket required.
39,000 Half of heated screen fails: screen replaced.
48,000 Would not run below 3000 rpm. Idle speed control valve replaced.'

Steve commented how expensive he found keeping the rear drive Sierra in tyres, but it was driven 'to its full potential'. That meant munching Dunlop D40s 'in as little as 6,000 miles. Even driven gently, 10,000 miles was barely attainable. A change to cheaper Avon CR28 turbospeed certainly helped with wet weather driving. Even with two tyres at most service intervals, the running costs were still considerably less than the Audis and Mercedes on our fleet, and they had a fraction of the Ford's performance,' concluded Steve of F514 SNO's service record.

The snags were well recalled by Rockingham, reminding me just how heavy that Borg Warner box became as the miles rolled by. In fact, when the car was cold, you had no chance of getting reverse to engage cleanly. That meant it was also a heavyweight pain in London traffic, the clutch also much heavier than the current Escort Cosworth and later MT75-equipped Sierra 4x4.

'My' rear drive RS Cosworth, nicknamed Odious after its ODX plate, was inherited at 40,000 miles with a variety of tyres installed and only months to run on a lease deal.

It was immaculate on the outside, but needed about £400 spent at Hartford Motors in Oxford before it would run without a misfire on boost. I took the opportunity to have the boost reset at the warranty maximum, sorted out the tyres and enjoyed the next 5,000 miles or so very much indeed. It was an awesome performer and marvellous fun. Especially when we lent it to Monsieur Delecour at a snowy Boreham Airfield track and forgot to tell him it was rear drive . . .

A brand new 4x4 followed in May 1991, one that cost about £23,000 of a then laughable £27,000 list price that *nobody* would pay in a stable mental condition. The car came from a Suffolk Ford dealer and had full RAC Recovery service plus extended cover, but did not have the leather trim and CD player that had been fitted to the Ford demonstrator that I had originally planned to own (stolen *before* I could confirm the offer!).

H335 GRT ('Gertie') was the worst Ford I have owned in respect of reliability, and the safest I have ever had to drive. In 12 months and 11,523 miles, it went for surgery at Hartford Motors in Oxford three times, each time with the engine failing to run: battery (this 'new' car was over a year old on delivery . . .), alternator, and a striking sensor were the causes.

Gertie was also afflicted by constant oil leaks and the dealer (faced with the car left over on the annual holiday) tried really hard to fix them, including an engine out session with new seals for the front drive shafts. Hartford did manage to stop the rear axle incontinence, but the front always soiled the garage floor.

I won't bore you with the other troubles suffered, as the car limped home from those. I did put on a standard size set of BF Goodrich TA/1 to replace

the original Bridgestone ER90s. The Japanese covers had worn badly on the inner edge of the rear covers (a problem suffered by other cars on the same fleet). I got a puncture that alerted me to their 15,000 mile uneven wear.

The BFGs were tremendous in terms of grip and I cannot commend the Sierra's speedy safety strongly enough, especially with such effective ABS braking from Teves as a back-up.

I hated seeing the Sierra RS Cosworth 4x4 go (July 1993 at 22,895 miles), but it is still in use for that London publishing group. I think it has been much better behaved in its middle age, although an AA engineer did confide that the 4x4 oil leak problem was a common warranty defect.

In my two years and 10 months in two Cosworths I suffered another attempt to steal one. That was the 4x4 from Wycombe Six cinema car park, and the Chubb locks defeated a punch, though the door skin was left with a dent. My unreliable experiences were not typical of other 4x4 Sierra Cosworth users on that fleet, although some had suffered engine trouble following increased power conversions.

Best until last? The Andy Rouse 304-R visited Castle Combe during my test week for the now defunct *Fast Lane* magazine.

Chapter 7

Rally warrior

The 4-dr Cosworth Fords were never intended as competitors, but they were rallied and raced with private and professional vigour.

The first edition of the Sapphire-bodied Sierra RS Cosworth was intended to compete for executive cash rather than dash for competition cash. As is the way for so many good Fords, it was drawn inexorably into the sporting arena.

The rear drive format obviously would do it no favours in rallying's slippery surfaces, so the factory eschewed building and entering such cars initially. Then the competition timing gap between the 3-dr and the 4x4 version of the 4-dr became too onerous, and Borham simply had to back some of their leading teams, or lose any rallying credibility.

Don't forget the 1988 season end had seen Ford Motorsport lose both Carlos Sainz (a Ford discovery who went on to win the 1992 World Championship . . . for Toyota) and Didier Auriol (also uncovered by the John Taylor/Ford Motorsport search across the Mediterranean for a new generation of drivers that shook even the Scandinavian establishment). To

Out on the streets: the rear drive Sierra Cosworth 4-dr was not intended as a competition car, but was widely used, particularly by those seeking a change in outline for sponsorship purposes. This was the Firestone series contender of Falklands hero Simon Weston in pursuit of £200,000 for the Weston Spirit charity, on the streets of Birmingham in August 1989.

retain any kind of presence in international events, Boreham simply had to back the efforts of crews such as the recently rehired 1989 Vauxhall RAC Rally star Malcolm Wilson.

As the factory had no direct plan to race the 4-dr Sierra Cosworth, whether in rear or 4x4 form, it was left to the privateers to continue the legend the 3-dr had established. As you would expect, this was in the more affordable realms of the production classes, although it must be said that there was no European title to compete for, post '88.

These formula are broadly categorized as Group N and national interpretations of the same. Those rules in Britain particularly favour the use of 'road' tyres rather than outright slicks, because the major Championship was sponsored by Uniroyal through much of the '80s. Competitors did not have to use Uniroyal tyres, so many front runners found backing from companies such as Firestone or BF Goodrich.

The road tyre habit in the UK was largely overturned for the '90s when the (initially Esso-backed, later *Breaking the Mould*) National Saloon Car Cup adopted full Group N rules, but Firestone backed a popular series until the close of 1991.

Overseas Group N series tended to stick to FIA Group N and the category was especially strong in Germany, Holland (the premier saloon series of the '90s), Sweden, Belgium (modified rules), France (unrecognizable rules), Spain and Italy.

From 1988 onwards Britain adopted turbo air restrictors, which were aimed at hobbling the Sierras (and latterly the two Nissan Skylines that appeared). Thus the BMW M3s and astonishing Hondas (wet weather wonders) could share the same photo frame.

For the Ford runners 1987/8 was all about the 3-dr Cosworths, and I cannot recall a production based race that they did not win in that period.

The 4-dr Sierra was so adaptable to racing and rally requirements that experienced international competitor (later Motorsport Correspondent of the *Yorkshire Post*) Chris Lord took one out to tackle a bit of both disciplines. Here is Chris, ignoring moorland sheep on the 1989 Autoglass Tour of Britain. They finished seventh and Chris got the 'Man of the Event' award for being a Yorkshireman.

The Ford winners of the period were a varied bunch: DJ Mike Smith enjoyed initial success in a very powerful Stuart McCrudden entry for Pirelli; former hot-rodder Sean Brown took a Uniroyal title in 1987 in his Castrol-liveried 3-dr, as did Kieth Odor in 1989, Jerry Mahony made his name in the category with a Roger Dowson example for Firestone, as did 1988 Uniroyal title winner Robb Gravett, of whom we hear a lot more in an RS500 connection.

Such Sierra Cosworth domination was only threatened at the Willhire 24 and 25-hour (1989 anniversary only) events, when the M3 BMWs, Mercedes 2.5–16 and similarly durable Golfs came into the picture. That was usually after 10 hours' racing or so, when the Sierra hordes ran into trouble (often wheel bearings, damaged discs/pads or head gaskets that had sucked too much boost, too long).

But the fleet Fords with the hobbled turbo motors still racked up the long distance wins, the more sensible preparation companies holding them down to 265 bhp on a conservative 1 bar boost. For shorter races 285 horsepower and more was easily available in the 1.2–1.5 twilight zone that threatened turbo life in air restrictor trim. I know, because I spent much of 1988 watching high boost turbos expire in the long distance (1-hour to 24-hour) 3-dr I shared with '90s Nissan star Kieth Odor.

For 1989 the big question amongst the Ford runners was weather to opt for the rear drive charms of the 4-dr (Sapphire style) Cosworth body, or stay with the original 3-dr. That winter I borrowed a 4-dr from SVE and Janspeed pitted it against a 3-dr, both running BF Goodrich R1s and the same turbo boost, but otherwise in road trim for a dry day at glorious Goodwood.

Kieth Odor and 1969 British Champion Alec Poole did the back-to-back driving and there seemed to be little (tenths either way) as the drivers swapped mounts. I was also able to drive both cars back to back and felt that the 4-dr was the tidier of the two under pressure, but the 3-dr was notably more stable as speed rose beyond 70–80 mph.

For 1989 Firestone front runner Mark Hales took the sponsored plunge and switched to a 4-dr, a decision he found challenging at times. Nevertheless bearded Mark of *Fast Lane* fame (the 1993 TVR Tuscan Champion), tussled with Odor's Janspeed 3-dr all season, scooped the Firestone title for the home team and scored what was arguably the 4-dr's finest victory.

The unlikely scene was the bleak Snetterton circuit in Norfolk, which annually transforms into a holiday funfair site and host for long-distance racers, eager to take on the only day and night race in Britain. In 1989, the June event was an elongated 25-hour one, marking sponsor Willhire's anniversary in business. Enlisting ex-Abba drummer Slim Borgudd's professional driving skills, Hales battled with Odor/Barrie Williams through much of the misty night (so misty they had the pace car out for $1^1/2$ hours) and came away with a unique victory.

The winning Dowson Sierra Cosworth 4-dr covered nearly 2,000 miles in the 24-hours (1,025 laps; 1,964.93 miles) at an average 78.54 mph, beating the accident-delayed Janspeed 3-dr by three laps. Behind were Mercedes, BMWs and a flock of other Sierras, ahead was a reputation for reliable speed at affordable prices that Ford emphasized in national advertising.

The rear driver RS 4-dr went as well on international rallies as you would expect on tarmac (for instance, Wilson was second on the 1990 Circuit of Ireland), but it was simply a holding operation until the 4x4 could be homologated.

Ford backing was primarily confined to Group N until early 1990 when Jimmy McRae's son Colin, paired with Derek Ringer, snatched outright victory on the opening National Championship round (The Cartel International). Driving an otherwise conventional Sierra RS in the 1,168 kg Group A Sapphire RS body, the 22-year-old had the honour of notching up the first British home international win for the Sapphire in rear drive form. On the same event Gwyndaf Evans conducted a 265 bhp Group N equivalent to sixth overall and an easy class victory, so the Sapphire's British forest potential had been proven long before the 4x4 could be homologated.

One that got away from Ford: Colin McRae was the youngest Briton to win an international (1990 Cartel), but Colin's greatest triumphs were saved for Prodrive Subaru.

Ford 4x4 Sierra Rally plan

Ford lifted the curtain on their rallying plans for the Sierra on the occasion of the Spanish press launch for the latest Cosworth RS 4x4 road car. We only had to wait about a month before experiencing the 'real' Group A and N rally machines at the Ford Motorsport HQ, Boreham. Thus we were allowed

Serious stuff: Boreham gets the 4-dr Sierra message in the opening months of 1990, largely a development year for the 4x4 with a few stop gap appearances for the rear drive 4-dr.

Ford exploited the no-homologation requirement of the Spanish rally series to slip an early victory for the Sierra 4x4. Mia Bardolet/José Maria Ferrer took the honours on the 24 March 1990 Alicante Rally.

to ride and drive competition versions of cars that were not quite in the showrooms.

Biggest threat to the progamme had been an industrial action by British electricians. That had a limited knock-on production effect at Genk, Belgium. This unrest could have prevented production of the necessary 5,000 Cosworths needed for 1 August 1990 homologation and the planned international debut in that month's 1,000 Lakes Rally.

Ford corporate colours, augmented by Q8 petroleum sponsorship, were out to build on the company's last Boreham-built World Championship win. That was the 1988 Tour de Corse victory scored by Didier Auriol/Bernard Occelli.

To usher in the new era in Ford Motorsport a lot of blue and white

corporate paint was splashed over the utility architecture of the Essex airfield, whilst the sporting stores section was moved in during 1989.

The usual quick 2.95 mile perimeter track framed the airfield, but it was the infield section that the rally engineers and 1973 European Rallycross Champion John Taylor so thoroughly redeveloped to push embryo rally cars to the limit, and check out each works car before it flew the nest.

The team for 1990 was normally reported around drivers Franco Cunico from Italy, a Group N champion, Cumbria's Malcom Wilson, Group N ace Gwyndaf Evans, and Pentti Airikkala, 1989 RAC Rally winner (for Mitsubishi). The programme was augmented with many more British appearances for the British-based Finn.

On 25 March 1990 Jose Maria Bardolet took the Marlboro-liveried Mike Taylor Developments Sierra RS Cosworth 4x4 to its first outright victory. Run in non-homologated Group A engine trim (40 mm turbo restrictor) and a Group N rolling chassis, it defeated a 280 bhp Citroen special and outlasted the official Volkswagen Group A G60 Golf 4x4. The VW had retired on the first stage, displaying some promise.

Then Ford Motorsport were also in the middle of an ambitious year-long session of World Championship event tests in which they assessed qualifying terrain in conditions as close to those expected as possible. In the early '80s a works team would do this by swinging an invitation as a course 00 car on a major event, comparing opening times with those of actual competitors. Today the international organizing body has banned such a front line reconnaissance (which benefited Audi in particular with the Quattro) and Ford used well-known Monte Carlo and Portuguese stages in similar weather conditions.

Ford Motorsport had the backing of 10 new Iveco Ford large support vans (intelligently doubling as tyre trucks) and up to 30 personnel marshalled by Peter Ashcroft and the gathering number of subcontractors who augmented the works efforts into the '90s.

The 4x4 Sapphires were progressed for several years, starting from the 3-dr base. When I drove the cars in 1990, John Wheeler was away engineering at SVE for the road version of Escort RS Cosworth.

John Wheeler's practical and theoretical chassis engineering skills were continued at Boreham by Philip Dunabin. It was then too tough a task to make a car to beat the multiplying Japanese and the entrenched Italian Lancia team with less than full-time commitment. Lancia were the Liverpool of World Championship Rallying. The Turin Delta team had then yet to lose a world title since the series went over to Group A in 1987.

The specification of the World Championship Group A Sierra 4x4 was heading steadily beneath the 1,200 kg barrier. A considerable achievement for a middle weight 4-dr with a bulky 4x4 transmission that was dubbed a turbo taxi cab by unkind commentators.

We also knew that the latest version of the effective 1993 cc DOHC 16V turbo (with replacement intercooler and considerable durability enhancements) was not going to yield less than 300 bhp in Group. 'More like 340 horsepower' was an insider estimate, but it was the massive torque that is even more important, and a lot less controversial.

As at February 1990, Ford Motorsport at Boreham had constructed three

---

WORLD CHAMPIONSHIP RALLY RECORD, SIERRA RS COSWORTH 4X4 (HOMOLOGATED AUG 1 1990)

1000 Lakes, Finland
DNF Franco Cunico, accident
DNF Malcolm Wilson, gearbox
DNF Pentti Airikkala, gearbox

Sanremo, Italy
11th Pentti Airikkala
DNF Franco Cunico
DNF Malcolm Wilson, accident but set five fastest stage times

RAC Rally, UK
9th Alex Fiorio (Italy)
DNF Malcolm Wilson, engine and crash
11th Gwyndaf Evans

1991

Monte Carlo, Monaco
3rd François Delecour
7th Malcolm Wilson
10th Alex Fiorio

Portugal
DNF Malcolm Wilson, crash
DNF Alex Fiorio, crash!
DNF François Delecour, crash!

Tour de Corse, Corsica
3rd Franco Cunico
5th Malcolm Wilson
DNF François Delecour, rear diff

Catalunya, Spain
3rd François Delecour
4th Mia Bardolet

Acropolis, Greece
DNF All three works entries for Delecour, Fiorio and Wilson had mechanical failures.

Sanremo, Italy
4th François Delecour
9th Alex Fiorio
10th Malcolm Wilson

RAC Rally, UK
6th François Delecour
DNF Malcolm Wilson, centre diff
DNF Gwyndaf Evans, crashed

In the 1990 factory engine bays, Mountune replaced Terry Hoyle. This is the second prototype works 4x4, still with a five-speed gearbox.

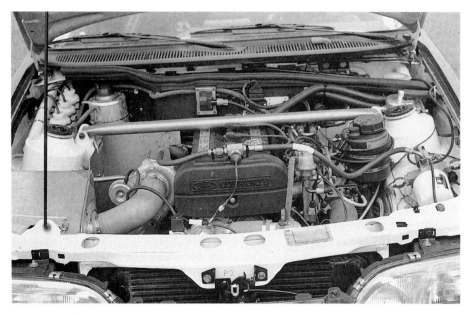

Opposite Interesting cutaway of the factory Ford Sierra prototype in 1990 displays the increasing complexity of roll cages and the usual Sierra rear end modification of 'coil over' spring damper units, but retains the uprated MT75 five-speed gearbox. Such a box was homologated for international Group A use in the Sierra, but not for the Group A competition Escort, so you were committed to the deployment of an expensive seven-speed at international events.

4x4 Group A test cars, the original February 1989 machine a converted 3-dr hatchback. A show car on Cologne plates was at the press launch badged 'Cosworth 4x4' and constructed by Gordon Spooner. For the press launch at Boreham in March 1990 two Group A cars and a brand new Group N machine — which had that weekend been debuted by Gwyndaf Evans/Howard Davies — were at a windy but dry Boreham.

Our boxed statistics give you a good idea of the 'potent mix' Ford operated initially. There are some passing references to cover the Group N machine in brackets, and note that the seven-speed gearbox was ready for 1 August 1990 to replace the five-speed MT75 uprates mentioned in this panel.

The Ford 4x4 had shown a modest 65 kg weight gain in competition trim over the 2WD 3-dr. 'It is a little bigger and heavier than the rallying ideal,' reported one engineer, but the cars shown to the media at Boreham were part of a programme designed to realize 1,150 kg. Not bad, but far from the 'homologated class minimum of 1,100 kg'.

Our engineering contact added, 'The aerodynamics at high speed need some further work compared to the 3-dr, but we are genuinely pleased with the car which is better not just on the loose but also for tarmac. He continued, 'The 4WD element gives the tyres a much easier time apportioning 299.9 bhp and some extra torque per wheel,' concluded our expert witness at this early stage of the factory 4x4 Sierra's development.

The biggest technical talking point during 1990 was the arrival of the seven-speed gearbox, one always intended for use with semi-automatic electronics. However, the money and development durability for that seven-speeder with planned steering wheel shift, or a sequential automated pattern, had not been forthcoming even when the Escort arrived. Such systems were extensively re-evaluated once more, before Delecour won the 1994 Monte Carlo Rallye with a conventional manual shift retained for the septet of ratios, more of which in a later chapter.

Ford started serious work on their seven speeds in December 1989. The non-synchromesh design was coded MS90. The revolutionary gearbox was fathered by Ford Motorsport engineers John Wheeler and Philip Dunabin and has proved good enough to develop further into the mid-'90s.

The initial manufacturing work was assigned to Ferguson Developments outside Coventry, but following the Finnish debut failure of teeth upon the input gears other subcontractors were employed, including Staffs Gears. When I had to write a preview of the 1993 RAC Rally for *Motoring News* a tour of FFD at Coventry showed FFD had far increased responsibilities for Ford factory car transmission supply, including assembling complete 4x4 layouts (front box to the tips of the four driveshafts).

The basic MS90 layout was that of a three-shaft gearbox, two of the four selector forks placed on the lay shaft. This further speeded the change action of the straight cut gears, which suffer no synchromesh hindrance.

Further features included a torque capacity of 500 Nm, rather than 360 Nm of a standard Ford MT75 five-speed. The Ford seven-speed also allowed quick change mechanisms to reduce complete gearbox replacement times to 10 minutes or less. It has such close ratios beyond the 'crawler' first gear that no more than 1,350 rpm is currently found between any ratio shift in the second to seventh plane.

Homologated as a six-speed unit plus an L-branded 'crawler' gear, the MS90 had the following internal ratios, the complete unit served by a separate oil reservoir:

L (first)	2.071	Fourth	0.866
First	1.529	Fifth	0.750
Second	1.263	Sixth	0.647
Third	1.037	Reverse	2.143

A new set of ratios, with the East African Safari Rally in mind, was sent for international recognition with far wider ratios. Here the first gear really was for crawling out of mud holes, seventh a motorway top, the complete set

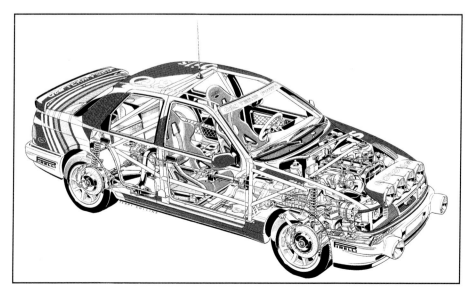

ORIGINAL 1990 GROUP A SPECIFICATION (GROUP N IN BRACKETS)

Motor: Cosworth Ford uprated RS500 production iron block; cast alloy sump pan; replacement inlet and exhaust manifolding; Garret AiResearch T3 and enlarged production intercooler; FISA mandatory 40 mm air restrictor and associated electronic management; 150 amp alternator; increased capacity water radiator and pump; developed in association with Terry Hoyle Ltd (Mountune).

Motor statistics; Inline 4-cyl, 1993 cc (90.8 x 76.95 mm); cast alloy head has 16V DOHC; reduced Group A compression 7.2:1 (8:1 production). *Ford-quoted Group A Power*: 295 bhp at 6,250 rpm (250 @ 6,250 rpm); 360 Nm (265 lb/ft) @ 4,500 rpm (300 Nm @ 4,000).

Body: 4-dr Sapphire with production RS uprates for 1990 plus seam welding; integrated steel roll cage welded into place; Kevlar sump; rear axle guards.

Minimum weight: 1,140 kg dry weight (1,210 kg dry weight).

Transmission: Replacement Ford Motorsport parts include MT75 competition gears (close ratios listed below) with direct fifth replacing production OD ratio; short gear shift with transfer box; front and rear drive shafts; 7.5 in front axle (and associated large sump pan) plus similar size rear replaced; limited slip devices engineered front, centre and rear; listed as Viscous Couplings but not available to privateers 'in 1991. Multiplate competition clutch; *Ratios*: first, 2.649 (3.608); second, 1.909 (2,082); third, 1.515 (1.363); fourth, 1.227 (1.00); fifth, 1.00 (0.829); final drive, Group A replacement of transfer and gearbox, plus rear axle ratios (4.44:1) to provide the equivalent of 5.36:1 on 'a conventional road car' when on 16 in diameter wheels and high profile tyres, compared to standard (Group N) 3.62:1; front and rear differential oil coolers.

Wheels: Ford Motorsport/ Speedline 16 in diameter: 6 in wide rims for snow; 8 in for gravel; 8.5 in for tarmac (6 in snow and gravel, 7 in tarmac).

Brakes: Options will include 315 x 32 mm fronts and rear 285 x 28 mm vented discs with four-piston callipers and adjustable F-R bias.

Steering: Power assisted rack and pinion; 12:1 high ratio rack for 2.4 turns lock to lock.

Pentti Airikkala (1989 RAC Rally winner for Mitsubishi) tests the Ford-FFD MS90 seven-speed gearbox on the 1990 Scottish Rally. Despite such high speed trials, the gearbox septet gave trouble when it made its World Rally Championship debut on that year's 1,000 Lakes in Finland.

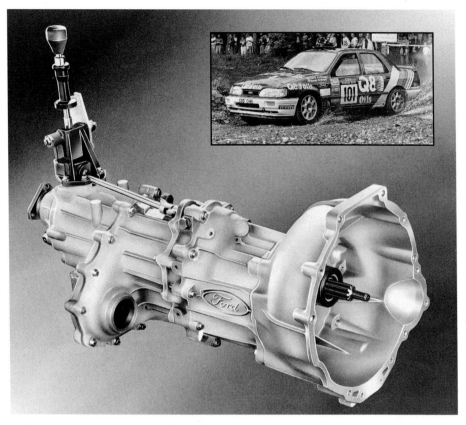

taking advantage of engine flexibility, boosting maximum speed and reducing the constant need for gear changing.

The Sapphire 4x4 RS Cosworth had featured in five World Championship rallies since its August 1990 debut on the Finnish 1,000 Lakes before I caught up with it again in February 1991. It had not been a particularly promising start. The seven-gear debutante drooped under pressure and forced all the works entries into retirement, leading to the rethink mentioned earlier.

Next came Lancia home ground and the Sanremo marked the dawn of serious speed from the Essex *équipe*: fastest test times were recorded by both Pentti Airikkala and Malcolm Wilson. Unfortunately they continued to be dogged by misfortunes and only Airikkala finished (twelfth), and that was after a fire had disrupted that Ford attack.

The Lombard RAC Rally was a triumph for Gwyndaf Evans in the five-speed Group N Sapphire. Both Airikkala and Wilson crashed out, whilst Alessandro Cesare Fiorio (son of then Ferrari GP team manager) looked to be struggling over oozing mud and the 124 mph straights, finishing ninth. A RED-prepared Sapphire for subsequent Subaru star Colin McRae was literally battered to the outline of 'a shed' in a spectacularly hard-fought sixth overall.

The 1991 Monte Carlo Rallye third place — which should have been a win — yielded the best post-'60s result Ford had then enjoyed since 1979 (when an Escort was an equally unlucky second). The only compensations were a final third place for Delecour/Pauwels and seventh place finishes for

Malcolm Wilson and a tenth for Fiorio.

That 1991 Sapphire rear suspension failure — identified as a bearing housing inner mounting bracket (Motorsport order code: 9093653) — robbed Delecour and Ford of victory against all the Toyota and Lancia establishment odds.

Portugal was not so kind in 1991, all three factory Fords crashing out of the running. But once again Delecour was battling with the front runners, underlining the world class of the Cosworth 4x4 in competition trim.

The company never challenged so effectively for the Monte victory again in the 4-dr Cosworth, although Delecour did lead briefly in 1992. It took the Escort finally to bring an overdue '90s win in the world's most famous motor rally.

Ford's Monte Army

For the 1992 Monte Ford dressed in corporate blue and white, some 85 personnel in total. They were there to serve two Sierra Cosworths, one occupied by the French crew of François Delecour (29) and co-driver Daniel Grataloup (27), and the other by Italian World Championship multiple winners, Miki Biasion (34) and his abnormally talented co-driver, Tiziano Siviero (also 34).

Siviero is unusually versatile, speaking on behalf of Biasion for the majority of interviews, picking tyres for the special tests and often supplying the driver feedback to describe car handling to the engineers.

The 1988/9 World titles achieved by the pairing for Lancia explain why I have good reason to believe that Ford paid $5 million over three years to retain their services. Compare this with 1991 World Champion Spaniard Carlos Sainz. The former Ford driver had an annual retainer of $3 million, of

Spirit of Monte Carlo. François Delecour/Daniel Grataloup urge their troublesome Ford to greater things on the 1992 event, when the 4-dr Ford was not consistently competitive.

No Brits required. The Ford line up for the 1992 Monte Carlo Sierra squad, two Italians and a brace of Frenchmen.

which he lost up to 25 per cent in paying his co-driver, a normal procedure in negotiating WRC crew fees for 1992.

Ford forces drove 48 assorted vehicles, and I mean 'assorted'. Ford rolled forward on wheels that varied from a Cargo 3224 with semi-trailer to Sierra Estates and a Renault Master that had been rented. Also on hand were Ford USA Mavericks, a Volvo truck and six Sierra Cosworth 4x4s in varying states of rally preparation to serve the ice note crews supervised by '60s Monte winning co-driver Terry Harryman.

There were just two factory Group A Cosworth Sierras with the personal registrations, A1 FMC (Biasion) and A9 FMC (Delecour), each car costing more than £150,000 to construct.

Each factory rally car was hand-built at Boreham, drawing heavily on the work of outside specialists. Just the parts to build such a Championship contender amounted to more than £68,500. A Sierra Cosworth that weighed approximately 1,190 kg (2,618 lb) was truly hand-built.

Official power quotes for the Mountune of Maldon-engineered Group A competition engine were the same horsepower (295) as Lancia, supported by 360Nm/260 lb/ft of torque. Even with the 1992 introduction of a 38 mm air restrictor on the turbocharger inlet tract, these are conservative figures.

The result?

On roads little broader than the Sierra itself, with drops up to 3,000 feet, Delecour reached up to 127.3 mph, flat in seventh, between the rock faces.

Sierra stage times were much the same with alternative gear ratios which allow up to 139.7 mph in top. The ability to zap to 60 mph in under 4 sec, and leap from 0–100 mph in under 10 sec, is emphasized with the lower top speed.

I was briefed about the 1992 Ford presence in Monaco by PR man Barry Reynolds and the usual 'Rally Bible', a fat Service Schedule compiled under the control of Boreham coordinator Jim (yes *that* Jim) Porter and the on-the-spot recce of Trevor Godden. For the event Godden would control three-channel communications from a Golden Eagle aeroplane.

A mountain of paper from Ford, the organizers, Michelin, Mobil 1 and Autoglass endeavoured to ensure we missed nothing. It took them three sheets to describe some of the key personnel involved from the new Director of European Motorsports Colin Dobinson, to Tyre Coordinator John Millington. Now contracted to Michelin, the Ford factory and their crews had more than 2,000 tyres at their disposal in 12 distinct types.

As for the old Escorts, it took fully six weeks to fabricate and hand assemble such a factory Sapphire contender. Unlike the winning old days most of the heavy hardware work — engine modification, body preparation — was the responsibility of outside subcontractors. The exception was the transmission which was designed in-house, manufactured outside and assembled by former Boreham employee Terry Samuells within a small department established at the revitalized Boreham workshops for the Sierra. Things changed again in the Escort Cosworth era.

A triple Viscous Coupling 4WD transmission (that means front differential as well) with the hardware set to give a basic 50–50 power split was employed in 1991. All three works cars had the now reliable seven-speed transmission, 16 in diameter wheels (changed for 6J x 15 in during my test at Boreham,

together with smaller cross-drilled disc brakes for snow work) and newly homologated, quadruple, Hella headlamps.

There were virtually two pages of alternative Group A competition brake sets listed. I started the test with the 330 mm front discs and 285 mm rears, those fronts as big as many road car wheels, measuring almost exactly 13 in in diameter!

The suspension was still based on MacPherson struts and trailing arms, but the latter were expensively cast in magnesium and redeveloped extensively during the Sierra's World Rally Championship life. The front suspension was located by a trailing link (homologated as a compression strut) back to the underbody, one that spreads the loads from the replacement single track control arm.

Monte Carlo 4-dr gallery: here we see just some of the resources Ford devoted to their assault on the 1992 edition of the world's most famous rally. It would be another two years before Ford and Cosworth grasped that victory with the Escort . . .

COLIN DOBINSON, DIRECTOR OF MILLIONS . . .

Reliable estimates put Ford of Europe annual expenditure upon tackling World Championship rallying at $11 to $12 million a year in 1991/2. I am further unofficially told that the company provided nearly $10 million of that operational budget. The extra was accounted for by Mobil 1, with Auto/Carglass scheduled to add less than $1 million when the tough talking was complete. The responsibility for ensuring those funds are effectively spent passed to the subject of this interview, Colin Dobinson, who had been at Ford for 26 years in January 1992.

Fresh from the legendary war zone that is Ford marketing, Colin Dobinson (47) faced his first event as Ford European Director of Motorsports on the 1992 Monte. A Ford employee 'straight from school', the bespectacled Dobinson is married and has two offspring, who are now in their twenties.

He freely admitted to no more previous rally experience than club rallying a Sprite in the '60s, and to being 'amazed at the complexity of World Championship rallying. It's one helluva shock, particularly the immense detail planning and the use of aircraft overhead to co-ordinate the army on the ground.'

Ford insiders say that 'Dobbo' Dobinson's proven ability to acquire relevant data quickly, and to manage up to 40 personnel effectively, will make a major impact in a short time.

Colin Dobinson treats suggestions that he worked in Ford's 'spy' department as irrelevant, but insiders say that his ability to acquire data about Ford's business rivals was taken into account in his appointment.

Both front and rear factory roll bars featured easy adjustment of preload to fine tune handling. Ford Motorsport did shift main suspension mounting points, albeit within the restrictions of plus or minus 20 mm in FISA ruling.

Mountune performance

The magnificent engine was valued from £7,500 upwards later in 1991. It was built by Maldon-based Mountune in succession to the previous Terry Hoyle link. Headed by David Mountain this concern supplied Robb Gravett with more than 560 bhp to win the 1990 British Touring Car Championship in the Evolution RS500 Sierra. In rallying the rules are far tighter and you cannot use the Evolution eight-injector RS500 layout, or the turbocharger fit for a truck! The official Ford quote was circa 295 bhp at 6,500 rpm, but I believe there was over 350 bhp present.

This was developed at 1.56 bar/22.2 psi boost and also provided up to 316 lb/ft of torque at 4,000 rpm. The highest torque reading then reached in the experimental units for the Escort Cosworth was circa 400 Nm, and such figures are common in the '90s, further motor development balanced by FIA mandatory turbo restrictors.

Racing onward

As noted elsewhere, the 3-dr went on to win again as a racer in the '90s; Andy Middlehurst took the 1990 Firestone title in the historic Dowson example. But when 3-dr homologation ran out at the end of 1992, the 4-dr was more than capable of exceeding its achievements, especially in wet races, because it had the 4x4 element.

However, the move to National Group N with slicks in 1990 Britain was not in Ford's favour, because Janspeed of Salisbury hurled a Nissan Skyline GT-R into the fray for the founder's son, Kieth Odor, and he won the first such title hunt. Matthew Neal attempted to repeat the feat the following season, but the battles were so intense (the Skyline clipped back on boost even harder than the Fords, but considerably heavier in this guise) that nobody was going to win the national title from the big class.

Thus the Sierra Cosworth RS 4x4 became the winning choice in 1992, but it was no longer a 24-hour winner, the BMWs just too agile and durable to beat as less ambitious Ford teams took up the challenge than those of the late '80s. For 1993 it was the Escort Cosworth's turn to star in proddy events, but Frank Greenway put up a committed assault on their supremacy with a Sierra 4x4 that either crashed or placed on the podium: a brave effort to close our account of the Sierra 4-dr's Group N-related track record.

There was an unhappier tale to tell when the 4-dr was pressed into 1991 British Touring Car Championship service. Stripped of its turbo, the £150,000 project Sierra (based on the 4x4 outline for a reported 6 kg downforce at the rear wing) was sponsored by Shell and Motorcraft for 1990 RS500 Champion Robb Gravett to conduct in rear drive trim.

The £20,000 motor was by Mountune, the normally aspirated version of the YBB family never able to perform in the same 270 bhp league as the BMW M3, mostly because it was never designed with the turbo-less competition purpose in mind, although Cosworth have plenty of experience of the motor in non-turbo competition format for the (mainly) American market using a variety of fuels.

The Sapphire's 1991 season was a disaster, initially because the car was fundamentally unstable in the chassis department (the gearbox was 6 in in front of the rear drive differential!), spinning more times than the proverbial top. However, after Trakstar had put in a monster effort and dispensed with the services of the original racing Sapphire designer, they did make some sort of sense of the car, managing a fine second overall at one notable Brands Hatch outing to establish their best (non-typical) result of the year.

Robb Gravett was hired as a professional by Peugeot for the ensuing seasons of monster BTCC popularity, the Thames Valley ace dropped abruptly in for 1994.

Meanwhile, Ford lost any interest in making the Sierra competitive for the TV arena, preferring to hold off until Mondeo was ready for a 1993 public debut — a dramatic tale we tell in our last chapter.

The way we were . . .

The works Sierra RS Sapphire Cosworth 4x4 never did allow François Delecour, or anyone else, an outright World Rally Championship victory, but I thought this piece, based on material that appeared in *Performance Ford* and *Autocar & Motor* in 1991, worth preserving for the flavour of François as he first arrived in the UK.

During 1991 his co-driver became Daniel Grataloup and for 1993 the car transformed into the sensational Escort Cosworth. It was this combination of car and co-driver that won the Portuguese, Corsican and Catalunya World Championship rallies in 1993. Their winning ways continued in 1994 with the 'Big One', winning Monte Carlo at Delecour's fourth attempt.

* * *

Mixed doubles

François Delecour is only 29 and has never won a rally in his life, yet he led World Champion Carlos Sainz by 41 sec going into the final test of the 1991 Monte. He was then robbed of rightful victory by *that* rear suspension camber adjustment housing failure.

To prove it had all been no fluke, Delecour put in a similarly storming performance on the rain-lashed and sometimes snowy roads of Portugal. François held second place, 46 sec adrift of Armin Schwarz (factory Toyota Celica GT4) when he crashed heavily. The Ford had covered 11 of 38 competitive stages. His leg was subsequently X-rayed but the French crew escaped without serious injury.

Since he was a teenager there have been two major loves in François Delecour's life: driving at impossible speeds on impossibly slippery surfaces, and an equal passion for partner Ann Chantal Pauwels. Delecour recalls with a grin that the seven-year affair with the lady who flies helicopters whenever she becomes bored with rallying is now ended; victims of living and rallying together.

Yet with Chantal of the same home village in the capacious Sapphire cockpit, a calm combination of calculated aggression and startling speed is

François Delecour was the driving force behind Ford's return to World Championship contention.

created between male and female, one that 1990 World Champion Carlos Sainz and his Toyota Celica could not match.

What fired the Delecour rallying ambition?

Certainly not his Father: 'He don't like this sport very much, all the time he is wondering why I do not race Formula 1,' observes Delecour dryly. Even though his brother was killed in a car accident, Delecour's mother let her 14-year-old son drive her car from Paris to Lyon.

'At night I would steal out with the car keys and try to find some ice or snow to drive . . . always I love the snow driving better than tarmac,' states the literally blue-eyed newcomer merrily.

Delecour's path up through French rallying could be traced by the machinery he drove to reach the limelight. His first mount was an Autobianchi A112, the second a Peugeot 104ZS, and Peugeot Talbot completed his ascent with 205 and 309 GTI derivatives. His sole rear drive mount was a BMW M3, but his best result prior to Ford was ninth overall in 1990 with the Pug 309, beating the Mitsubishi of Ari Vatanen.

That feat impressed former Ford Escort World Rally Champion Vatanen, who passed on the good word to Ford Motorsport director Peter Ashcroft. Both Delecour and Ashcroft were slightly surprised to be talking to each other, sight unseen.

Yet the Lancastrian Ford boss took the big chance and put Delecour out alongside two other team cars for the 1991 Monte. The rest, as all the best hacks say, is history.

* * *

Here is how I recalled driving the factory 4-dr Ford for *Autocar & Motor* in the winter of 1991. My thanks to the editor for permission to reprint the iciest track test I can ever recall. I should point out that this is the longer original text and is written in original 'WaltonSpeak', not as skilfully translated by A&M sub-editors.

* * *

Seventh heaven?
Courtesy of Cosworth, Ford have the most powerful and flexible of current World Rally Championship engines. So why mate it to a seven-speed gearbox? Jeremy Walton drives with the team that so nearly won the Monte Carlo rallye.

Ford at Boreham looked like a set from *Scott of the Antarctic*. It was time for us to drive one of their Monte Carlo team Sapphire 4x4 RS types and meet François Delecour, the man who led the best in the world and so nearly scored a sensational debut win.

Despite swirling snow, the former aerodrome was a warm place to be. Now that the Ford team know they have a truly world class car and driver, there is a cheerful determination about the workshops that has not been seen since the Escort won the 1979 World Championship.

The Sapphire 4x4 RS Cosworth has tackled four World Championship rallies since its August 1990 debut on the Finnish 1,000 Lakes. It was not an auspicious premiere, the septuple gear ratios disgracing themselves and forcing all the works entries into retirement, but that has now been amended.

A winning pace was not maintained until the 1991 Monte Carlo Rallye yielded the best result Ford has enjoyed since an Escort finished second in 1979. The 1991 heartbreak was a rear suspension failure (bearing housing, at the inner mounting bracket) that robbed Delecour and Ford of victory. The breakage left the bitter-sweet memory of a final third place, one that was backed by seventh place factory finish for Malcolm Wilson and tenth for Alessandro Fiorio.

Back at Boreham, Delecour's demonstration of Cosworth Ford prowess was as memorable on the outside as sitting alongside the changing face of World Championship Rallying. Spectating, the Cosworth looks like a demented and inflated toy stunt car. It spills flame at frequent gear changes, jinking through the artificial obstacles of the Boreham track with astounding speed.

Ford insiders estimate that 0–60 mph should occupy less than 4 sec, the official maximum at 7,500 rpm in seventh a quoted 134 mph, a speed Delecour reached regularly over dark and icy Alpine passes.

Merely watching the Q8-coloured Ford buck its flighty path across the bleak backdrop allows an appreciation of the engineering skills that make this the first £100,000 plus Ford Sapphire we have assessed. That estimated replacement cost sounds almost reasonable as you learn that the seven-speed gearbox accounts for about a quarter of the total value, recalling that it takes six weeks to hand assemble a works Ford.

Every major item is the subject of at least major modification. Former Ford employee Gordon Spooner crafted the body and its integral alloy roll cage. The welded cage not only serves the obvious safety purpose, but also strengthens the body considerably by absorbing many of the incoming suspension loads via front and rear suspension mounting points. Kerb weight is not that different to the showroom car at 1,205 kg, but the uprated engine will allow more than 270 bhp per unladen ton.

Ford Motorsport totally replace suspension, steering, and braking and

February 1991 at Boreham Airfield and the press were allowed out in these conditions to drive or be a passenger in the seven-speeders that so nearly scooped Monte Carlo in January.

implant a triple Viscous Coupling 4WD transmission. The suspension is still based on MacPherson struts and trailing arms, but the latter are expensively wrought in magnesium and there are almost two pages of alternative brake sets listed. These reach beyond the diameter of many road car wheels, the largest option listed at 14 in diameter and 1.25 in thick. Even then, Ford Motorsport engineers may add the refinement of water cooling to the giant AP Racing callipers. The magnificent engine (less than £8,000) was built by Maldon-based Mountune. Headed by David Mountain, this concern also supplied Robb Gravett with up to 580 bhp to win the 1990 British Touring Car Championship in an evolution RS500 Sierra.

As a factory Ford passenger, the impression of inflated slot racing speed is reinforced by blurred vision and the forces on your body. However, the sound-track is purely mechanical; whinging gear teeth and forceful engine are joined by pungent exhaust fumes.

The first driving task is to acquaint yourself with the reverse collar protected shift pattern. You have to lift the collar to obtain clonky access to first on this non-synchromesh box. The change pattern on Malcolm Wilson's Monte machine was hidden by Ford at Boreham humour: a four-speed 'repmobile' gear lever knob, dimpled in the cheapest of plastics, topped a gearbox reputed to be worth almost as much as a complete Sapphire RS road car: £25,000.

The gear double H-change pattern is as you would expect, laid out as follows:

R	2	4	6
1	3	5	7

The collar makes mountain pass storming slightly slower in the Ford than for a Toyota or Lancia, for when first gear is required it takes longer to select on the Ford. Indeed Delecour reckoned that this feature — and the Ford's understeer reluctance to negotiate truly tight hairpins — had cost some 3 sec versus the World Champion's Toyota on the final *Col du Turini* ascent.

François Delecour left the fixed Recaro within intimate proximity of the three-spoke suede steering wheel rim, and we also had to sort out the right small black button to press and activate the Championship contender. You have to concentrate fairly hard not to stall against the sharp action of the twin plate clutch, but the engine electronically compensates for a stranger and we manage a debut clean pull away.

Immediately the need for a gearchange becomes apparent. Out of that short first slot, it is important to push the lever fast and confidently across the gate, for the reward is a shift that is noisily rapid. Hesitate and you are marooned in neutral with only your embarrassment as a result. Up or down, the box should be managed without the aid of the clutch, but I reserved that only for straight line occasions where I was sure I would not miss a vital swap.

Overall the whining Ford seven-speed came across as a fine competitive unit that offers swift acclimatization in all but the ill-defined gate. Unlike the six-speed Group A Toyota (Xtrac), Peugeot and BMW (Prodrive) that we have enjoyed, it was possible to meander between cross gate changes such as third to fourth. Otherwise the change was a model of rapid fire delights. The steering and handling of the production Sapphire Cosworth is one of its prime attractions. The factory car builds on that base to provide astonishing ability in adverse conditions. Geared at just under two turns lock to lock, the competition power steering is frequently called upon to balance the comparatively slim snow tyres and wheels against the arrival of maximum torque in mid corner. The factory Ford slews easily from lock to lock with a balance that is neutral on all but the slowest and tightest corners. Then it ploughs wide with all the unwieldy finesse of an old Audi Quattro.

Despite the unfamiliarity of '70s quadruple headlamps within a Sapphire aero generation beak, this works machine remained a recognizable Ford Sapphire. The tickover and noise levels were elevated but it was not the anticipated rowdy ride, absorbing bumps gracefully over 40 mph.

At 89 mph and 5,000 rpm in seventh, the vibrations and whines are generously amplified versions of the noises familiar to many Cosworth owners. The performance is exceptional yet (unfortunately) many aftermarket specialists provide more horsepower with less safety and durability than Ford assembles to withstand worldwide rallying rigours.

My thanks to Nigel Fryatt (editor) and Martin Sharp (Nigel's deputy) at *Cars & Car Conversions* for the research that inspired this brutally abbreviated adaptation of a 1993 article by Martin Sharp.

∗ ∗ ∗

Malcolm Wilson: development driving force

Malcolm Wilson will always be linked with rallying Fords, right back to his teenage days in an Anglia with Mum and Dad in close attendance. Since then we have seen him compete in front (RS1600i, tenth on the 1983 RAC) and rear drive Escorts (mostly RS1800). These as well as all kinds of Cosworth powered Sierras and Escorts, although he only tackled one event in the 3-dr Sierra RS.

Out of the limelight there have been thousands of test miles put in on the RS200 supercar or the ill-starred RS1700T, before he came back into public Ford view with the Sierra Cosworth in two-wheel drive (2WD) and 4x4 form. The Escort Cosworth was made for Malcolm's development driving talents, owing much of its 1993/4 success to the Cumbrian proprietor of Malcolm Wilson Motorsport.

The young sensation matured away from Ford, first becoming a World Championship driver for Rover and their Metro 6R4. Malcolm took Vauxhall Opel into the points on World Championship events, a memorable 1989 RAC seeing Wilson beat all the Cosworths with that front drive Astra, which also netted him a third overall during that Championship season. Malcolm also drove for Peugeot during the mid-'80s, when Ford had no programme beyond testing.

Of the Sierra Sapphires, Malcolm recalled that the FIA-backed decision to eliminate the 00 numbered course opening cars that were completing manufacturer development programmes was very significant to the 4x4 Sierra Cosworth's rally record. 'That was a bit of a shame really, because I think we could have probably speeded up development, because there's nothing like

Ford Motorsport at Boreham owes Malcolm Wilson much for his consistent development work on all types of faster Fords. He was not a fan of the 4-dr Sierra in rally format, but never stopped trying to find the winning formula for the car.

actually doing events. I think we would have ironed out a lot of the reliability problems, a lot sooner.'

What was Wilson's chief driving memory of the rear drive 4-dr?

'I've got to be honest and say that I found it a very difficult car to drive. I never felt at ease with the car. You couldn't use an exuberant style like you could with an Escort and get away with it.' At the heart of the problem was the size of the car and the fact that 4-dr did not respond to running the same damper and spring settings as the original 3-dr rally competitor.

Of the 4x4 Sierra era, Malcolm commented first on the seven-speed gearbox. 'As time progressed, it improved and the gearchange now is absolutely fantastic. I mean, its the best gearchange of any rally car I've driven. Now it's perfect.' The handling was not so easy to sort. Wilson was quick to point out that mild damper setting changes would result in 'no traction' and a marked 'difference in the amount of oversteer you got out of it'.

Overall Malcolm likened driving and developing the Sierra 4x4 most to the Audi Quattro: 'very similar in a lot of areas. To get the best out of it you had to have a stiff (setting for the) centre diff, which meant you got quite a bit of understeer and could not use the handbrake. On the '92 RAC I did lose out quite a bit on the tight stuff, but I think I more than made up for it on the quicker bits, where the car was more stable than it would have been with a soft set central diff. You had to move it, you had to be aggressive with the car. And that was just the case for the Quattro too . . .'

Compared to the 4x4 Sierra that debuted on the August 1990 1,000 Lakes, or the cars I wrote about at the beginning of this chapter, just about every dynamic aspect was changed by the time Sierra Cosworth 4x4 made its works swan-song on the 1992 RAC. Malcolm cited the example of 'magnesium rear suspension arms. We still run mag arms to this day, but they are not the same arms that were on the 2WD Cossie: they just look the same.

'We found that everything had to be reinforced: compression strut brackets, the compression struts themselves, camber brackets. Even the 2WD magnesium uprights we could not run on the 4WD. All these things, like the joint that broke on François' car in Monte, *everything* had to be re-engineered.

'Once we'd got all those bits, you knew you could just get in the car and drive it to the maximum. That's what I did on the '92 RAC. Then the car was competitive, it was a bloody good car by the end,' summarized Ford's quiet development star thoughtfully.

Russell Brookes scored his fourth Manx international win, and the first international victory for the Sierra 4x4 Cosworth, when he won the 1990 edition in this R-E-D example with Terry Hoyle power and Dunlop tyres. As for his victory in 1989 (when he won on a Team Orders basis versus Mark Lovell), it was a controversial result. Russell completed a promising Ford weekend as the Escort also won its first event in unhomologated form in Spain and Robb Gravett was headed for the British Touring Car title with another RS500 win at Donington. Russell was third in another 4x4 in 1991 for the Manx, the Brookes Ford by then outpaced by two Prodrive Subarus.

Chapter 8

The executive express

Built to rectify the more obvious defects of the pushrod iron Ford V6 for the '90s, the 24-valve Cosworth conversion spread its charms more widely by 1994.

'The 24-valve V6 for the Scorpio actually started outside Cosworth,' recalled Chief Designer Geoff Goddard in 1994. 'Brian Hart had prepared a prototype for Ford to examine. At the time Brian was in the Cosworth fold and so the project was inherited within Cosworth itself,' explained the Cosworth motor maestro.

The project was drawn under the FB designation. It amounted to dressing a bare Ford iron block with completely new ancillaries, including alloy DOHC heads with four valves a cylinder. It thus became 'a totally in-house project with a 100 per cent commitment to producing a better, more efficient, *road* engine,' says Geoff Goddard.

After extensively overhauling the basic 150 bhp Ford unit (more details in the 'period piece' that follows), Cosworth released the unchanged capacity 24v V6 at 195 bhp for series production. By 1994 the performance gap between Cosworth 24v and the FMC 12v iron had increased: Ford rated their cat-equipped unit at 145 bhp on 5,500 rpm (as high as you would want to

High in the Austrian foothills, the first production Scorpio 24-valve displays only the diminutive '24v' badge to advise the populace that the pushrod iron V6 has been revitalized and reborn as a DOHC unit of broad power band.

take the production 12v unit) and 228 Nm by 3,000 rpm. The Cosworth creation was rated at 195 bhp by 5,750 rpm and had a massive torque increase too: now 275 Nm by 4,500 revs. In UK torque readings that means 202 lb/ft at 4,500 rpm. This compared with the 12v production output of 172 lb/ft of torque in 1991.

The effect on performance was equally forceful; top speed closed on 140 mph (up 16 mph, according to Ford) and 0–60 mph, with the handicap of Ford specifying only their automatic transmission accompany the Cossie V6, was down to 8.2 sec. That was some 2.4 sec faster than the traditional 2.9i Ford could manage.

Furthermore, still using Ford figures, the Urban and steady speed fuel consumption figures were little altered; indeed *Autocar & Motor* returned 21 mpg overall versus 18 mpg for their standard car test format in 1991. My 1994 experience saw 21.4 to 22.6 mpg recorded over 600 miles.

Impressive though the figures were, they were not the heartland of why Cosworth supplied 10,250 such FB units from October 1990 to the end of 1993. There were two key reasons for this 24-valve vitality to Ford: 1, it set excellent standards in increasingly tough emission tests; 2, media enthusiasm for the revitalized Scorpio 24v of April 1991 gave the valued 'halo effect' to the rest of the range.

Aside from the cleaner exhaust breath of the 24v motor and its obvious performance edge, the car wrapped around it was superior, too. Better braking, massively uprated suspension (details in our contemporary piece, but note that the changes were so effective many made it lower down the range in 1994). All this accompanied an equipment list that would make a Jaguar driver's eyes bulge.

The most obvious 24v goodies over the usual Scorpio norm of power-assisted everything were the standard fitment of air conditioning, cruise control, automatic four-speed gearbox and a Viscous Coupling limited slip differential, one shared with contemporary Sierra RS Cosworths. It is worth pointing out that the Pirelli tyres referred to in my launch piece had been replaced by outstanding Michelin Pilot series MXV2 items of 205/50 ZR 16 on my 1994 UK test car, but the alloys remained the smoothly finished five spokes for saloons. Those with a sharp catalogue eye will note that the estate runs a 205/60 x *15* sizing on a 6 x 15 alloy, whereas the saloon operates on a 6.5 x 16 ledge, with the 16 in Michelin sizings quoted above.

Electronically monitored Teves GmbH disc braking with ABS action was common to the Granada Scorpio line, but the discs, pads and callipers were specifically uprated for the Scorpio Cosworth.

Prices and Scorpio 4/5 door saloon availability in 24v trim were maintained from the April 1991 UK launch at £27,383 (for either hatchback or saloon) for most of the early '90s. Both models dipped under £27,000 for the latter section of their J plate 1992 availability in Britain, but were back over £27,000 by August 1992 (K plate registration) and had reached £27,775 by the close of 1993.

I would stress that these were official list costs. The British market of 1992/3 had drifted far away from official costs. I suspect most of these cars would have been sold as part of a Granada Scorpio discount package to larger car fleets (over 25 cars), so that Managing/Sales Directors could enjoy a burst

Quietly packaged, the Ford Scorpio and Granada 24v suspension influenced settings throughout the range. The near 200 bhp motor was offered in 4, 5 and estate car bodies.

of speed not available to their minions.

If private owners or small business entrepreneurs bought them at anything like list price, there was a very nasty first year depreciation curve that certainly saw £10,000 lopped off their market value. Unfortunately for such a good product the motoring magazines did spot the trend, and any enthusiasts would have been forewarned that a low mileage, second-hand, purchase made more economic sense.

Early in 1994 Ford revised the availability of the 24v unit to take advantage of 24-valve showroom appeal, allowing Granada buyers their first chance to specify the unit (£26,845 on Ghia 4-door) as well as the original Scorpio 4 and 5-dr at an almost unchanged cost over the original launch: £27,765. The 1994 Scorpio Estate was also allowed to haul beyond 132 mph with Cosworth heart and a £28,685 tag.

By 1994 the showroom equipment list maintained items such as the standard AC and cruise control, but these were now part of the Scorpio showroom deal, along with a CD player alongside the usual stereo radio/cassette player. Also on all Scorpios was a convincing burr walnut 'wood effect' appliqué, multi-function fuel computer and ten-function, electrically assisted operation of the seats, for which leather was standard in UK by 1994. At the launch seats were cloth trimmed, but leather at an optional cost of £510 was listed in 1991.

The sunroof was, and is, powered on all Scorpios. So there were few items the 24v buyer could opt for, beyond personal upgrading of stereo systems and cellular phones, tow hooks and the like.

There was no original intention to build a competition engine from this base, but Cosworth did later conceive an FBE descendant for the BRSCC ProSports 3000 sports car racing series. This formula was not a huge success at the time of writing, entries having sunk beneath a 10-car grid in 1993, but the competition motor was an interesting development, offering 300 bhp at

6,750 rpm and 248 lb/ft of torque by 5,500 rpm.

As for the mass production FB (well, nine a day at press time), the FBE had chain drive for the overhead camshafts, a reinforced version of the iron cylinder block and retained nodular cast iron for the crankshaft, although it was further balanced by the provision of an extra central counterweight. However, the crossover injection system and dry sump lubrication were all new for life in the pit lane.

The V6 proved a comparatively low speed but torquey racing unit, one that will doubtless one day be transplanted by bright sparks into Capris and Sierras for use in racing formulae where DIY initiative is encouraged.

Contemporary comment

Just prior to the 1991 sales launch of the Scorpio 24v, I was allowed a preview of the car in Austria. Here is what I wrote for *Performance Ford* at the time. My thanks to editor/owner Dennis Foy for permission to quote excerpts from that material.

Scorpio goes for the Cossie treatment
Jeremy Walton drives the 24-valve version of the Ford V6 that is now allowed out in a £27,000 plus Scorpio. It's no racer, but gives the big Ford executive suite cred . . .

The plummy five-door Scorpio 24v stood outside the equally ritzy Austrian hotel, ready to prove to the press that Ford had chosen to inject some civil Cosworth speed into their range leader. At £27,383 we hoped the 'Cossie' Scorpio would be worth our time and a more credible place in the executive classes.

Spring 1991 and Austria was the venue chosen to introduce the international press to the Cosworth Scorpio. Nobody doubted that this was a very much better Granada Scorpio and a few wondered why all examples of the big executive Ford could not be made this way.

A day of *autobahn* and hill motoring at 18.2 mpg proved that all the extensive mechanical changes, excluding the mandatory automatic transmission, had wrought an all round improvement in the big Ford.

Available on five hatchback or four-dr saloon Scorpios (the latter accounting for some 50 per cent of all sales today), the Cossie treatment extends a long way outside the engine bay, including a long list of electrical goodies, stronger brakes and a beefier chassis.

External clues are confined to five-spoke alloy wheels wearing Pirelli P700s of 205/50 ZR-16 profiles and a modest 24v badge on the boot lid. No drainpipe exhaust, no bi-plane wings, no external Cosworth badge (the V6 engine, alone, carries that message).

Natural centre of attention is the massively reworked 2.9i 60° V6. Normally an all iron unit with a single camshaft trapped within the block, Cosworth created a 34 per cent gain in horsepower and a 24 per cent advance in torque.

The new engine is mated only to the Ford 4ALD automatic gearbox. The rumour machine tells us that this is because 1, the MT75 has no torque capacity to accommodate the more muscular motor, and 2, 'people in this category do not buy manual transmissions anyway'.

The 24v Scorpio will now reach from rest to 60 mph in a series of coarse ratio swaps within 8.8 sec; maximum speed is equally credibly claimed at 140 mph. We saw the equivalent of 137 mph indicated in our LHD demonstrator on the *autobahn* and had no quibbles with a Ford V6 that was equally at

The motor was one of the first Ford units to be packaged for showroom appeal, with hidden spark plugs and the kind of 'clean appeal' that the Japanese pioneered.

home around town. The idle is very carefully stabilized at 750 rpm, and it is only when exploring the new 4,000 to 6,000 rpm ability that you are conscious of this engine's rough upbringing.

The Cosworth Ford delivers its power bonus with an ease that extends to allowing a momentary 6,150 rpm from a short stroke (93 x 72 mm) 2935 cc. A continuous rpm limit of 6,050 rpm is advised. The torque curve looks peaky on the Ford graph, but more than the standard output is available just beyond the usual 3,000 rpm torque peak and the peak of 4,500 belies its all round ability.

Ford and Cosworth performed the kind of cost conscious engine durability modifications that echoed some past programmes. For example, the cast iron crankshaft is fillet rolled, a process employed on the 2.8i V6 when it travelled from '70s Granada to injection Capri. The 60° block is strengthened around the webs to support the four main bearings securely, a faint reminder of the thickwall blocks that have characterized turbocharged inline four-cylinder progress with Sierra RS types, notably the RS500.

Ford told us, 'Some machining operations are deleted to provide extra strength in the new application and there are now external oil drains from the heads to the oil pan.' Naturally the water radiator core has enhanced cooling capability and an oil cooler is complimented by an aluminium sump pan.

All four camshafts are driven by a single duplex roller chain. Replacement pistons compress the Ford EEC-IV managed mixture at a 9.7:1 ratio. Cheaper grades of unleaded fuels are digested by the catalytic convertor-equipped unit at the rate of 18.7 mpg. Outside town, Ford expect 28 mpg at a constant 75 mph and up to 33.6 mpg at a traffic-infested 56 mph.

Outside the engine bay there are effective changes to the brakes and chassis. The front spring rates were modestly uplifted (as is the roll bar; (27 to 28 mm)), but those of the rear climb a whopping 23 per cent to associate with an 18 mm rear anti-roll bar. Gas damping rates were also described as 'uprated by 15 per cent' front, or a massive 75 per cent at the back. The handling is further modified by the action of a Viscous Coupling limited slip differential, one that can clearly be felt at work when exploring the 6,000 rpm

As installed, the Cosworth version of the Ford V6 was neatly surrounded by plastics and a clear indication of routine checks required.

abilities of the revitalized V6 over damp mountain roads.

Fighting with the RS4x4 Sierra for the honour of being the most expensive UK listed Ford, beyond £27,000, the Scorpio 24v has an extensive list of showroom items to offset its lack of the 4x4 ability. All come to Ghia trim levels, plus a bonus in showroom orientated goodies.

The usual Granada benefits of a big cabin continue, particularly strong rear legroom for a rear drive design. What has changed is that the steering has reacted to the change in wheel and tyre equipment to become quite sensitive to cambers and bumps at slow speeds, allowing the Scorpio mildly to follow its own way if left unchecked over adverse cambers at town speeds. Consequently the steering also 'nibbles' at the driver's palms in a restive town manner that is reminiscent of the older Porsche 911s.

On the road this Scorpio comes across as a very disciplined executive indeed. The 50 per cent aspect ratio Pirellis do their best to absorb the bumping and thumping generated by such vastly stiffened rear suspension, so the ride does not become as comfortable as that of its contemporaries until it is beyond 45 mph.

In motorway use some 112 mph and 4,000 rpm seemed an amiable amble, not a comment that would be likely of the standard Scorpio. When the accelerator becomes intimate with the carpet 130 mph comes up readily enough, but we did not see the LHD km/h speedo indicate more than 220 km/h (137 mph) of the claimed 140 mph.

Acceleration is the compensation, but the rough action of the Ford automatic on all but the gentlest running spoils Ford aspirations to belong in the £27,000 classes. Even manual gearchange selections do not make the problem disappear as the plastic lever moves through an obstructively serrated gate.

We liked the Scorpio 24v immensely. It stood up well in a week that also contained the 174 bhp Audi 100 V6 launch on to the UK market (their 4x4 variant is less than the Ford and still reached 135 mph). That suggests Ford have made a much more competitive customer proposition of their flagship.

What a pity that only 6,500 will be made annually, just over 50 per cent coming to Britain. Maybe, one day, all Scorpios will be made this way, leaving the Granada to soldier on with the iron age V6s?

Motorsport professional's choice

Kevin Shortis, for many years a guiding light in the Ford RSOC club and the owner of such collectible fast Fords as the RS1600, had operated a Scorpio 24v for 12 months and 26,000 miles when this was written. He told us, 'I have had many performance cars in my 47 years, but this one gives me the lot.'

Kevin established Motorsport Management International upon his retirement from the Kent police force and needed a long distance machine to transport his 6 ft 5 in, 16 stone frame. He recalled, 'Having driven a Vauxhall Senator 24v I decided that the choice would be between Vauxhall and Ford. Although the Vauxhall scores in economy, I did not like the wandering

steering and felt that the body styling was not as pleasing as the Scorpio.

'Finding a suitable Scorpio 24v was a problem. I found the car advertised by the Brundall Motor Co in *Motoring News*. I came, I saw, I purchased. With its 195 bhp engine it is not slow. The firm suspension and replacement Yokohama AVS tyres give superb traction and the luxury leather chairs (as opposed to mere seats) keep me in my place.

'Other appreciated creature comforts include air conditioning, heated front and rear screens, heated front seats and a CD player. I love the sound quality in this car and must compliment Ford for producing such an acceptable sound quality for such a low price. A year on, I still find the leather smell a thrill, not a fetish!

'Petrol consumption varies between 23.6 mpg around town to a creditable 27.4 mpg on a long, but high cruising speed, journey.' Kevin was also pleased to note that servicing cost him less in 1994 than 1993 as 'Ford have reduced the price of many stock items'. His bill was down £30 at Jermyn & Sons of Seaford in Sussex.

This 1991 J plate Scorpio 24v was bought in February 1993 for 'a sum approaching £15,000'. Kevin concluded, 'I have been offered in excess of £11,000 as a trade in against another new Ford, which represents excellent value for such a large car over the year, especially with a total mileage in excess of 45,000. I may keep the car a bit longer and see what the new Granada and Scorpios look like.

'Don't suppose the Cosworth badge will be on the engine though — pity.'

In fact, I think there was good news for Kevin and Cosworth on the way, for a new supply contract had been signed. Cosworth looked certain to bring their expertise to further emission-conscious versions of the V6 in the mid-to late '90s.

Unique alloy wheels and 24v badge were the only clues to the extra power provided in the 1994 Scorpio with 2.9 litre Cosworth heart.

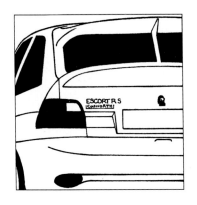

Escort with Sierra heart

The rallying logic of Escort size and Sierra Cosworth hardware was impeccable, but to build 2,500 required over 400 unique parts and exceptional international co-operation outside Ford.

Incroyable! The Escort Cosworth makes its Luxembourg public production bow in the spring of 1992.

T he Escort Cosworth RS was a courageous corporate act in a world full of politically correct players. The world's first mass production car with downforce aerodynamics, it rewarded Ford with five World Rally Championship victories in its debut year. The company also scooped their first Monte Carlo Rallye win in the 41 years that had elapsed since Maurice 'Gatso' Gatsonides in the straight six Zephyr era of the '50s.

Unfortunately the competition success was not accompanied by equal commercial viability. In Britain the near 140 mph Escort RS Cosworth was

sold in three trim levels at prices fixed in May 1992, ranging from £21,380 to £23,495. That was considerably less than the Sierra predecessor had officially reached in its heyday (over £27,000 before the £6,000 'slash-back' of 1992), but still the even more advanced Ford Cosworth was haunted in the showroom by tales of gargantuan insurance premiums and the recessionary climate then prevailing in the UK. Just 310 were sold in 1992, another 576 in 11 months of 1993.

LHD Europe was not so keen on the Escort Cosworth either. It took from March 1992 to February of 1994 to build a total of 5,186 of the YBT power units found in every road-going Escort Cosworth, considerably slower than the build rate on the original 3-dr.

In fact the bulk were built in support of the minimum 2,500 homologation run (more of that in the competition chapter) and a total of more than 4,000 were constructed in 1992, supporting the suggestion that most of the road cars stood a while before finding customers. It would be at least a year longer than Ford originally anticipated before the planned smaller turbo/Ford EEC engine management supplanted the original T04 turbo and Weber-Marelli electronic injection/ignition layout.

The initial public road specification of Escort RS Cosworth had three trim levels (Motorsport, Luxury and Lux plus leather trim), but all shared the torsionally toughest body shell ever wrought in production Escort, including the later safety bodies. Ingredients embraced the usual Ferguson patented Ford 4x4 system (34 per cent front, 66 per cent rear power splits) with two FFD Viscous Coupling differentials and a modestly uprated Cosworth Ford YBT version of the 2 litre turbo, which retained its steel crankshaft and virtually unburstable associated hardware.

Complete with hybrid Garrett AiResearch T35 turbocharger and trick two-stage intercooling, public highway power output peaked at 227 bhp, more than had been offered in any production Cossie, even RS500. True top speed was down in the 137 mph region, a product of those effective aerodynamics, but 0–60 mph was faster than that recorded by *Autocar & Motor* for its Sierra 4x4 predecessor at 6.2 sec.

To my mind it was the best Ford Cosworth yet, combining incredible handling and braking abilities with scintillating acceleration. Only the steering failed to thrill, being simply 'dead accurate'.

The bigger surprise was that Ford managed to pull together such a car at all, for its parentage was the wackiest yet of the performance production Fords.

Road or track, there is only one person to talk to about the gestation and continued development of the Escort Cosworth, and that passionately committed engineer is John Wheeler. Former Porsche engineer Wheeler joined Ford Motorsport in October 1980, and oversaw both competition and road development of the latest Ford Cosworth product, having previously created the Escort RS1700T, RS200 and overseen the Sierra RS Cosworth rallying programme.

John was involved in the first creative Cosworth Escort discussions of 1988 at Ford Motorsport and subsequently was appointed manager of the Escort Cosworth development programme; he was then 43 years old.

I interviewed Wheeler several times in pursuit of Escort Cosworth lore and had the privilege of driving both pre-production and Corsica-winning variants

Escort Cosworth team leader, road or track, John Wheeler in push-button mode at Boreham.

of the breed to build a 3D view of this extraordinary Escort's evolution. Before we get into the timing and technical details, I should stress that the Ford engineer was always quick to point out the role of other individuals and companies. It was simply a journalistic convenience to channel all the information through one man who had seen both sides of the story.

It is also relevant to say that this modest man drives to a level at which he can interpret the feedback from a 600 bhp evolution RS200, the latest 360 bhp works Escort or pack in the daily road miles in pursuit of elusive pre-production quirks. He cannot tell you all that, so I will, for these abilities resulted in an outstanding Ford Cosworth.

Our tale starts back in 1988. In the largest Boreham administration office at Ford Motorsport, needed to house all the wallcharts and diagrams needed to monitor this complex programme, Wheeler recalled: 'There were discussions and concept studies from February 1988. But April 1989 was the start of the real work on the car we have today.'

The basic concept was that of combining Sierra Cosworth RS mechanical components and Escort body, but before that stage was reached many other concepts were evaluated against the known opposition, particularly Lancia's all-conquering Delta. The Ford Motorsport personnel present included Stuart Turner, then Boreham boss Peter Ashcroft, John Wheeler and Mike Moreton, the latter bound for TWR Jaguar Sport.

The team looked at possibilities including 'the nightmare' of transverse motor V6 machines. Yet the principle of mounting the engine longitudinally would be the one that marked them out against their World Championship opposition, most becoming based on 4x4 conversions of previous front drive machinery.

Ultimately — and here I am talking about a programme that hit its planned sports debut date of January 1993, some five *years* after these initial discussions — this insistence on the north-south engine location would give

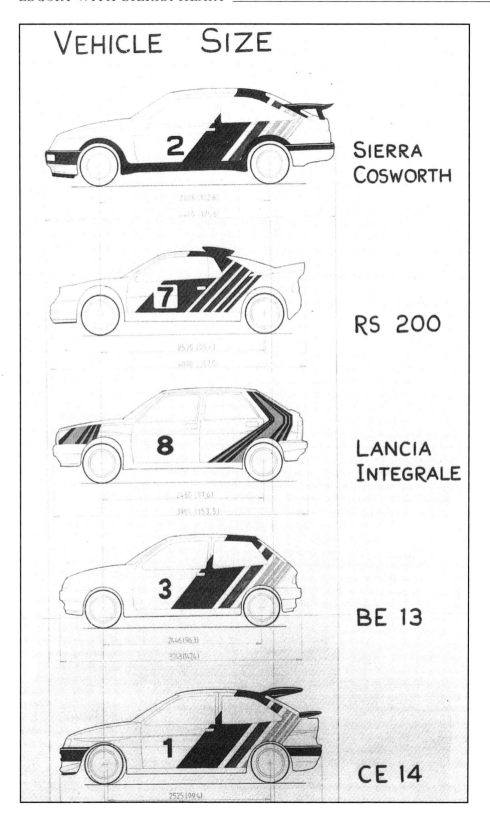

VEHICLE SIZE

2 — SIERRA COSWORTH

2608 (122.6)
4460 (175.6)

7 — RS 200

2530 (99.6)
4000 (157.5)

8 — LANCIA INTEGRALE

2480 (97.6)
3900 (153.5)

3 — BE 13

2446 (96.3)
3763 (147.4)

1 — CE 14

2525 (99.4)

Original thinking: this was part of the Ford at Boreham presentation of how the Escort (CE14) and Fiesta (CE 13) would fit into the World Rally Championship. Illustrated versus the Lancia Delta Integrale and previous Ford experience with Sierra and RS200. The wheelbase of the Escort was actually extended considerably after this prediction (made five *years* before production commenced!), up from 2,525 mm to 2,551 mm. Overall Escort length also expanded in this period, from a planned 4,037 mm to a final 4,211 mm, both still considerably down on the Sierra 3-dr (2,608 and 4,460 mm respectively) official statistics at this stage.

the Escort a distinct edge over the opposition. It would also drive Delta integrale into well deserved retirement as the most successful World Rally Championship winner to date.

The two key sports advantages were improved handling balance under pressure (less terminal understeer) and the quick service ability of that proven engine layout, which left the Boreham team with better access to key items such as the gearbox/clutch and engine ancillaries.

Authorization to build a first prototype around a contemporary Escort front drive shell came in June 1988. The work was completed by a subcontractor: TC Prototypes in Northamptonshire, who have also created Formula 1 alloy monocoques for the biggest names in the business. Coded 'ACE 14' ('A' for Group A, plus part of the new Escort CE14 internal code), ACE was the name most used prior to the launch within the company and its subcontractors.

It was August 1988 when that first prototype was submitted for management appraisal in the second front drive generation Escort body. It was reportedly 'very nice' to drive and their enthusiasm was soon communicated to outsiders, *Autocar & Motor* publishing a commendably accurate account that year. However, journalistic emphasis on the original conversion led a lot of people to assume the car was some kind of motor sport kit car, rather than a full blooded production car that would have to pass through all the usual manufacturer tests and homologation procedures.

In fact a new body had to be created, rather than cutting and shutting until Escort mated with Sierra. John Wheeler was adamant that the body priorities for the showroom product should not be compromised: 'The body is substantially stronger in torsional stiffness than the majority of current hatchbacks in its category. I wish to emphasize that this comparatively small, but very sophisticated package has been engineered with safety as a high priority. This is not a converted car in any way. It was engineered, drawn from scratch for over 400 unique components, not a cut and shut marriage of Escort and Sierra,' Wheeler reported at my Boreham briefings. At the time,

Production cutaway from Studio Collins emphasizes the blow-moulded plastic fuel tank and the separated coil spring/telescopic damper layout.

the company were unwilling to discuss a torsional strength figure, but I later learned that 6,000 Nm was attained, more than double the figure of the contemporary Escort.

Ford estimated that 'some 50 per cent of the Escort RS Cosworth's body panels are new, the remainder derived from existing Escort and Sierra components'. I would say that the line below the doors owes most to Sierra, allowing a central 4x4 transmission tunnel and engine bay accommodation for the north-south Cosworth unit. Some parts were redesigned so heavily that the Escort-Sierra references was untrue. John Wheeler highlighted the lower chassis rails as of vastly stronger Escort stock, partnered by a beefy centre transmission tunnel that naturally did not exist on the contemporary front drive Escort. Hatfield Polytechnic Engineering department crush-tested 14 samples of front side members to uncover the optimum deformation characteristics, for the installation of the north-south 2 litre would obviously effect crash barrier test performance.

Ford Motorsport had to find a specialist to build at least the 2,500 homologation minimum, for there was no Ford facility that would be allowed to face such a specialist challenge in the '90s.

By November 1988 they had the body design, which was a combination of Motorsport briefs (such as enormous torsional strength, the downforce aerodynamic requirements and wheelarches to clear 18 in diameters) and design sensibilities. These were tackled by the UK Ford Design Centre at Dunton with practical work, including Clay predictions of final outline, executed by MGA at Coventry.

I was impressed by Karmann personnel. Their good humoured persistence, especially when engineering a cheaper alternative seat to the beloved Recaro seat against fierce internal opposition. Equally persistent was Cosworth engineer Paul Frick. This genius resisted constant barracking for more power whilst mating that oversize T35 turbocharger with a lag-free road car response to the accelerator: an impossible brief, but Paul was used to pressure having worked on the Sierra Cosworth engine programme almost as soon as it was in appreciable production volume.

When the body design was approved it had amassed 200 hours, most of them in the Cologne wind tunnel. Tests at that site reported an 0.38 Cd with aerodynamic spoiler package (front 'beard', three-position front splitter and upper rear wing) in place, and downforce. An 0.33 Cd, minus top wing and front spoiler, was recorded.

Cladding the unique Escort RS was the first mass production wing set to generate rear *and front* aerodynamic downforce. Ford had achieved *rear* downforce with the Sierra Cosworth and (notably) with the RS500, but company engineers admitted that these cars were not balanced by any reduction in downforce effect at the front. That led to appreciable front end lightness at higher speeds, an effect Ford Motorsport were determined to eliminate.

John Wheeler sketched and commented: 'The objective was to turn considerable front end lift into a small level of front downforce, combined with twice that downforce figure at the rear. This without any great sacrifice in the drag coefficient. This package was to give a centre of pressure, behind the centre of gravity (C of G) and minimal changes to allow small yaw angles. These are the ingredients for ultimate dynamic stability.

Roadrunner. Dynamic
roadholding was the prime aim
of the Escort Cosworth over top
speed, the first mass production
car to benefit from significant
aerodynamic downforce
generated front and rear.

'The rear spoiler is a genuine inverted wing profile, which has the effect of shaping the air stream off the back of the roof. Thus creating laminar flow down the rear screen. This laminar flow then passes over the lower rear spoiler, creating further downforce, with minimum drag,' explained Mr Wheeler.

So determined were Ford Motorsport and Karmann to create the ultimate aerodynamic advantages for the 'Escort' outline that the rear body side elevations were lifted 30 mm (1.2 in) to ensure that the lower of the two rear spoiler blades was effective.

At 180 km/h (112 mph) down forces were listed as 45 Newtons at the nose, 190 N on the double wing rear. This compared to 164 N generated by the original 3-dr Sierra Cosworth at 200 km/h (124 mph), rear only. At the front, the old three doors still had a degree of uplift, only reduced on the RS500, not turned into appreciable downforce.

Most aero data was collated under the leadership of Eberhardt Braun from Ford Motorsport in Germany, who had also played such a significant part in the creation of the first Cosworth Sierra/RS500 outline.

Escort Cosworth aerodynamic aids were the deep front spoiler, slowly adjustable (in three bolted extensions) front splitter, the Resin Transfer Moulding upper rear wing and a lower air dam to complete the rear downforce process, as was the case for RS500. Also part of the body cladding were side sills and rear, under bumper, panel extensions in conventional Polyurethane by Phoenix. Not so obvious, but equally important, was the management of air in the engine bay. This included an undertray, traditional bonnet louvres and air escape paths engineered into the front wing louvres (at the back of the arches). At the rear, the Sotira Resin Transfer Moulded (RTM; 50 per cent lighter than using polyurethane) upper spoiler was employed. Another innovative material use was that for the plastic, blow-moulded, 65 litre Kantex fuel tank, 10 litres larger than for a contemporary Escort.

The Escort Cosworth would finally draw on three production centres, but it

Not much in common! The front drive Escort (J685 WOO) alongside the press fleet Cosworth derivative in the Scottish summer of 1992.

was December 1988 before Karmann, at their Rheine plant, were selected as ACE assemblers. Note that even the basic pressings are modified with further stamping work at Karmann, the heaviest work carried out at Osnabruck. Most of the Escort upper structure had to be fundamentally modified (particularly the top mounts, bracing used from the turret tops and inner wings). Only the Escort roof, bare tailgate and doors made it through unscathed.

Why Karmann?

Ford certainly looked at all the companies the RS200 subcontract build programme had explored (including Lotus and Reliant), but Karmann always had the strongest hand. Ford had such positive experience of the Escort Cabriolet production record. It also subsequently helped that the Special Vehicle Engineering staff (SVE) had worked on the Escort convertible as well, so the two sides had a record of co-operation that would prove invaluable in bringing such a sophisticated Escort to fruition.

Dimensionally Motorsport wanted a compact overall length like that of the Lancia Delta to follow Sierra, but as much wheelbase as could be squeezed in to retain RS200 standards of ride and stability. The result was an interesting comparison with the standard transverse engined Escort of the period and Sierra: the Cosworth Escort was broader than either, a fact highlighted by the stretched front and rear arches. Of all steel construction, the front wing was a particularly tricky one piece Karmann stamping.

The Escort Cosworth was a little taller than its standard Escort and Sierra stablemates, resting on a wheelbase 57.5 mm (2.3 in) shorter than Sierra, 26.5 mm (1.4 in) longer than front drive Escort. Against its production namesake, the Cosworth measured 175 mm (6.9 in) longer, 50 mm (2 in) broader than an Escort. Back to back against the Sierra, overall length was clipped some 284.5 mm (11.2 in).

Escort Cosworth wheelbase was cropped around 60 mm (2.36 in) versus Sierra, the latter figure varying upon the ride height used for the Escort. In road trim the homologation form reported 2,551 mm (100.4 in), but the Ford

Side by side: SVE engineers
pause for thought as the second
Motorsport prediction and the
production prototype work their
way through 1991. *(Picture
courtesy SVE/John A. Hitchins)*

Side by side: SVE engineers pause for thought as the second Motorsport prediction and the production prototype work their way through 1991. *(Picture courtesy SVE/John A. Hitchins)*

Motorsport Escort was drawn on 2,550 mm (100.3 in) versus 2,608 mm (102.8 in) for their Sierras. The Escort cropping treatment ensured a much more manageable car, road or track.

Official launch kerb weight was just 5 kg lighter than the 4-dr Sierra RSC 4x4, totalling 1,275 kg/2,805 lb. Later catalogue figures were 1,300 kg (2,860 lb) for the Motorsport version and 1,375 kg (3,025 lb) for the Luxury model, almost 100 kg up on the original 3-dr Sierra RSC and an indication of the extensive reinforcement body and running gear had received.

It was April 1989 before the pre-production programme was approved and the first complete road car prototype assembled. It is worth remembering just how many corporate steps the Escort Cosworth had to tramp before it was given the final go-ahead, committing millions of dollars.

Altogether there were eight European and American committee reviews that this special Escort passed. These included the November 1989 Ford of Europe approval for the full programme and (January 1990), the Ford USA parent finally approving programme in respect of a production run and the competition cost implications: my understanding is that more than $20 million are required annually just to run the works cars, but I have no idea what it would cost to construct the cars for sale and homologation. Unlike most rivals, Ford would aim to make money on the showroom bases for competition cars. That may be why the Escort Cosworth had such a long commercial life planned at announcement time, one that took it into the late '90s.

It would be August 1989 before Ford Special Vehicle Engineering (SVE) were formally requested to further develop the public sale Escort Cosworth. There were 15 heads assigned to the job inside SVE at Dunton, but up to 26 company personnel had some other regular involvement. Wheeler added, 'That takes no account of those who helped us at Dunton Design Centre, or at the Lommel Belgian track and all the other facilities of a major manufacturer that we could draw on.

'Outside the company we were assigned regular engineering/design help from MGA Coventry, Cosworth and Karmann, plus our other suppliers,' recalled John Wheeler. Escort Cosworth raw material and design sources were as varied as Ford factories and engineering centres in Britain (Halewood,

Dunton and Boreham), Germany (Cologne and managerial control over the Belgian activities listed), Italy (Ghia) and Belgium (Genk production, Lommel proving ground) to co-operate with major outside suppliers.

These outsiders were headed by Karmann in Germany, Cosworth in Northampton and Wellingborough, Fichtel and Sachs shock absorbers, Germany's Phoenix and French-based Sotira (both firms provided aerodynamic body panels). The unique white on black instrumentation was the work of Aston Martin supplier John McGavignan & Co Ltd.

Ronal five-spoke 8 x 16 in wheels were to Ford at Dunton Design drawings, and were not initially released on the aftermarket. Their dimensions suited Ford Motorsport, who wanted to run up to 18 in tyre diameters under the 2 in gain allowed by FIA Group A regulations. So far as I know these covers were not actually used in public until the 1994 Monte, when Biasion complained the car felt unstable, so the team reverted to 17 in diameters.

Pirelli were the Original Equipment (OE) tyre suppliers, with a P Zero in 225/45ZR-16 sizing of asymmetric tread pattern. I was told Dunlops would follow, but have only experienced an oversize (18 in wheel diameter) Yokohama A008R, standard size Bridgestone Expedia SO-1 or equivalent Goodyear Eagle NCT.

Most of that non-standard tyre wear was experienced at Castle Combe or Oulton Park race circuits and I would nominate the Yokohama for sheer grip, Bridgestone for all round ability on a thoroughly updated tyre design (they have paid serious attention to road noise and ride requirements). Goodyear was the most underrated cover I have come across for the Cosworth, within fractions of the Bridgestone around a track and extremely consistent.

Most cars (Lux and Motorsport specs) came with Recaro seating, so far as the press were concerned, but Karmann had worked very hard on a cheaper alternative that was acceptable by launch date for the standard road Cosworth. Behr take the credit for the sophisticated intercooling, a system that was to be aided for Motorsport by an additional water spray with a Bosch pump and ancillary plumbing living in the boot.

Ford reported building over 2,600 Escort Cosworths with the plumbing lines supplied in the boot (not connected) to fulfil FIA homologation requirements. More about the unsporting row that lurked through much of 1993 and into 1994 in the following chapter, but it is worth commenting that Ford Motorsport traced precise build numbers at Karmann. Ford found that the first 427 cars had been allowed out without the water spray plumbing, so concours judges will have to be beware of making hasty judgments in this respect.

Exterior styling inputs were co-ordinated by Dave Turner, Director of Design then based at Ford in Britain. Paul Coucill and Ian Callum — known for the Ghia Via and the Aston Martin DB7 — supervised the work carried out by MGA (in this case MGA stands for Mike Gibbs Associates) with additional input from Steve Harper.

There were some fine drivers consulted. An SVE chassis engineering team was led once more by Mick Kelly, but had experienced engineers such as Fiesta racer Colin Stancombe and considerable outsider inputs from Jackie Stewart, '60s European touring car champion Sir John Whitmore, and contracted rally drivers Jimmy McRae, Malcolm Wilson and Gwyndaf Evans.

It is worth recalling the speed at which the Cosworth Escort was

The body hardly had a smooth panel in it, but was immensely strong and perfectly suited to its international motor sport brief. The glass tilt and slide sunroof was fitted to all but Motorsport bodies in the first series.

progressed to production, despite these multiple inputs. From the full allocation of funds in April 1989, it took 12 road car prototypes and two Motorsport/Show and rally car forerunners three years to bring the Escort Cosworth into production. It is also worth emphasizing how far ahead a major manufacturer has to think, for February 1990 was only the start of Sierra Cosworth 4x4 production.

By July 1990 road prototype number 12, was complete at Karmann, so it is worth looking at how some of these forerunners had been employed. At that point there were 17 SV-prefixed prototypes (including clay models on rolling chassis and interior models), plus six assorted functional ACEs.

These ran on 700 series codes, where SV-700 was a design study of the north-south longitudinal engine installation, then mounted in the old Escort shell. SV-701 was assigned to wind tunnel work in Cologne, SV-703 was the Clay that MGA worked with to execute external appearance, SV-704 was a bare shell study and SV-705 ended up in the barriers as a crash test victim. The first full working prototype of June 1990 was assigned SV-710. Motorsport used the system of MS001 and so on, more of which in the next chapter.

The subsequent SVE development cars had to perform missions such as general durability, structure testing, brake development, chassis (handling) development, production wind tunnel evaluation, cooling runs, hot climate performance (at Nardo on the southern toe of Italy), cold climate performance and handling (Finland), noise vibration and harshness (NVH) research (the latter was a cause for concern just months before launch) and crash tests.

The SVE development Escorts were seen widely, testing at domestic venues such as Castle Combe besides traditional Ford haunts such as Lommel and Nardo. The Cosworth went through four editions of the 40,000 km (24,800 mile) Ford General Durability programme at Lommel. Plus a more severe improved durability schedule, seeking out company duplications of pave, country lanes and sustained high-speed running on the banked outer circuit.

Perhaps the toughest tests were reserved for the basic body, which

Early 1991 Escort Cosworth on test in Germany heads for a morale-boosting visit to Saarlouis plant.

withstood the equivalent of 62,000 miles (100,000 km) duress over a 66-hour cycle on the hydropulse rig at Dunton to probe its worth.

To meet their 'best in homologation class' aspirations, SVE conducted comparative Escort Cosworth test drives. They took along the Lancia Delta Integrale 16v and 238 bhp BMW Sport Evolution M3, the trio visiting venues as varied as the Ford test tracks in Belgium and Britain (Lommel and Boreham airfield), plus the challenging Nurburgring and a lot of comparative public road miles in Britain and Germany.

One prototype crosses over our road and competition chapter divides. The first publicly seen prototype rally ACE was built in May 1990 by subcontractor and former Boreham employee Gordon Spooner. This car (coded MS002) went on to score the Escort Cosworth's first rally win, long before homologation was secured (September 1990). It was then also used for static publicity purposes at Escort introductions before becoming a genuine rally car again.

Motor work

Production of a specific Escort YBT-coded derivative of the 2 litre turbo Cosworth motor began on 23 March 1992 and ended almost exactly two years later, superseded by the similarly powerful YBP unit, after 5186 had been built.

Graduating from YBG engine specification in the Sierra 4x4 RS Cosworth to the Escort YBT unit involved no dimensional changes in the short stroke 1993 cc (90.8 x 77 mm), which continued to run an 8:1 compression in its belt drive, DOHC, 16-valve, cylinder head of aluminium. The iron block had been beefed up since the original 3-dr Cosworths, but was not the 'full heavy metal' thickwall special of RS500 application.

As for the Sierra Sapphire RS 4x4, an MT75 gearbox did its best to resist

Most powerful production variant (227 bhp) of the Cosworth YB-series to date was the revised Escort application with mid-range overboost facility.

an extra 10 lb/ft of torque (now 224 lb/ft) of torque generated for the Cosworth 4x4 Escort, but these gearboxes do appear to be on their production torque limits in these applications, never mind modified. In production saloon car racing, weakness has been found in third gear which is lifed for replacement around 500 to 750 km, but this is in association with approximately 300 bhp.

The big production changes were external, centred upon fitment of a Garrett T3 turbine and T04B compressor wheel in association with a three-way catalyst with closed loop boost control. This 'T35' turbocharger was coddled by two-stage water/air, plus conventional air to air intercooling. The complete ignition and injection system was managed by Weber-Marelli (with some licensed Bosch parts) and the software programme allowed substantial mid-range overboost. The latter was an attempt to disguise the Motorsport mismatch between bigger turbo and 2 litre road car engine.

Ancillary engine changes under a new blue rocker cover embraced a considerably lightened flywheel (better for competition multi-plate clutches, as well as lower inertia), more effective oil pick up and baffling for the alloy pan wet sump, replacement cam belt covering and considerable work on the engine mounts to reduce the cabin reverberations that were such a severe development mileage problem.

Power output was not sensational on the road, just 7 bhp more allowed (227 PS at 6,250 rpm) than for its 4-dr Sierra predecessor, this alongside a 14 Nm torque bonus (304 Nm at 3,500 rpm) by Cosworth. Initial (up to 2,200 rpm) and top end (over 4,500 rpm, to the 7,000 rpm limiter) boost was the traditional Cosworth YB conservative setting of 0.75 bar (10.7 psi). Depending on climatic conditions and the throttle opening applied to the engine, you could have a Lancia Delta-style mid-range overboost to a maximum of 1.25 bar (17.8 psi). The overboost built between 2,200 and 3,000 rpm, contributing a carefully tailored thrust to 4,000 or 4,500 rpm.

Virtually every panel of the
Escort RS Cosworth exuded
performance, but the car was a
civilized road companion in all
but the inevitable lag of the
oversize turbocharger.

It took a lot of development miles to make this mid-range boost offer civil
support: right up to pre-production examples it would droop abruptly.
Despite those conscientious miles, and maximum co-operation from
Cosworth, neither press nor public were convinced. The dreaded
turbocharger lag was present until 3,500 rpm, or more. In turn, this led to a
number of popular road conversions, some of which went to the huge
horsepower overkills of the Sierra. My favourite, by Brooklyn at Redditch in
Worcestershire, saw them meet customer demand early for a smaller
turbocharger. They used a Sierra-sized T3 to generate amiable mid-range
pulling power and a sizzling 320 or so horsepower. Even in circuit use, it was
faster than the standard-size turbo cars of other customers, which nominally
had 15–20 bhp more . . .

On the production statistics front, *Autocar & Motor* reported 0–60 mph in
6.2 sec, a 137 mph maximum and 21 overall mpg. Full results are in the
appendix, but I used the industry standard Correvit test gear and Millbrook
track to record 0–60 mph in an average 5.78 sec, 0–100 mph in 16.48 sec and
the standing 1/4 mile in 14.66 sec at 95.1 mph. Top speed around the banking
was under the 140 mph claimed by Ford, but the 0–60 mph time was as
claimed.

The official fuel consumption of cheaper 95 octane unleaded was reported
as 8.4 litres per 100 km (33.6 mpg) at 56 mph; some 9.4 litre/100 km (30.1
mpg) at 75 mph and 12.4 litre/100 km (22.8) by the tortuous urban trail. I
managed 19.5 mpg, over 519 hearty miles logged for *Motor Sport*.

Chassis lore

Fichtel and Sachs provided gas-filled shock absorbers, as they have for so
many SVE fast Fords. A considerable amount of development work went

into the front and rear suspension compliance package. Particularly successful were the newly designed bi-directional bushes for the rear suspension subframe. This allowed taut control of suspension geometry without sacrificing the longitudinal compliance required to absorb shocks.

Braced mounting points for the rear crossmember, and the reinforced trailing arms and stiffened front suspension mounting bushes, were carried out in association with Ford Motorsport's Terry Bradley. The idea was to make sure the car performed well in 'showroom' Group N guise. Mission accomplished.

John Wheeler confirmed that the interchangeability between Sierra/Sapphire and Escort chassis components was exceptionally high and that he saw 'few reasons' why owners of the older cars could not update to Escort road or competition specifications.

Mick Kelly listed out the following significant showroom changes over the Sierra RS 4x4 chassis for the Escort replacement:

	Sierra 4x4 RS	*Escort 4x4 RS*
Front bar, mm	28	29
Rear bar, mm	18	22
F/spring rate, Nm	23	21
R/spring rate, Nm	51	62

The same source also supplied 1991 homologation material that showed how much effort Ford had put into the recalibration of the variable ratio servo-assisted steering and its Cam Gears rack. Working through 2.45 turns lock to lock and an overall 13.05:1 ratio (12.5:1 to a maximum of 16.67:1) steering feedback was being adjusted even in the summer of 1991: the result was precise, more precise than many pedigree performers, but the feeling of instant communication with the driver that the earlier Cosworths conferred was absent. The Boreham works competition rack, also power assisted, needs only a kart-like 1.9 turns lock to lock and runs a straight 12:1 ratio. If money is no object and it checks out with your RS Dealer, buy it.

The handling was also modified, as was the action of the Teves anti-lock brakes. Worthwhile advances in the software logic for the anti-lock system were made, and an overall stiffening in the action of the central and rear Viscous Coupling differentials was carried over from otherwise unchanged Sierra 4x4 hardware. The rear limited slip differential went from 85 to 125 Centistokes (up 55 per cent), whilst the central unit went from 30 to 50 Centistokes (over 30 per cent). For the customer, the effect was to ensure that the limited slip differentials worked for a living, rather than being backed off to ineffective levels to promote the unhindered action of ABS.

More subtle changes concerned steering pump characteristics to increase sensitivity and response. There were stiffened callipers and replacement, ecologically sound, pads for the four-wheel disc brakes. The discs themselves featured fresh design with improved air cooling flow, ducts built into the front spoiler for motor sport use.

Those 278/273 mm front and rear discs were allied with ITT Teves Mk 2 anti-lock electronics and 'an additional mercury swipe switch type deceleration sensor'. It was only in circuit use that any braking limitation was apparent, the system notably effective for road demands and totally replaced for works rally cars in Group A.

By March 1991 all 400 unique production parts had been designed and approved. It was August 1991 when the Escort Cosworth was passed fit for production, 10 'functional build' road cars made for publicity and service department use. In the run up to full production, the landmarks included the January 1992 creation of '4P' pre-production cars on production tooling. There were 58 of these, plus other preproduction Escort Cosworths: 66 in total. They were assigned as follows:

2 for Geneva Show
25 press cars
31 marketing, emissions & homologation
8 bare bodies for Ford Motorsport, UK.

There were actually two press launches, one in LHD format from a Luxembourg base pre-dating the actual volume availability in Britain, when a RHD exercise was held in Scotland. The 25 cars referred to above were for the first LHD exercise, the RHD models being full production specification, which meant they had three key development problems eliminated.

These developed as two months frantic work to sort out a very nasty overrun boom that most of us thought was an exhaust mounting problem in Luxembourg.

Fortunately then SVE boss Dieter Hahne (now with chassis engineering in Britain) had considerable transmission engineering experience. Dieter supervised an investigation that traced the sound paths down to the clutch stimulating a rear axle crown wheel and pinion resonance, only to be soothed by replacement springs and dampening for the clutch.

Also occupying the team on the run into production was the unique instrumentation, or more particularly the 'banana' pod in which the three auxiliary dials were housed. The black plastic cowling carried the capital lettered COSWORTH badge. This would not sit snugly upon the rest of the fascia, drawing attention to uneven fit lines. There was no answer except constant rectification work to achieve tighter tolerances.

Some SVE members thought the cost of the unique white-faced

1.5 bar) by 2,800 rpm, which makes it a lot easier to drive on UK roads.

Other modifications include a Swedish export specification battery to cope with the draining loads imposed by triple anti-theft systems, 8.5 x 17 in Speedlines with Yokohama A008s and a Momo steering wheel. The suspension has now been overhauled to a tauter Group N specification with Graham Goode springs lowering front ride height 12 mm and the rear 25 mm.

Although Niland is displeased that Ford discount the car he paid £24,000 for, meaning that depreciation leaves him with £10,000 dealer offers for his car in 1994, he is otherwise extremely pleased with his Escort Cosworth.

The aptly 'K-AR' registered Cologne Escort Cosworth provided early 1992 driving impressions and witnessed the endorsement of the RS badge in the German market (the RS comeback came with the 1991 RS2000). At this stage the Escort Cosworth still suffered pre-production glitches, but these were eliminated before RHD output commenced.

instruments would have been better spent on further development engineering this very special Escort RS. Others (including Dieter Hahne) supported its unique showroom appeal. At least the instruments were legible, and were widely imitated for lesser Escorts. Their unique 'electroluminescent' instrument panels, in which no bulbs are employed, cover a conventional speedometer, tachometer, petrol tank contents and water temperature.

These are all displayed in front of the driver, whilst supplementary dials in the same finish spoke of battery volts, turbocharger boost and oil pressure. Both units adapt their lighting output to ambient, brightening as you enter a tunnel and fading in daylight conditions. The system works, according to the PR people at Ford by 'using a composite material for the surface, which includes a phosphor-coated layer. A 115–120 volt AC current is applied to this layer, which causes it to glow.' If you are wondering how they make DC battery current become AC lighting energy, the answer is 'a small inverter at

The RHD Escort Cosworth is shown with the correct leather trim, original three-spoke steering wheel and 'Cosworth' appellation in the 'banana' instrument console, but has the wrong instruments in the official press picture. The LHD model has the correct seven white-faced dials that were imitated in the 1994 Escort Si for style, but not content.

the rear of the instrument'. Is an inverter a politically correct transformer? I'll never know . . .

We do know that series production begun, on 25 per day at Karmann on 27 April 1992. The official European press and public launch was dated 5 May 1992 and 22 May 1992 was the public sales date for the UK. December 1992 saw 2,500 examples of the Escort RS Cosworth inspected by the FIA for Motorsport Group A and N recognition, that month marking the decease of the 4x4 Cosworth Sierra 4-dr. Dropped when more than 12,000 had been sold, nearly 4,000 of those coming to the UK.

The Escort Cosworth was not a stripped out homologation special, unless you specified the MotorSport or Standard versions. Even then all models had items like power steering and ABS braking that was hydraulic pump-assisted, rather than servo-boosted.

The 75 kg extra quoted in the Ford RS catalogue for the Luxury Escort underlined that the cheapest variant, saving up to £2,416 on the most expensive Cosworth Escort, was intended as the basis for competition. It therefore lacked the Luxury model features as follows: no electric operation of exterior mirrors and side glass; no glass tilt and slide sunroof; no 'Quickclear' front screen and heated washers; Hexagon fabric trims only. Karmann seats were reserved for the Standard model, minus rear map pockets, instead of Lux-spec Recaros. There were no rear seat head restraints and no facility to optionally order air conditioning (made available first on 1991 Model Year Sierra RS 4x4), leather trim, heated seats or a CD player.

An alternative seat from Karmann (used in the Standard model only; the Motorsport 'stripper' came with Recaros) highlighted the quality of Karmann personnel involved. Karmann persisted until they had 85 per cent of a Recaro's attractions, but saved hundreds of dollars per front seat. The same large savings to the company result when offering the updated Ford EEC IV engine management in place of Weber Marelli.

Writing this in early 1994, with benefit of knowing that just 310 of the 800

Highlight of a full test week for *Motor Sport* was a Brands Hatch outing. The 4x4 system loved this weather rather more than that of the rear drive BMWs that were sharing the session. *(Courtesy LAT/Motor Sport)*

allocated to Britain (1,000 for Germany) had been sold in 1992, plus 576 in 11 months of 1993, it could be seen that the dealers would do well to attain further revised June 1993 list prices of £22,050 (Motorsport), £24,240 (Lux) and £25,590 (Lux + leather).

You had only to flip through *Motoring News* or *Autocar & Motor* to find dealers offering new and unregistered Lux examples of Escort RSC at £20,995 to £22,295. Any Cosworth RS with 800 to 2,000 miles on the clock descended into the £19,000 bracket, with the occasional standard car, or private deal, hovering around £17,000. By 1994 prices had softened slightly: new Lux spec Cosworths were put on offer at £21,495, second-hand prices ranged in the sub £14,000 bracket (rarer 1992s) to £18,000 plus for dealer 1993 models with leather trim.

At least five variations of Escort Cosworth body and engine were originally planned for public sale. These met Motorsport's needs (as above), plus that 'Luxury' package. Then, initially planned after the first 2,500 were made with all aerodynamic aids fitted, there was optional choice of deleting such downforce aerodynamics. The latter 'wingless' format was demanded by the Swiss authorities from the start and was officially available in the UK during 1993, although the dealers I spoke to had all deleted the wings from existing customer/stock cars rather than ordering such cars officially.

Without the front and rear aerodynamic package there was an 0.33 Cd and 145 mph maximum, according to Ford engineers. The promised Ford-

Shape of the mid-'90s? The Escort Cosworth without its aero-pack was thoroughly tested in the original development programme. Safety changes, including the latest in steering wheels, accompanied the 1994 arrival of the predicted 'small' turbocharger and Ford electronic engine management.

engineered EEC-IV injection/engine management, to replace the Weber-Marelli electronics (which would continue in Motorsport use) with a smaller T3 turbocharger from Garrett, had proceeded no further than promises and the 1993 Geneva Show editorial news columns of *Autocar & Motor*.

In fact Cosworth built no such production engines in 1993, and it was March 1994 before a more comprehensively engineered YBP-coded successor was placed in production. This had the smaller T25 Garrett AiResearch turbo in conjunction with updated Ford-Cosworth microprocessor electronics, that were still stamped EEC-IV. I am told the car itself incorporated many of the later Escort safety moves in its structure, including door beams, and this accounted for an anticipated 30 to 40 kg weight gain in 1994.

Writing all this has made me want to buy one all over again and envy Jeremy 'BBC *Top Gear*' Clarkson with renewed frenzy for the two such cars he has operated. I can't face asking him how it went, frothing jealousy would slash my vocal chords in milliseconds, but I do know the televisual Jeremy managed a parking year on the South London streets with no problems on the first car, then had the second extensively vandalized.

In May 1994 Ford allowed us to see and drive the Escort Cosworth that would be offered to the public for the remainder of the '90s. The biggest changes were to the engine (over 20 modifications listed) and wider public access to the no-cost option of deleting the front and rear downforce wing/spoiler equipment. Prices were unchanged, and total 1992-4 (May start and finish dates) Escort Cosworth sales were reported as 2,666. The biggest markets were the UK and Italy (640 each), Germany (399) and Switzerland (340). Despite strong rallying links with Ford Motorsport, Spanish Escort Cosworth customers numbered just 280 and the French took 160.

That is enough of Escort Cosworth's engineering success and showroom tribulations. Now let us see how it performed in its element: motor sport.

Handy hatchback format for the Escort Cosworth was often overlooked amongst the paeans of praise for its grip and grunt performance. *(Courtesy LAT/*Motor Sport*)*

From racer to shorn spoiler format: Ford concept designs for '94.

Ready for the off: Luxembourg press fleet are readied by Cologne and Karmann personnel. The verdict was far more favourable than before, because of improved engine response at public road speeds.

Side view reveals the loss of the front splitter and spats as well as the upper rear wing.

Not just a prettier (concealed spark plug) cosmetic 'face'. Among 20 listed engine changes were the 'small' T25 Garret AiResearch turbocharger, Ford EEC-IV electronic engine management, individual coils for 20,000 mile lifed plugs, 10,000 mile service intervals and an enlarged catalyst. Power and torque retained the same peak values, but maximum power was now at 5,750 rpm (rather than 6,250 rpm) and 90 per cent of maximum torque could be obtained from a 20 per cent broad rpm range. On the road; it meant the Cosworth started to pick up by 1,900 rpm instead of 3,500 . . .

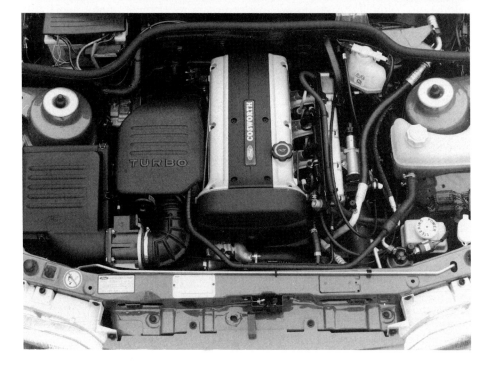

Above left 'White-out' instruments were retained, but the air bag steering wheel was new. Our LHD test cars lacked the lower spoke Ford oval in the rush to get the latest safety equipment publicized.

Above Rear wing loss could be felt at speed, but was sensible for those wanting a lower profile Escort Cosworth.

Still the best driving machine produced by Ford, and the most thoroughly engineered Cosworth Ford yet . . .

Chapter 10

Escort Cosworth: the winner

The protracted development period for the rally version of the Escort Cosworth proved totally worthwhile, as the car was on winning form for the first World Championship Rally it contended. As a bonus, the Escort also became a very worthy saloon car racer, both in production format and the prestigious German ADAC GT series.

Corsica has always been good to the French, Ford and Cosworth. Scene of the Sierra's only World Rally Championship victory, the Mediterranean island also demonstrated the 4x4 Escort's tarmac agility with a win for François Delecour/Daniel Grataloup. Note how upright and far forward the driver sits, whilst the navigator lies as far back as possible!

'. . . The Escort has acquired all the virtues one used to associate with the Delta.' David Williams, Editor, *Rallycourse*, 1993.

Praise comes no higher in World Championship Rallying circles than this, for there has never been a more successful WRC marque than Lancia, and the Delta was the most successful of a line that has included the fabled Stratos.

In our previous chapter, devoted to the road car that had to be built before the company could homologate a vehicle for world class competition, we saw that Ford broke new ground in the Group A and N formulae that currently prevail. Ford achieved this by purpose-building the basis for a competition car, the bias firmly on World Championship rallying.

This dedicated formula did not give them the huge advantages enjoyed in

the '70s by the mid-Ferrari-engined Stratos against a field full of Escort RS clones. Yet the basic recipe of a longitudinal engine and downforce aerodynamics did reap the service and anticipated handling advantages that the Ford Motorsport executives had discussed five *years* before the Escort could compete in world class competition.

From its first non-homologated appearances in 1990 to its amazing run of five WRC victories in its 1993 debut season, plus 1994's 'Big One' at Monte Carlo to celebrate 12 months' World Championship experience, the Ford Escort RS Cosworth has established itself as a benchmark for the rest to beat, especially as it won one of those WRC rounds (Sanremo) with a discarded ex-works driver (Franco Cunico) and a specification that was far from the ultimate in factory Ford terms. In 1990 it was a comparatively crude

---

TIMETABLE FOR THE ESCORT RS COSWORTH

May 1990: Gordon Spooner constructs MS 002, first Group A prototype, registered H930 JHJ; MS 001 was a 'weekend racer' project car seen at motor shows late 1990.
September 1990: MS 002 wins in Spain for Joseph Mia Bardolet; Talavera Rally, Spain.
1 January 1993: Escort RSC homologated, Groups A and N.
21–27 January: WRC-1 Escort RSC finishes 2–3, debut Monte Carlo; Delecour leads all but last two stages, Biasion second and Escort wins Group N: J-B Serpaggi.
12–14 February: WRC-2 Swedish Rally receives no works Fords; neither Malcolm Wilson nor Sebastian Lindholm in semi-works Escorts finishes.
3–6 March: WRC-3 Escorts of Delecour and Biasion finish 1–2 in Portugal; score 26 fastest stage times.
8–12 April: WRC-4 No Escorts entered on Safari.
2–4 May: WRC-5 Delecour wins Tour de Corse by 1 min 2 sec; 15 fastest stage times. Biasion 7th, and Ford Escort RSC wins Group N (Giovanni Manfrinato).
30 May–1 June: WRC-6 Biasion wins Acropolis; Delecour retires (motor).
14–17 July: WRC-7 Biasion 2nd, Argentina; only works Escort entered, but Carlos Mennem 5th (Mike Little-prepared) and Escort RSC wins Group N (Mohammed bin Sulayem).
5–8 August: WRC-8 Delecour 2nd, New Zealand; Biasion retired.
27–29 August: WRC-9 No Boreham Escorts for 1,000 Lakes; Wilson 5th before crash, Lindholm finishes 6th.
18–21 September: WRC-10 Delecour 3rd in Australia, Biasion retired.
11–13 October: WRC-11 Both works Fords retire; Franco Cunico 1st, Sanremo, Italy, for Ford Italia/Malbrun; Patrick Snijers 3rd; Escort RSC wins Group N (Renato Trevaglia).
2–4 November: WRC-12 Delecour 1st, Biasion 4th; 15 fastest stages; winning Group N Escort disqualified.
21–24 November: WRC-13 Wilson 3rd (semi works), Delecour 4th in sole Boreham entry on RAC (UK); Group N to Gwyndaf Evans.

FIA World Rally Championship (Manufacturers): Ford Motor Company 2nd. FIA World Rally Championship (Drivers): François Delecour 2nd, Miki Biasion 4th.
FIA Cup, Production Car Drivers: Antonio Coutinho (Group N Escort RSC).
FIA European Championship (Drivers): Patrick Snijers (RAS Sport) 2nd, Robert Droogmans (G. Spooner) 3rd.

*Escort RS Cosworths won five of 10 WRC rounds; Snijers won more Euro events than champion Pierre Cesare Baroni (Lancia Delta Integrale). French International Championship: Bernard Beguin (Group A; Snobeck) 1st. British International Championship: Malcolm Wilson (MW Motorsport) 2nd Gwyndaf Evans (SBG, Group N) 3rd.

22–27 January 1994: WRC-1 Delecour wins Monte Carlo, Biasion 4th, Thiry (RAS/Boreham) 6th: Escort RSC 1–2 in Group N; Escort Cosworths fill 50 per cent of top 10 places.

The first test car scored the first works Escort Cosworth win two years and three months before homologation. This Ralph Hardwick photo (its brethren frames sold to Ford for worldwide distribution) records Mia Bardolet/José Ferrer winning with H930 JHJ in the September 1990 Talavera rally, just as they had with the Sierra 4x4 in pre-homologation trim. The seven-speed Escort was part of the massive Ford display at Birmingham Motor Show by the following week . . .

After persistent criticism of their modesty in 1993, Ford ensured that Europeans got to hear about the Escort's Monte Carlo Rally success in January 1994. *(Poster courtesy Ogilvy & Mather, London)*

The Ford Escort Cosworth

The driver was brilliant. In fog, snow and ice, he took an early lead and kept his nerve to finish more than a minute ahead.

The engineers were magnificent. The months on the drawing board and weeks of preparation proved the point: that the Ford Escort has got what it takes to take on the best and beat them all.

There is, however, more to winning rallies than champagne celebrations and victory advertisements like this. Because, win or lose, we take part in motorsport to learn.

It helps us develop better engineers and they in turn develop better cars for you.

There are hundreds of examples of the lessons paying off by improving the Ford cars you can buy.

Four-wheel drive, advanced multi-valve engines, fuel-injection, anti-lock brakes and turbocharging were all perfected in the heat of competition.

And one day you might be driving cars with push-button gearchanges, carbonfibre body parts and interactive control systems.

When we win rallies the ultimate victor is you. Because you get the results.

We race. You get the result.

amalgamation of seven-speed Sierra Group A running gear and hand-made Escort outline, now it is a very thoroughly developed competitor that repays the input of original thought and high technology.

The Cosworth Escort has achieved more than its creators could ever have dreamed when they sat down to simply create a World Rally Championship contender that would 'give the Delta a run for its money', in the words of one modest insider. In fact it was so good that the company were forced to fund additional 1993 sorties to Argentina and Australia, chasing Toyota and Juha Kankkunen hard for the title for three-quarters of the season.

Outside the premier league of WRC, the Escort Cosworth also exceeded expectations. It proved an outright winner in rallycross as well as circuit racing, particularly suited to Group N (showroom) track use in the UK with drivers such as Charlie Cox, Frank Greenway and Peter Clarke. The power to weight equations of German GT Championship events, also attracted Escort Cosworth entries.

Wolf racing effectively fielded privateer examples at a little over 320 bhp for drivers such as former RS500/Zakspeed Capri star Klaus Niedzwiedz; Ralf Kelleners Jnr showed top six form as well in another distinctly non-works Cossie. In the UK some 300 bhp was the norm but race wins were

Old generation hangs on, newcomers charge. The Sierra 4x4 was an obvious privateer choice in these conditions, but the Escort was even quicker. Frank Greenway/Kurt Luby resist the tide of change at Donington in 1993 with Mountune power. *(Picture courtesy of John Gaisford)*

It was not all rallying in the Escort Cosworth's competition life. The top class of the British saloon car cup was dominated by the Escort Cosworth in 1993 and here's a similar specification Escort of 300 bhp (1.4 to 1.5 bar boost) from Kevin Maxted. I tried this car at Goodwood, where it would average over 102 mph for a lap. In 1994 this car won the Snetterton 24 hours for owner Nicki Torregiani and three co-drivers, its first 24-hour win.

common, whereas BMW mopped up most of what was going in Germany with a factory team and the talent of Johnny Cecotto.

As to the World Rally Championship itself, the Escort Cosworth and its Boreham-based personnel acquitted themselves with distinction.

The Ford flew to five victories outright (four to the works, one to Ford Italia with local preparation and Motorsport parts of varying specification. Only once did Ford fail to fight for the lead, when in works specification.

The Escort was always on the pace, actually setting the standard for rivals Toyota and company for all but the vital final stages of its Monte Carlo debut. Only in Australia did the Escort fail to thrill. My information was that this could be traced to a combination of fuel/tank glue ailments, as could some time-consuming delays in Acropolis.

It was obvious that the original north-south engine recipe was right (only Subaru had the same layout, and that was a flat four turbo), as was the decision to test, test again, also ignoring the lure of the mega-expensive East African Safari, with its attendant requirement for a radically different technical approach, in the dream debut season.

The handling balance of the Escort was owed not to its front engine/rear drive basics (weight distribution still saw 58 per cent in the nose, front drive style), but to the aerodynamics and team familiarity in extracting the best from their MacPherson strut systems and FFD 4x4.

The loss of rear overhang compared to the Sierra certainly helped the driver perceptions of how well their Escorts handled versus their 'edgy' predecessors, but the weight mass distribution was only 1 per cent different between the two vehicles, the Escort bearing that slight extra bias toward nose end weight distribution.

Because of the change in FIA regulations from 1992 to 1993, the competition Sierra actually went in the record books as lighter than the Escort Cosworth counterpart: Sierra managed 1,140 kg in the 1,100 kg minimalist era versus 'just over' the 1,200 kg mark for its descendant; both cars in Corsican 4x4 format. In the case of the Escort, the desire to save

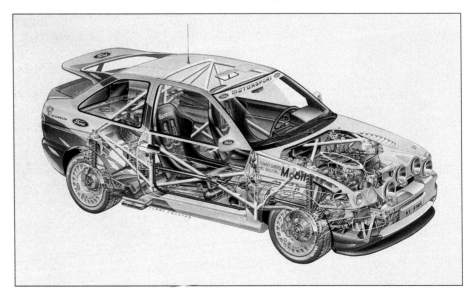

Drawn to win. Incorrectly registered as A1 FMC (the 'personal' Ford plates did not make it from the Sierra to Escort era), the 1993 works Escort for Miki Biasion displays the usual Sierra-Group A style 'coil-over' rear suspension, extensive roll cage and side exhaust.

weight was best expressed in the 'very expensive' provision of carbon fibre casings to the fire extinguisher canister!

The fixed mechanical power split allotted by the central differential and its epicyclic gear set favoured the allocation of 45 per cent front power and 55 per cent rear during the season, but they ran at other times with 40, 50 and 55 per cent fed to the front wheels.

Were there any weak links to the Escort armoury of WRC advantages? Some, and the team were always honest enough to discuss the need for a diet in association with more grunt. Weight loss measures were implemented later in 1993, once the gravel road specification had become routine, but the way in which more power would be obtained baffled me.

The Mountune engine is already highly developed, releasing 180.5 bhp a litre even with the mandatory 38 mm restrictor. Ford/Mountune were already running truly phenomenal boost levels in 1993 (3 bar/42.7 psi in Corsican trim). The major steel reciprocating components, such as the crankshaft and rods, remained. Yet the complete motor was stripped and rebuilt around replacement pistons, camshafts with substantial extra lift and a cylinder head running a leading edge 7.5:1 cr (sky high, in view of the boost employed).

The engine management electronics were key to obtaining clean performance from such constricted hardware. Most of what I saw was Weber-Marelli, but the cabin and John Wheeler revealed that a small consultancy called Pectel had reprogrammed the commands issued. The results were sensational in the 3,500 to 7,800 rpm high boost band. The motor was at least as well mannered as the showroom item in delivering drivable performance, only the fast idle and intimidating note from the oversize single tail pipe telling you that shattering performance was available, upon further request.

The result of all that motor work was revealed when we tested for *Autocar & Motor* in the summer of 1993. K832 HHJ had a privately acknowledged 360 bhp at 6,800 rpm. A whopping 450 Nm of torque at 4,000 rpm was reported by *Autocourse* as the norm. Other sources quoted 4,500 rpm as the peak for torque, and 450 Nm at 5,000 rpm was also the quote for *Autosport* in 1994.

Three years Escort engine bay progress: the 1990 test car used this straight turret brace that hindered engine access and was not so accessible as the V-pattern used on works cars through 1993. Power output was always diplomatically referred to as 300 bhp or less by Ford people. Research to support my *Autocar & Motor* tests of three Sierras and one works Escort revealed 340 to 360 bhp. More important was massive torque and superb electronic engine management (from Pectel in 1993).

Such engine output figures were enough to fling the Escort from 0–60 mph in less than 4 sec and certainly seemed competitive (within the bounds of competition bullshit) with all known rivals. As ever the drivers and listening media reported that there was a need for more power in late 1993, but the Escort entered 1994 with winning pace displayed in both Monte Carlo and Portugal, only Toyota apparently right in the same power league.

Beyond those outline comments and subsequent technical analysis, I'll leave the debut season record of the Escort Cosworth to speak for itself. For what it is worth I believe that what was achieved was as influential as the Mondeo programme of the Rouse squad, but the results were grossly understated by the less pervasive TV coverage and appalling marketing/PR of WRC. UK cartoonists such as Jim Bamber were actually begging Ford to blow their own trumpet. I don't think the media have ever made that request to a Ford sales centre before: usually Ford beat us to death with their achievements, even when they are rather less significant than taking on the best of WRC manufacturers and emerging with honour . . .

Rally development

Our primary interest here is to trace how the Ford Motorsport facility at Boreham developed the competition version of the Escort to a regular WRC event winner. Although the car was seen in prototype form from 1990 onward (see our Timetable/Results table) in both Britain and Spain, the pace of development naturally sharpened as the official homologation debut date of 1 January 1993 drew closer.

Essentially the first prototype Group A cars was based on the latest in Sierra seven-speed hardware in an ingeniously married Escort and Sierra suit,

The new face of Fast Fords at tarmac test work in the hands of François Delecour and Malcolm Wilson. The allegiance to Pirelli and rectangular headlights would go before the cars made their World Rally Championship debut in 1993.

the ceremony conducted by former Ford Motorsport mechanic Gordon Spooner at his Witham, Essex base. At this initial stage the car did not wear the quad individual round lamps that had first appeared on the later Sierra 4-drs, but these were in place for 1992 forays and its factory rallying debut, Monte Carlo 1993. John Wheeler recalled of the early development days.

'The May to June construction of MS002 was the true starting point, and it was pleasing when it won in Spain, later that year. But we were still a long way from the car's homologation and 1991 was a quiet year whilst the road car progressed. However, we had proved the basic layout and cooling system in Spain,' felt John Wheeler.

'In 1992 things picked up and we went testing with MS002 in Sanremo and Corsica over WRC stages. Spain (again) came back on the menu, but this time we competed through a co-operation between Ford at Boreham and Mike Taylor Developments of Northallerton. In the UK Malcolm Wilson did both the Centurion and Scottish rallies, again with very encouraging results [especially in the stage time speed of the Escort versus the McRae/Prodrive Subaru *JW*).

'By June 1992 we were ready to freeze the specification, designing and building Escort Cosworths to a 1993 specification. In August of 1992 we went tarmac testing to develop the car for Monte Carlo and gravel road running.

'Over that 1990–93 development period, I would say the biggest changes were in improving body strength and stiffness, particularly with regard to the triangulated and welded in TG45 steel roll cage. As regulations changed we had to respond as well. Here I am thinking of the fact that tyre diameters and widths were controlled more rigorously in 1993. Previously the diameter was free — now it is 658 mm (25.6 in) maximum and the overall 10 in width went down to a 9 in tyre tread width,' recalled John.

Maintaining maximum competitiveness, Ford developed a wider track suspension system, 'one that takes us to the limits. In round figures the track stretch was 45 mm (1.77 in) and an obvious number of new components were engineered to support that increase, front and back,' said Wheeler.

Speaking in the summer of 1993, the Ford Motorsport engineer continued, 'Talking of tyres reminds me that Michelin were our contracted suppliers,

Below left The 1992 rendition of the front layout for the Group A Escort included the massive brakes, replacement hub/upright castings and the drop link front roll bar linkage to the replacement lower track control arm.

Below Rear suspension castings for the Group A works Escort with their ball joint mountings and massive hubs.

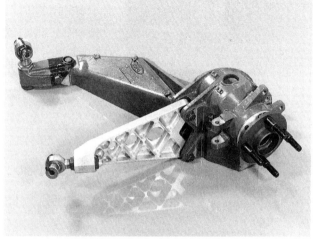

and that meant we could run their anti-puncture (ATS)/Mousse tyres, which deal so efficiently with punctures.'

Following that extensive testing, the Escort was homologated into Group A. The 1 January 1993 reference number was A-5466. There were then 12 sheets of Group A alternative equipment, and a mass of photographic evidence supporting their existence and permitted outline. In Group N the modifications are tightly controlled, but still Ford Motorsport needed 11 more descriptive sheets (N–5466). During the season seven more homologation amendments or options were added in Group A and the track dimensions for Group N were corrected (vital for competitors on the wider wheel choices).

All this additional paperwork naturally meant a far more competitive car, so what were the principle changes?

WHO ARE FFD?

FFD stands for Ferguson Formula Developments Ltd, who have rather imposing offices just outside Coventry. FFD is the descendant of the British 4x4 pioneer (in racing and rallying terms) that was born from the post-war genius of Harry Ferguson.

During 1971 FFD was founded as an amicable breakaway from GKN, who had acquired all the rights to mass manufacture (then defined as runs of more than 500) of Ferguson-patented hardware in 1969. Tony Rolt was rewarded for his years of work on Ferguson's behalf by the right to develop further and license for sale Ferguson innovations, and his son Stuart ran FFD into the mid-'90s.

The GKN deal led to the establishment of overseas Viscodrive factories (initially, but briefly, in alliance with ZF). The largest is now in Japan, whilst Europe is served by an Italian factory or the Austrian Steyr concern, who also have a mass production licence from GKN.

By the early '70s, Ferguson had proved capable of converting not only the thunderous works rallycross Capris for Roger and Stan Clark, plus the rapid Rod Chapman, but also public road Ford Zephyrs, Capris and Opel Monzas.

The mass production possibilities for 4x4 systems were 'totally the result of the 1980 Audi Quattro,' in Stuart Rolt's opinion. He explained, 'Suddenly companies like Ford and BMW needed our help to make their own 4x4 road cars. They just had to have them, *quickly*. So we gladly did much of the prototype work here for both.

'In production terms that led to the Sierra XR4x4 and a similar system for the Scorpio and Granada, plus the LHD only BMW 325iX [all no longer available *JW*]. These 4x4 designs were quite different in their detail execution, but both Ford and BMW allowed a distinct power bias to the rear, which allowed quite exciting power oversteer handling,' concluded Stuart Rolt. That system lies at the heart of every Escort Cosworth too.

Ford became the champion of the Viscous Coupling for all reasons and remains a prime user into the '90s. Escort Turbo, RS200, all the Cosworth Sierras and on into the present 1993 world class winner, Ford has been a big league competition customer for FFD. Even the prototype rear transaxle RS1700T ran a VC from April 1982, so this is the longest works rally team link for FFD.

Ford also employed the Viscous Coupling for production road cars, first debuting on the 1984 Escort RS Turbo.

Today FFD do not just make hardware for Ford Motorsport. In race or rally terms, Lancia, Alfa Romeo and Audi have also been big customers, along with 'practically every team in the 1993 British Touring Car Championship, including the Rouse Mondeo'.

FFD 1993 production versatility extended through the design of five-speed front drive boxes for mass production at 7,000 units daily to the 'two or three units a week' of the massive five-speed needed to resist the torque of the twin turbo Jaguar XJ220 V6. In the name of durability FFD also tortured the BMW/Weismann/Murray six-speed box that served the McLaren F1 road car and its 627 bhp.

A more accurate prediction of the works Escort came from this May 1992 win on the Centurion Rally of Northumberland. The crew was Malcolm Wilson/Bryan Thomas and the 100 miles of Kielder stages helped test both durability and 'different suspension settings to gain data for future events. The Escort is small, light and very nimble, the ideal rally winning package,' commented Wilson prophetically at the time.

In Group A the extensive re-engineering of the car becomes apparent when the first sheet tells you of a replacement gearbox (with its own 1 litre remote mount oil supply) and therefore body shell apertures and gear linkages, needed to accommodate the seven-speed from FFD at Coventry (see 'Who are FFD?').

Developed under the generic MS90 coding and first seen in the Sierras of our earlier chapter, Ford Motorsport and FFD have not stood still on their MS90 through to MS93 seven-speed box development: the code simply means Motorsport and the season it is specified for, but after the original redevelopment (post 1,000 Lakes, August 1990 in the Sierra) it was matter of steady evolution, not revolution. From the start the Group A rallying Escort was homologated with two sets of ratios (see Appendix 2) which were colloquially referred to as 'Long' and 'Short' referring to the overall gearing. It is important to note that the previous Sierra close ratio five-speed set up, an uprated MT75, was *not* homologated for the competition Escort. That alone made the cost of preparing a top line Ford for international Group A leap by at least £20,000 (roughly £17,500 of that for the gearbox by 1993).

It is easiest for me to identify the two seven-speed gear sets by the difference in maximum speeds given. Philip Dunabin, the overlooked and overloaded Ford Motorsport engineer, quoted me 155 mph in seventh at 7,800 rpm for the longest set, or 127 mph in the same circumstances on the shorter ratios; this for the slick shod Corsican tarmac road racer.

However, for the drivers the differences in homologated gear sets do not start until you have changed two gears, for its only from third to seventh that the ratios differ. Some of those differences are fractional, borne out by the fact that sixth gear on the taller set (0.654) matches seventh on the long ratios (0.653) in all but the third decimal place.

The transmission work extended to the choice of six gearbox-mounted final drive reduction gear ratios (from 1.263 to 1.688) and seven ratio choices for three types of front and rear axles: the 9 in crown wheel and pinion unit for the rear, its 8.8 inch Group A counterpart at the front, or a more cost effective

Cursed: save for an
extraordinary performance on
the 1993 RAC Rally (when they
beat Delecour to third overall),
Malcolm Wilson/Bryan Thomas
and the attractive Michelin Pilot
Escort Cosworth (built by the
driver's own Cumbrian
preparation company) had no
luck in the UK, Sweden (shown
here) or Finland. In 1994 the
livery and MWM preparation
enjoyed more initial fortune
with Stephen Finlay winning
the first two UK home
internationals of the season.

and less durable 7.5 in front. In all cases the spread was from 4.63 to 3.25:1.

Some 156 assorted examples of the MS90 to 93 gearbox had been made when I called in at the close of October 1993. At that time the further logical development and homologation processes for the seven-speed was being concluded with a sequential (pull forward and back, like a motor cycle or typical BTCC racing saloon) seven-speed ready for Monte Carlo 1994 pre-event testing. This was successfully carried out, but François Delecour and company were obviously not convinced, because the cars ran a conventional — gated — septet to that emotional victory. The double H-pattern gated layout is recalled in my retrospective piece on driving the works Sapphire in a previous chapter.

The rest of the transmission was of equally heavy duty Ford Motorsport/FFD creation; by 1993 FFD were also assembling the works 4x4 transmission systems complete, Viscous Couplings to shafts (see 'What is a Viscous Coupling?'), ready for complete matched set replacement or installation in Boreham-built Escorts.

What is a Viscous Coupling?

Patented by Tony Rolt Snr and Derek 'Tyrrell' Gardner in 1969 on behalf of Harry Ferguson Research, the VC or Viscous Coupling is a versatile limited slip device, one that can be used in front or rear differentials to control wheelspin, or in a central differential role to monitor front to rear power proportions.

How does it work?

Thin metal plates run in a silicone-based fluid that remains stable up to extremely high temperatures. The plates are machined to provide differing characteristics through holes and slots spaced to provide a progressive fluid coupling that is based on the shear properties of the fluid and speed differences registered via two input shafts.

The action of the VC can be primarily altered in two ways: properties of fluid used (viscosity) usually expressed in centistokes (or Newton metre (Nm) torque pre-loads applied in FFD assembly) and the number/physical shape of the plates. The plate permutations are particularly interesting to the competition engineer, who may even straight line sections of the disc to obtain the torque curve required.

The VC is *not* the answer to every differential difficulty, but it has proved exceptionally sympathetic in its 'soft' snatch-free action for front drive cars.

German 1993 Champions Alfa Romeo are FFD regulars, inheriting much of the original 4x4 drive train for the Italian (1992) and German Championship 155s from the Lancia Integrale rally cars.

For rallying purposes, Ford Motorsport are the VC's biggest fans, but other teams have also utilized its properties, publicized or not!

Today Ford employs the VC on production Escort Cosworths (centre and rear diffs), but FFD also enjoy the prestige of VC fitment on the Range-Rover and other large 4x4s.

The European days of big production runs of the classic Ferguson 4x4 layout with Morse chain for Sierras, Scorpios and BMW 325iX could be over. Instead, FFD have the compensation of a growing USA market, especially with Jeep's high production run use of the FFD 4x4 drivetrain and VC units.

The Corsican winner I drove had a trio of Viscous Couplings and — I believe — the works used the trio of VCs through most of 1993. Their settings varied from event to event, driver to driver, but Biasion seemed to have sorted out the gravel suspension and VC settings that both drivers could use for forest racing. On tarmac they both went very different ways and John Wheeler commented that Malcolm Wilson faced 'a fairly unenviable task' when carrying out the majority of testing chores in 'working to the taste of not just one driver, but two'.

By 1994 Ford had sorted out alternative (mechanical) limited slip differentials for Monte Carlo 1994, but John Wheeler remained 'very happy' with the 4x4 system, which he reported as substantially similar to that of the 1989 Sierra.

At first glance the factory engine bay looks pretty normal. The homologation papers tell you they have to stick to a precisely calibrated 1994.5 cc, but for FIA purposes this is multiplied by a factor of 1.7 to give 3390.6 cc. In 1993 the minimum weight had to be 1,200 kg, so the engine needed to have pulling power as well as bhp to shift its compact bulk.

The Garrett T35 turbocharger had to remain (it was cross-bred for competition reasons anyway), as did the Weber-Marelli engine management, although the homologation form does reveal the presence of some Bosch components.

Controversy arose not over the effective Mountune horsepower and torque released, but the way in which the Fords were built at Karmann with water injection for the intercooler. This was fed from a 20 litre reservoir in the boot via two Bosch headlamp washer pumps and a filter, and plumbed on to the three-stage Behr intercooling at the leading edge of the engine bay.

Tricky stuff. Inevitably a scrutineering row in Corsica was triggered when some privateer cars were found not to have the water injection system, which was applicable to Groups A or N. Ford initially felt this could happen where customers built Escorts up from a Sierra base. When a full investigation was demanded by the FIA, a senior Ford engineer told me, 'there had been a bit of a cock up.

'We had built more than the 2,500 required *with* water injection — 2,634 actually — but some 1992 production Escort Cosworths had initially gone through without the water injection plumbing, 427 to be precise,' said my source as the row rumbled from 1993 to 1994. Finally the FIA did find in Ford's favour, but not before some pretty nasty insinuations had been made that lightly tainted even the afterglow of 1994 Monte victory.

In production the water injection kit was simply stowed in the boot, not hitched up to spray, close to the intercooler joint with the inlet manifold supply pipe. Such a water spray could damage an engine not running the appropriate Motorsport microcomputer. When installed properly it cools intercooler air further and provides a consistent power bonus under high boost temperature conditions.

The initial homologation papers then dived into the extensive chassis engineering that is demanded when setting world class times over any surface, repeatedly. That means even the crossmembers were replaced, the front available in steel or cast alloy. The rear was replaced as well, the emphasis on new mounting points (allowed on a substantial 20 mm radius tolerance by the FIA), but this time only a sheet metal derivative was homologated.

All primary suspension components — particularly front TCAs, rear trailing arms and adjustable anti-roll bars (from the cockpit, from the start) — were replaced by dedicated designs for rallying. Details included the provision of magnesium or alloy trailing arms (a material choice also offered

Deserved test break: the first of a new works Escort generation (MS001) in March 1991 assessment for Sanremo. Registered H930 JHJ, this car had an extraordinarily busy life, participating in rallies as well as motor shows. Note the sturdier girders that now form the rear section of the steel roll cage and OZ wheels to Ford Motorsport Design specification.

for the associated drag links), a front compression strut that could be welded or bolted in position to locate the replacement TCA. The rear suspension was run with a concentric coil spring wrapped around the strut/damper body, the original separate coil spring removed.

Naturally, replacement sets of dampers (Bilstein) and springs (Eibach) were available to fine tune alongside roll bars and suspension geometry for each event. The wheels were by OZ to a Ford Motorsport design and rarely used the full 2 in bonus diameter granted by the FIA, 18 in wheels proving tricky to handle on the 1994 Monte Carlo. Wheel spacers from 3 to 10 mm thick allowed all kinds of offsets to be accommodated.

The brake equipment could be drawn from either Brembo or AP and occupied three sheets of the homologation papers in Group A (not permitted in N). Availability embraced four or six pot callipers in association with slotted/radially grooved discs in diameters from 270 to 380 mm; you'll realize from that the biggest discs would not fit behind the smaller diameter wheels! All this equipment was only homologated *if* it carried the Ford logo as well as that of the maker.

A hydraulic handbrake and replacement pedal box (with drilled pedals and front top rear bias, cockpit-adjustable) were more obvious Group A moves, but Ford also went for a water cooling option that was homologated in one move as 'water cooled brakes and/or shock absorbers, comprising pumps, filters, water jets, Reed switch, relay sensors and mini computer with fuel feed pipes and reservoir of 10 litres each'.

This wet move did not attract the controversy of the water cooling arrangement for the intercooling, but was very effective. By that I meant that the performance in hot and rough conditions such as Acropolis in Greece (where the drivers are lucky if cockpit temperature is *below* 35°C) or the Australian qualifier is retained under duress, rather than ultimately improved.

There was plenty more, particularly to provide a competition version of the power steering, complete with quick rack (1.9 turns, lock to lock!) but our piece on driving the Corsican winner should give you a better idea of what was done, and (partially) how much it cost. Here I will just say that the works did not plan to sell off their used cars under £160,000 (well-used) in the summer of '93 . . .

Contemporary comment

Iam obliged to Michael Harvey of *Autocar & Motor* for permission to reproduce my test of the Corsica-winning Escort Cosworth which appeared in the issue of 21 July 1993. Full performance specification data appear in Appendix 2. As before, the story is as submitted; it therefore includes some additional cost paragraphs that were unpublished.

* * *

Three times a winner
The Ford Escort is back winning World Championship rallies. Exclusively for Autocar & Motor, *the victorious RS Cosworth hurtles through its paces, dismissing 0–60 mph in less than 4 sec.*

K832 HHJ awaits blast off at Boreham. The 1973 European Rallycross Champion John Taylor took the wheel for the acceleration runs and showed that he had lost none of his quick getaway skills in the intervening 20 years, scorching from 0–100 mph in less than 10 seconds . . .

The four-eyed Ford, worth in excess of £160,000 squats and awaits our command. Inside the stark metallic cabin there are two dashboard dials and seven forward gears, clattering sympathetically in response to a constant 1,150 rpm grumble. Mechanical complaint emitting from the most potent 2 litres to rest behind a Ford factory registration plate. This is the summit of Ford Escort Cosworth RS engineering, a machine to conquer the world. Or at least the world of rallying.

Outside, white and swirling metallic blue paint are powdered black by the fishtail side exhaust, which has spent a day puffing out spent high boost energy. Flashy extrovert the factory Ford may be, but it also delivers the performance goods (0–60 mph in 3.8 sec, 0–100 in 9.9 sec) to pack alongside that outrageous road warrior appearance. This turbocharged 1994.5 cc Escort accelerates faster than *any road* car we have tested over the 0–60 mph span.

If we wanted to simply dish out 0–60 statistics, specialists would serve us with any number of allegedly 500 horsepower Cosworth Fords, but such machines do not have to surmount the tough engineering exams which Ford's 24 Boreham Airfield employees have so successfully passed. Under the managerial eye of Colin Dobinson and the engineering skills of John Wheeler and Philip Dunabin, Ford Motorsport have won three out of four 1993 World Championship Rallies versus the best that Japan Inc and the legendary Lancia Delta can muster.

Ford should feel robbed about the 'one that got away'. In that astonishing Escort international debut, François Delecour led most of Monte Carlo from his team mate Miki Biasion, only to succumb to a last night charge from Didier Auriol's Toyota and the unpublicized ills of a clogging fuel system, so the Ford newcomers finished second and third. Fuel delivery problems also effected team performance in the Acropolis Rally, but the Greek event joined Portugal and Corsica as Escort World Championship victories.

Now Ford of Britain have a serious chance of scooping the World Rally Championship, tied with Toyota on points at the head of the table post-Acropolis. Delecour led Biasion and Toyota's Juha Kankkunen, when we drove this authentic works Escort. One that Delecour took to victory, guided over the tortuous tarmac maze that is Corsica, by Daniel Grataloup.

From the multitude of fuses, switches and buttons that cling to the 'centre console' you need only click on the ignition and stub the black button to set the Cosworth mumbling. There is no need to use the throttle during or after the start. Ford Motorsport modified Weber-Marelli management takes care of reliable ignition and a stable idle speed, one that sounds like distant small arms fire.

Strangled by the sports authorities and their 38 mm air restrictor, Escort number 3's menacing version of the Traffic Light Snuffle is delivered contemptuously. For this car has stood three days of unreasonable demands from a Frenchman, one who regards the 7,600 rpm limiter as the start of gear change negotiation, and rock-faced goat tracks as suitable terrain to exercise a maximum of 136 mph at 7,600 rpm. 'Our' 700 mile Corsican rally victor wears its front end scrapes (a gravel spin aptly described by the hard working mechanics as a 'Scuffette') with insouciant pride.

Corsica was followed by that head-butt set of acceleration and deceleration runs (see our panel) in the hands of 1973 European Rallycross Champion John Taylor. K832 HHJ is hardly going to beg for mercy as a mere motoring journalist climbs aboard.

The cabin comprises a competition collection of bare metal and T45 HG steel scaffolding supporting the roll cage foundations. The integrated cage is now so comprehensive that it is nearly as difficult to drop into the left-hand seat as that of an American stock car.

The driving position is that of a contorted garden gnome, perched way in front of the laid back navigator, but the 'tools of the trade' are excellent. An anti-sweat suede rim for the three-spoke OMP wheel, enveloping Sparco seat and six-point Sabelts are backed by gridded foot pedals. These positively seduce slim feet, encouraging the most intricate of interrelated left foot

Of the works drivers in 1993, Miki Biasion's only win came (*below*) on the Greek Acropolis, whilst Delecour took three victories in Portugal, Corsica and Spain. Former Ford contractee Franco Cunico (*below left*) grasped the Italian fifth win of a magnificent debut season. In 1994 Cunico tackled Corsica for the factory, subbing for the injured Delecour.

Bliss at Boreham: the author with the winning Corsican Escort of François Delecour in the summer of 1993. The exclusive test appeared in *Autocar & Motor* and the sensational performance figures are in our appendices.

braking, or heel and toe manoeuvres, without a second thought. In fact they seem to do the job for you.

The superbly wrought footrest looks as though it would serve as an airframe spar, whilst the co-driver is braced by a footwell filled with kevlar composite construction, materials which are also (*very* expensively) used to encase the fire extinguisher! I also pause to admire the neat twin roof hatches that provide the majority of ventilation on a thunderous 20° day.

Each hatch is spring loaded to notch through a variety of air intake positions, individually tailored to suit driver and co-driver, with a choice of draught patterns achieved with an internal metal slide for the co-driver. Yes, Ford was the company that brought a '60s market Aeroflow . . .

The electronics age made obsolete the traditional rallying competition dash panel, one suffused with black and white dials. Just two analogue instruments survive in front of the driver. Yet Ford has not gone for the digital displays that adorn the leading BTCC racing saloons. Pectel Control Systems — an innovative UK company — provided an eight-mode digital readout. This was switched to monitor turbocharger boost, rpm, air and water temperatures.

Cinch the belts a little tighter. Dip the clutch through most of its travel. *Cccluuunk*. Its collar felt, and raised, you can access the only dogleg alley in the H+2 gate. The non-synchromesh gearbox now offers the first of seven speeds. On the move you barely need the twin plate AP clutch; the gearchange is the fastest and sweetest I have used in any kind of saloon. The only danger is that of getting lost within three main alleyways to the shift pattern.

Subsequent practice proves that a light throttle and just 1,200 Stack-indicated rpm is enough to set the plot rolling. Even with a constricted engine air supply, the 1993 Escort runs 0–60 mph a full second faster than Didier Auriol's rear drive Sierra managed in 1988. Today's factory Ford equals the eye-rotating 1.2 sec stride for 0–30 mph exhibited by the full blown Group B RS200 of the Supercar era.

Fabulous acceleration statistics are not the primary point, which remains the manner in which this Escort shrink-wraps around you. Hauling the farthest tarmac horizon, preferably one a dozen dirty bends and more away, on to an instant zoom lens magnification. Manipulate pedals, levers and wheel in the right micro second sequences, and there is no faster way to traverse tricky *terra firma*.

Even at 3,000 to 4,000 rpm for photography, the steering feedback promises instant gratification: more power steered pleasures than a man can decently accommodate. Although the regulations lopped an inch from overall tyre widths this season (now 9 x 17 in), the 'quick rack', one fractionally under two turns lock to lock, prods this Michelin slick-shod Escort on to lock with the alacrity of a Caterham Seven snorting steroids.

Considering there is the aforesaid power assistance, 58 per cent of vehicle weight over the front wheels, plus a trio of Viscous Couplings to serve the 4x4 system and its epicyclic centre differential, such alert reactions are rather more commendable than for the simple Seven.

The complete chassis and its suspension system has been rejuvenated. Sure, there are MacPherson struts and semi-trailing arms. Yet the freedom allowed in selecting the optimum mounting points, the replacement of key components with magnesium (ie, the trailing arms) and alloy castings that support a big (355 mm fronts with *six* pistons) brake layout, all travel a new dimension.

They transform the already impressive Cosworth Escort road car into a two-seater competitor with racing car grip (such G-forces leave you with a

Interior of the works Escort is a cross between basic creature comforts and essential safety defences embodied in the roll cage and automatic fire extinguisher systems. This is Delecour's Portuguese winner.

WHAT DOES IT ALL COST?

Ford are notoriously shy when it comes to revealing multi-million Dollar competition expenditure, but Ford Motorsport Parts, Boreham Airfield 26/200, Chelmsford, Essex CH3 3BG exists to serve the needs of those who are prepared to pay for a competition Ford.

Excluding the UK VAT rate of 17.5 per cent, typical Group A Escort component prices are dominated by the Mountune-assembled engine and FF Developments of Coventry seven-speed gearbox.

Both are priced at £18,500. The enormously strong seam-welded body — complete with integral welded high grade steel roll cage — amounts to £7,500 in LHD. That stainless steel side exhaust, a must for *Serial Poseurs*, is hand-made from four sections that total £1,450.25.

Smaller items eat up the cash, too. A 150 Watt alternator demands £805.10 and a single one of those AP racing disc brakes costs £288.20.

Judged by previous sales of second-hand works Escorts — three more of the seven built so far are scheduled for release this summer — we can tell you how much the international Group A Escort costs to duplicate. Or as closely as Ford will permit (which is close enough to score sensational results).

Buying a second-hand works Escort also brings in items such as the £300 apiece Magnesium OZ wheels that Ford Motorsport do not sell.

Depending on specification and your status with Ford the price for a full blown Group A rallying Escort can be from £130,000 to 'more than £160,000' in the words of one experienced insider. You can also build a car from scratch for the lower figure, but it will be built by an outside specialist; Ford Motorsport at Boreham does not build customer cars.

sore neck as a passenger) and rally car standards of flawless 4x4 traction. Its ability to claw tarmac is soothed by a Bilstein-damped ride that only deteriorates below 35 mph on concrete blocks.

As John Taylor whips through 25, 62 and 81 mph in the first three gears, threading the Escort through the concrete complex infield of Boreham at fourth gear speeds up to 90 mph, we gain an insight into the sheer breadth of forces generated and absorbed in such spectacular progress.

Water cooled brake callipers, damper cases and injection intercooling (all with separate boot-mounted containers) shrug off our attentions. They can maintain consistent temperatures in 40°C ambient, underwriting six water, oil and air radiators packed behind those quadruple lamps. The 7,500 rpm shifts and the constant need to flick the alert Escort from 90 mph fourth gear to 25 mph first, highlight two more outstanding attributes and one defect. There is a superbly managed engine and a motor cycle quality gearchange, but also a propensity to understeer, drooping off boost when shuffling back and forth to first from second in tight corners.

Boost, more than thrice constant showroom boost, was managed flawlessly. From 3,000 to 4,000 rpm, the works Escort packs a 3 bar (42.7 psi) punch, one that flings the Ford forward with addictive dependability. Such turbo boost software, by Ford Motorsport staff in association with Pectel and hardware assemblers Mountune of Maldon, has been remapped since that first win in Portugal.

Now the accent is on 3,000 to 7,500 rpm drivability and premium access to bundles of torque. The Mountune figures culminate in a minimum of 360 bhp at 6,800 rpm and a whopping 550 Nm (404.4 lb/ft!) of torque by 4,500 rpm. These for an engine that would cost £18,500 (ex-VAT) to duplicate with its trick camshafts, pistons and lightweight steel crankshaft. A shaft now ducking and diving alongside 'a seriously modified engine', in Chief Ford Motorsport Engineer John Wheeler's words.

This truly factory fresh Ford reminded us that rallying really does improve

the breed, for it was certainly the best works car for its purpose that we have driven, including the legendary supercars of the Group B '80s. Not the fastest, nor the most dramatic, but the most able all-rounder.

No other competition car expands so thoroughly on a production base than the Group A Escort RS Cosworth, courtesy of Ford Motorsport. And none promises so much for the durable speed and safety of future road cars.

Author's footnote
In July 1994 Ford of Britain confirmed rumours that the Boreham-based Motorsport team would no longer field its own competition cars. The last event for Boreham-built and managed machines was set as the 1994 RAC Rally. From 1995 onward Boreham was asked to develop cars for others to enter and compete in World Championship Rallying, FIA 2-WD rally formula and touring car racing. Truly the end of an era, and one that made many dedicated insiders very angry.

Opposite If you could not afford £150,000 for the real works car in 1993, this was the model makers' option for less than £130.

This page Reconnaissance (L421 NHK) for a snowy Monte and François Delecour, shown winning (L730 ONO; up on two wheels over sheet ice!) the most prestigious victory to date for Ford and the French crew. Once again it was François Delecour/Daniel Grataloup who 'did the business' for Ford Motorsport, earning a richly deserved 1994 Monte Carlo win after three years of disappointments with Sierras and the 1993 Escort. Just two months later Delecour was badly injured in a road crash (driving a Ferrari F40) and was destined to be sidelined for much of 1994, abandoning any realistic chance of earning the driver's title. Ford fought back to give the Escort Cosworth a Manufacturers' World title opportunity with a variety of drivers, including Franco Cunico and Malcolm Wilson. *(Monte victory picture, courtesy Bilstein in Germany)*

Chapter 11 _____

Race track wiles

For 1993 Ford and Cosworth were allied again on the race track, working with Rouse Engineering to turn the Mondeo into a world class winner.

T he flexibility of 2 litre formula touring car rules allowed Ford to order and Andy Rouse Engineering (ARE) to deliver a worldwide winner, within 12 months. The partners achieved this with a unique front drive variant of the 1993 Mondeo Si 4-dr that relied on Cosworth Engineering for a very special V6. This 24 valve aluminium six came from Mazda, but was eligible for use by Ford as it was also employed in the Ford Probe Coupe.

Prodded by Cosworth to yield over 290 bhp and mated to the ubiquitous

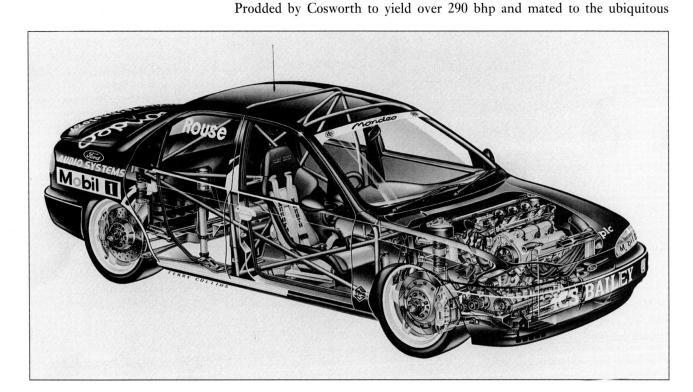

Xtrac six-speed sequential gearbox, the reborn Mondeo put Paul Radisich on the podium in its second race, won its fifth event, and went on to sweep up the FIA Touring Car Challenge at Monza against a 40-car field of the finest opposition (BMW alone had 11 of those cars!).

On the first anniversary of its belated go-ahead as a Ford-authorized project, the racing Mondeo lifted the ironically titled Nissan Mobil 300 in New Zealand; truly a remarkable debut season, a story to show that the Ford Cosworth alliance is a living association, not just (admittedly fabulous) automotive history.

But it was not an easy RS500 powerhouse ride to victories against a feeble opposition. Rivalry amongst the mass manufacturers contesting these 2 litre, 4-dr, events was intense as the Mondeo was readied. It looked an impossible task to squeeze another tenth of a second from the 4-cylinder, front drive format that all but BMW used.

So Andrew Rouse drew up the bold prototype Mondeo with rear drive, even though the tiny Mazda V6 had to remain in the transverse position. Thus a power-sapping gear drive was inevitable, to take drive through 90° to feed the back wheels.

To discover the background to this rapid fire winner with a drive dichotomy, we must travel to the British Midlands. Herald Way, threading through the Binley Trading Estate on the outskirts of the British Motor Industry's traditional Coventry birthplace, is just another industrial artery. 'Quick-fit' tyre emporiums vie with Nissan dealerships and undistinguished factory units to interrupt any postal address logic.

Then you see a giant Ford Iveco transporter, one carrying the massive Mondeo/ICS logo. It looms beside the 11,000 sq ft HQ of Andy Rouse Engineering. Inside around 18 skilled staff have concocted cars to set world benchmarks for their winning ways since 1988.

As ever, there is no chance of parking without a double degree in craftiness, but it's worth the hassle to step inside. Within these utilitarian walls were created 30 of the mightiest RS500s, 80 of their monstrously powerful motors and the sophisticated Rouse 302R (10 built)/304R (95 built) Sierra 4-dr road conversions.

But these dedicated premises are not a museum. In fact the last of the 1990 ICS RS500s was consigned to nearby Coventry Transport Museum, leaving the stable bare and ready to tackle (whisper it) Toyota Carinas for 1991/2. ARE won seven races with these 285 bhp four cylinders. When that Oriental interlude was drawing to a close ('TOMS underbid us substantially for the contract, just to keep some of their Formula 1-hired designers in work,' observed Rouse dryly), our tale began.

'For months back there in 1992, it looked like we hadn't got a deal with anyone at all,' recalled 47-year-old founder/boss Andy Rouse early in 1994. When Andy spoke to us, the Mondeo with the Cosworth V6 heart had proved its world class.

Andy reported that unfamiliar 1992 major manufacturer contract hiatus, amidst a mini-boardroom full of trophies and racing RS500 photography; 1988 was his big RS500 year, beating Steve Soper in the Eggenberger RS500 the favourite action subject. Meanwhile ARE staff were readying *nine* racing Mondeos for 1994. These to Ghia rather than Si spec, for the 1994 season.

Opposite Terry Collins gave us this graphic insight into the racing Mondeo, one I suspect demanded hasty redrawing as the car itself switched from rear to front drive. Big brakes, refabricated strut suspension and on board jacking are clearly shown here. The transverse V6 engine is shown with a good guide to the wrap-around front bank of exhausts and the simple induction arrangements of 1993, both aspects considerably updated by Cosworth for 1994.

'We simply haven't got the capacity to build any more cars this year,' said Andy wistfully. 'But' — a lengthening pause as the biggest of grins lights up the grey-topped features of Britain's most successful touring car driver — 'I have to say we will have the satisfaction of supplying cars to our old RS500 rivals at Eggenberger this season, and those cars are likely to appear in the German 2 litre series.' Otherwise, it seemed as though the main EC countries would also be seeing the racing Ford in 1994/5 action.

When and how did the Mondeo renew Rouse's links with Ford, setting them all on the historic path to Ford's 200th BTCC victory?

'In the Summer of 1992 we were one of the outfits asked to quote for a Mondeo touring car programme,' Andy reported. He added, 'We looked at complete pre-production cars that were running around at Dunton [the car was not on sale until March 1993 *JW*]. It must have been late summer before our evaluation was complete.

'At that time we were dealing with John Griffiths at Ford Motorsport, Boreham. Nothing much was happening, but we heard that *if* there was a Mondeo Touring Car effort, we would be the outfit doing the work. At the beginning of October, Ford was looking likely.

'Then we heard from Toyota that TOMS would take over the Carina racing programme we had undertaken for 1991/2. That took us into November, by which time we had heard Ford, or at least Ford Motorsport, were not interested in taking it further.'

But a new possibility was emerging within Ford. Marketing and Merchandising Manager Nick Palmer, with the support of senior Merchandising Manager Peter Townsend, had become the proprietors of an enormous promotional and advertising budget. At this stage they were the only Ford of Britain staff to command sufficient budget to undertake such a major programme. Early in 1994, Nick Palmer let me have his thinking as to how and why the project progressed within Ford.

'We knew 26 per cent of new cars buyers follow motor sport closely and that a further 28 per cent take a further interest in motor sport. We could see that interest had grown in the past five years and that TV was the most popular way to follow the sport.

'We also knew that motor sport could provide the emotional message (reason) to buy a car. This had traditionally been the role of advertising, but there is now a requirement to provide an environmental and safety message. Advertising Standards restrict the blatant speed/aggressive messages,' reported Mr Palmer.

I knew there had been an earlier programme punted around the Ford UK HQ to develop a racing Orion. That was during 1991 and other sources told me that one subcontractor had envisaged running with a central driver; an idea adapted by Peugeot and seen at Monza in 1993, but with the LHD driver nearly 2 ft inboard of the door, rather than fully central, as was this Orion proposal from a British specialist, one used to winning at every level from Le Mans downward. It would have made lap speed sense, but could have been banned so swiftly that everyone wasted money following suit . . .

Nick Palmer continued: 'In May/June 1992, when we were debating the Mondeo racing programme, Ford of Britain was conscious that the 1990

Escort launch had been disappointing. Then there had been no sporty model or immediate motor sport programme (it would be 1993 before the Escort went World Championship rallying). We could have the same situation with Mondeo. There was no doubt that all our immediate competition were entering Mondeo class cars in the BTCC.

'Ford Motorsport were always supportive of a touring car programme, but an individual national sales company would have to fund it, such as Ford of Britain, Germany and so on.' Ford Germany wanted to go in for the big class for their home market, but the budgets were far too expensive [only Alfa Romeo and Mercedes contested the 1993 title *JW*],' recalled Nick Palmer.

The original Mondeo touring car paper was written by Palmer, then a newcomer to his job, but Peter Townsend pushed it around senior management. Ford Competitions Manager Colin Dobinson was another supporter, along with Ian McAllister (Ford UK Chairman).

The 1991-debutante sports manager, Dobinson, started the team selection process in June. As for every other UK supporter, Colin knew the money could only come from the marketing budget of Ford in Britain.

Some concerns were raised over the choice of engine (solved by appointing Cosworth as consultants) and (by senior European executives) over whether Ford should invest in another form of motor sport while the company was going through a tough time; this especially as Ford were already represented in Formula 1, IndyCars, NASCAR and the World Rally Championship. The latter argument delayed the decision by half a year.

Rouse confirmed, 'There would not have been a Mondeo racing car without the support of Palmer and Townsend. But the first time they put it up, the Chairman of Ford of Europe (then Lindsay Halsted) rejected it.'

Just when things were looking really hopeless, Lindsay Halsted moved on. Lebanese Australian Jacques Nasser took over at FoE. To Andy's immense relief Nasser 'ticked the job off' as one of his first decisions. This story was not corroborated inside Ford, insiders telling me, 'Lindsay Halsted had no input on this issue, either positively or negatively.' The same source did acknowledge, however, that 'a change in management, seeing Jacques Nasser arrive as chairman of Ford of Europe, made the process easier. Mr Nasser had supported the Ford programme in Australia to go touring car racing and saw the benefits.'

It was the first week of December 1992 when the Ford go-ahead came through. Andy Rouse barely had time to celebrate his birthday (he was born 2 December 1947) before hurling his workforce — and that of major subcontractors such as six-speed transmission aces Xtrac in Berkshire — into a flat out design, fabricate and assembly routine, one that would yield two *rear drive* Mondeo racers, converted from complete Dunton pre-production test vehicles.

Why *rear* drive?

Andy grinned. 'Well, we were offered a clue as to the way to win in BTCC by BMW. They had won 13 races in a row in the formula and the previous two titles into the bargain. We knew the rear drive BMW was kinder to its tyres [a point that really matters in a tightly controlled formula like BTCC *JW*]. At the heart of our RWD concept was the Cosworth prediction that they would provide a 5 per cent improvement on the best power then offered

Public debut. A Ford test day at Brands Hatch in March 1993 saw Rouse fit in a few laps with the rear drive Mondeo sounding wonderful.

by our rivals, all of that needed to offset the 2 to 3 per cent we were going to lose in power transfer losses with a double 90° bevel gear drive to switch drive from our front mounted V6 to the back wheels.'

As you will probably know, the Mondeo never raced in that initial rear drive format, so our next question had to be, why did it not work out?

Pause for thought. Andy still thinks there is development life in the rear drive format, but 1993 regulations and circumstances were against him as he explained.

'First, there was an obvious shortage of sheer horsepower to make the rear drive gamble work. We tested at Snetterton, Brands, Pembrey and Silverstone, but Snetterton was the significant one. Using a speed gun on rival cars and our own, we discovered we were 8 to 9 mph *down* on our rivals. It was pulling the cornering speeds OK, but the 285 bhp we had initially was just not enough to roll the lap speeds we needed.' At this point we should say that the car was not a disaster by most team standards, but Andy had agreed that he would not race the car until it was comfortably capable of top ten times, and that was not happening at the Snetterton benchmark circuit.

'The second factor was the BTCC regulations. If the car is not homologated in Group A, and the Mondeo initially was not, the RAC require that the model raced is based on a model of which at least 1,000 examples are made in a year. When we set out on the project, we thought that Ford would be making the 4x4 Mondeo variant by April/May 1993.

'When we got to the last week of April of that year with our rear drive project, it was obvious that Ford were *not* going to be making the car for some time yet [a wise move: the car would not be available, until 1995! A similar RS2000 4x4 was sold from August 1994. *JW*]. Our rear drive racer,

based on the premise that Ford would mass manufacture a 4x4, would be illegal. If we wanted to race by our target Grand Prix July date, we would *have* to go the front drive route.'

Rouse does not grimace, or shake his head in woe at the memory of asking the workforce and subcontractors to make another massive effort. As at the time, he simply gets on with the job in hand . . .

'We took one of the two rear drive cars we had made and turned that into the front drive prototype. All done in-house . . . in 14 days! Basically we just used whatever we had around to make it work, to get it running so that we could see just how quick a front drive Mondeo could be. We used a gearbox that we had from another project, adapted strong drive shafts to suit, and so on.

'It felt good at Snetterton, straight away. In fact it was quicker than the rear drive car, straight away, so we knew it had potential,' Rouse recollected. It certainly did, and two other significant competitive factors — a new source of body shells and engines — were about enter the equation . . .

As ARE completed their Snetterton evaluation, Nick Palmer's enormous internal gamble had been backed by another personal contribution toward a better racing Mondeo: he had backed the production of seven special bodies. Rouse commented that these Mondeo race bodies 'have all the things you do not need for racing— brackets to hold trim, underseal, even undercoat paint — deleted from the build process at the plant. The paint may sound minor, but a coat of primer adds 4 to 5 kg. So eliminate many of the production processes, and the cars are raced in three coats, including etched primer, undercoat and the colour you see.

'The only strengthening is that the Motorsport bodies receive are double spot welds. The additional strength a car needs to go touring car racing really

Looking for a time? Andy Rouse at Snetterton with the rear drive original racing Mondeo. At this stage it was only able to run times outside the top ten and that was not good enough to race in the eyes of Ford and Rouse. The Snetterton sessions forced the fundamental rethink to the lower weight, front drive, format.

comes from the changes we make here at ARE, especially in the purpose-built roll cage.'

Authorizing these special builds was a brave move from a man with a career on the move, because the hassle within the Belgian Genk factory was considerable. The popular Ford had to be removed from the line at an unorthodox point and every build requirement thought through on the weight/strength basis, rather than high speed production.

I do not believe Ford created an unfair advantage over rivals, for this practice is quite common amongst BTCC contenders. I recall Janspeed commenting how helpful the Sunderland factory had been over the production process for Primera GT. But I do believe that the Mondeo would not have got down to the front drive weight limit in the UK series (950 kg) if it had not had the benefit of the unique production body as a foundation.

The second critical element was engine supply. The basics of using the ex-Mazda 626/MX-6/Ford Probe 24v V6 remained constant. ARE created all these 60°, aluminium units for the rear drive prototypes and Cosworth those of the front drive racers. It was not planned quite so tidily as that. Rouse recalled, 'We have our own engine building department with three technicians, under the control of my business partner Vic Drake. Initially the plan was simply to get the car up and running on our version of the V6.

'Then we found out that Cosworth had only been assigned the further development of the motor with a start date of January 1993. Incidentally, our first motor ran in the third week of January: a much bigger achievement than redeveloping the RS500 since we had to design, freeze specification and order basic parts like the steel crankshaft and rods. In fact every internal part was redeveloped, leaving just the basic head and cylinder block from the road car.

'The Ford Cosworth contractual agreement for the racing V6 was to

Below Even the massive Ford-IVECO articulated truck carries signwriting for the Michelin man, as well as the racing Mondeos . . .

Below right Feedback: Andy Rouse (*right*) and Paul Radisich communicating at Silverstone on Mondeo's racing progress.

deliver the first racing engines in August that year. When we learned of this we had to say "Forget it." None of us need bother if we are not going to have competitive power until August. It'll all be over by then!'

Rouse and Ford applied pressure to Cosworth, 'constantly' in Andy's recollection. The team of draughtsmen and engine builders under Chief Designer Geoff Goddard turned up the wick (see 'The Cosworth connection'). Remember that Cosworth were already up to their necks in corporate pressure in 1993 Formula 1. At the time, McLaren strove to turn the amazing winning abilities of Senna plus HB Grand Prix V8 into engine supply parity with contracted works HB runners, Benetton.

The politics of Ford-Cosworth teams employed to beat the dominant Williams-Renault reverberated around the Big Buck board rooms. Cosworth then got the message that this full racing version of the compact (18 in long!) V6 was *that* important to their long serving competition and commercial partner for saloon car racing.

Rouse continued, 'We got the first Cosworth engine in late May, but there was not a big power difference when we switched over. At that point I reckon we had about the same as the best of the Toyota four-cylinders did at the end of our development: about 285 bhp. In fact we ran one of our engines and one of theirs at Pembrey; the cars were nose to tail at one point, so I have no doubts about the respective power outputs.

'The big difference with Cosworth was that during the summer they were able to concentrate on our engine supply and performance. During the year I would say it gained about 10 bhp, but it's always had good top end power. In fact it would be fabulous if we could run it 10,000 rpm, but the BTCC 2 litre rules [which Andy helped frame *JW*] stop us at 8,500, of course.

'Initially the V6 was very "top-endy" and really liked life above 8,000. Further development in association with our preferred engine management system from Zytek [used by ARE, Cosworth, also Mazda in their similarly powered 1993 Xedos V6 competitor. *JW*] filled in some of the early gaps. Standing starts required replacement electronic programming and they filled in the 7,000 to 8,000 band a little more strongly.

'Torque? Our target is to get 200 lb/ft, and we can do that. Then the power drops right off, way below what is competitive . . .' Andy's voice trailed off thoughtfully. For perspective I should add that BMW race the 100 kg heavier 318i/318iS UK touring cars at 'only' 275 bhp, but do allow a good mid range as a deliberate policy: 190 lb/ft was reported as far back as 1991 from two rival BMW specialists.

Was the rest of the racing Rouse Mondeo-Cosworth up to scratch? It mostly certainly was, according to the moaning from most rivals.

Even in rear drive format the all-strut suspension system (with transverse double arms at the rear, two piece lower wishbone to the front MacPherson layout) proved formidable. When Rouse changed hurriedly over to front drive, it was not nearly as bad as Andy feared and said rivals hoped . . . In fact, the Rouse Mondeo looked absorbingly capable from the Pembrey start. It is in the car's immense wide track, low overall height, high cornering capabilities, that the astonishing parity with RS500 lap speeds (equalled or beaten at Thruxton, Donington and Brands) lies.

Rouse was not about to vouchsafe more than the bare facts that the company fabricate the suspension, and its key mounting points, from scratch. ARE, like any other leading competitor, merely uses the principles of the road car, as demanded by regulations, not specific Ford parts. Thus the suspension arms are entirely new, ARE made the twin bearing race hubs and stub axles (taking single wheel nut and four peg Dymag alloys), along with the cockpit-adjustable blade and link anti-roll bars. Utilizing a bell crank action and Bowden connection cables, a 40 per cent change in roll bar stiffness can be dictated by the driver 'in-flight'.

Spring rates were not discussed, but Rouse acknowledged, 'We use the Dutch Pro-Flex pressurized shock absorbers.' However, they take extraordinary care to make sure that the settings are their own property, taking the dampers in directly and reworking the valving according to ARE requirements on these remote oil reservoir units.

Other key chassis speed elements were the change from initial Yokohama to Michelin tyre use, a later swap to a Viscous Coupling (VC) limited slip differential and the pros and cons of power steering. The tyre contract had deliberately been left open, so that Rouse could pick whatever cover gave them the most consistent lap speed; the 1987 RS500 had underlined the worthlessness of qualifying and opening lap tyre specials.

ARE evaluated the merits of tyres in a post-Pembrey session, Rouse commenting, 'I knew that both Dunlop and Michelin were coming along well. It was also a factor that the works Escort rally team also used Michelin and I knew they would work very hard for us. In fact there was no dramatic difference in lap speed initially, but the Michelins were more consistent in the heat. I am not going to tell you what the problem with Yokohama was, but the Michelin solved it. We also gained in lap speed as we dialled the car to the tyre, rather than any trick compounds, or any of that stuff.'

The limited slip differential change from a multi-plate unit to the almost local supply of the Ferguson Formula Developments (FFD) patented and supplied VC assisted that historic first victory in the car's fifth racing appearance at Brands Hatch. Again, settings were a fiercely guarded secret, but this time FFD prepared and supplied the unit, as they did to many other leading UK and overseas race and rally teams. (Monte Carlo '94 looked like being the first time Escort would rally with some plate differentials installed.)

Finally, there was the question of power steering. Paul Radisich commented in the summer of 1993 at Silverstone: 'It was OK going from rear drive RS500 to rear drive Mondeo. But when we switched to front drive for the Mondeo . . . Boy, was it ever hard work! We've no power steering and getting all the power and torque down to the ground and steering it, well, that's a tough job. But I just love it. I think third place on our second outing is a great credit to Andy and all his staff.'

From that moment on, power steering was back on the agenda. Rouse told us in January 1994, 'It's a tricky one to solve. Sure you want to take out the effort of manhandling the car around slow corners at circuits like Knockhill and the hairpin at Pembrey. Even at Thruxton, where I averaged over 106 mph in pre-event practice, you have to put a lot of steering effort into holding the car over those long corners, and there are still a lot of bumps down there. So power steering is certainly worth having, but balancing sufficient driver steering feedback against the low effort is hard. It involves

Spick and span: the interior of the Mondeo is kept just as clean as the exterior, protected by criss-cross roll cage and guided by four-spoke MotaLita wheel.

fundamental engineering, including a new rack. I am sure we'll have this in 1994,' said Andy. They did, from 29 May at Oulton Park.

One key attribute that the Mondeo has that the RS500 could never match (because of the restrictive sheet metal on its wings) is the ability to run the lowest possible ride heights. Rivals commented that when the Mondeo came up to pass, 'I could only see its roof aerial, not the car itself.' That was totally unlike anything else in 1993 BTCC, save the kissing cousin Mazda Xedos 6.

As ever Rouse was not just content with a car that already ran nearly 2 in lower at the headlamp upper leading edge than the winning BMW 3-series. Andy told me in 1994, 'After the 1993 Grand Prix we did investigate the aerodynamics at the MIRA wind tunnel, but it's always the same. These tests are useful for the best cooling layouts and so on, but for lap speed they just tell you how you cannot run the car!' A twinkle and then he continued, 'A

Above The Dymags grew vanes for 1994, but the low ride height remained a key factor from 1993.

Above right Another 1994 tweak was brake air intake allowed by deleting the Ghia's auxiliary lights in the lower spoiler.

tunnel will tell you how you should rake the car for maximum speed. *But* if you do what the tests tell you, the thing won't go round corners.'

To give us an inkling of the alternatives that ARE calculate, Rouse revealed that they had studied the commercially available Ford RS parts body kit. 'It did help. It cut the Cd factor fractionally and offered *slightly* more downforce. But it wasn't worth the extra 10 kg weight penalty, the differences were *so* marginal.'

However, one crude aerodynamic consideration was worth a substantial body change for 1994. 'The rules allow us to remove fog lamps and fit air scoops,' explained Rouse. Therefore we decided to race the Ghia-bodied Mondeo for 1994, not the Si. Even though we lose the Si rear spoiler, it's worthwhile to increase cooling air flow to the brakes.' Andy did *not* say it, but it also means that standard rear spoiler does nothing worthwhile for rear end stability at any speed.

Braking ability was always going to be considerable, given that the Mondeo was down to the front drive weight limit of 950 kg. The same AP braking layout (minus water cooling) was installed as the 1,200 kg 4x4 rally Escort: 14 in diameter ventilated discs, clamped by six piston callipers. At the rear 12 in units are used with four piston callipers, front to rear bias being cockpit adjustable, as for every other serious BTCC entry.

Paul Radisich educated us about braking power at Silverstone during July 1993: '. . . from about 125 mph, the brakes are something else on the Mondeo. A good hard pedal, but the retardation is stunning.'

I agree with Paul, but I think the 'stunning' verdict applied to the complete car which redefined the performance of a front drive 2 litre racing saloon. Now let us have a look through the results this stunner achieved in its debut mini season. Cheats can simply mug up on the handy results panel provided . . .

Following a February 1993 sneak preview of the racing Mondeo in its original rear drive format at Ford's Dunton research establishment (courtesy the Guild of Motoring Writers), I wanted to follow the progress of this superbly presented and crafted car.

I could not believe the gleaming standards achieved in minimal time. If this low rider went as well as it looked, in its swoopy suit that was just about knee-high to a Sierra, then I wanted to be around.

Ford returned to a series they had vacated with honour in 1990 and with back door dishonour in 1991. By 1993 the intense competition from seven manufacturers in the pioneering 2 litre British Touring Car series was the best supported in a motor racing world that was adopting this realistic category. Even in the German Fatherland of 2.5 litre mega-budgets they had 2 litre supporters (even if Audi and BMW ventured to France and Britain respectively to win those national titles).

Those who catered for the formula and approved of the 8,500 rpm limit (effectively equalizing the difference between a thoroughbred racing engine and a unit designed originally for family fare), plus a 4.2 metre minimum length (designed to keep hatchbacks out and attract the maximum number of motor makers), stretched from Scandinavia to the Antipodes, and back via Japan and most of Common Market Europe.

Ford were latecomers to this formula. Rouse was well aware of the frantic pace being established as BMW sent their Schnitzer forces to wrest a third consecutive UK title from the jaws of Toyota, Nissan, Vauxhall, Peugeot, Renault and Mazda. Schnitzer BMW were beginning to blitz the results sheets as Rouse readied Mondeo, but outside the PR talk from Ford anyone who saw the Rouse Mondeo fighting to return a front running time against the opposition in those preliminary practice day skirmishes would have realized it 'simply wasn't doing the times', in racing parlance.

It certainly puzzled me. It was not *that* far off the pace and you could see that there were no savage handling vices, unlike the pogo-action Peugeots, Vauxhalls and Renaults exhibited. The motor sounded wonderful and there was an obvious aero advantage over the other upright 4-drs from all but Mazda. Meanwhile the race season was flying by and BMW were looking totally unbeatable.

At one particular Snetterton session I cornered Andy and spoke for all those frustrated Ford fans.

'When are we going to see this car out *racing*?' I asked.

'Not until it's doing top 10 times,' was the crisp answer.

'Why is that not the case now?' (it was lolling around the 15th to 11th slots at most sessions) I persisted.

Andy was too diplomatic to say more than 'There's just a little bit to come from each area of the package.' By 1994 he was more open and confessed they just did not have the planned power to offset the 1,050 kg weight and transmission power losses. Thus the 950 kg front drive format was swiftly adopted, satisfactorily tested and two new cars readied from Motorsport racing body shells to join the UK star car wars from round 8 of the *Auto Trader* backed series, Pembrey in South Wales.

It was tough debut, for Paul Radisich's car was being completed in the Paddock prior to official practice. Both Vauxhall and Toyota dipped beneath the psychological 1 min barrier to establish the first three on the grid. However, Rouse was right there in fourth place, his 1 min dead scant tenths away from the 59.78 sec pole of Ecosse Cavalier charger, David Leslie.

Paul Radisich's position looked worse than it was, for 11th on the closely contested grid in 1 min 00.41 sec was actually less than 1 sec from the front spot on the 0.456 mile short circuit.

From the off Joachim Winkelhock blazed a trail from fifth on the grid to the front, before the first corner! Andy Rouse was pitched into the thick of battle: if there was any sentiment at seeing him back at the wheel of a Ford, it didn't show in the battle scars inflicted on the third-placed Ford. Five cars bounced by before Rouse was forced to pit with accumulated damage, topped off by a bump from Kieth Odor's Nissan.

That left Andy out of the running, but Paul Radisich showed that his only previous race appearance of 1993 was no fluke (at Oulton Park he scored a hard-fought Fiesta win). Paul eased his barely race-ready Mondeo through the carnage to take eighth with the sixth-fastest lap to his credit. Not bad for a debut in a machine that had been totally rethought and prepared from scratch in less than two months.

Then came the most prestigious British race of the year, the Silverstone GP support event. Now equipped with Cosworth V6s for both cars, Mondeo's fleet form became more apparent on the longer (3.25 mile) track. At five points around the track the Mondeo was exceeding 130 mph and the maximum logged was close to 150 mph at the 8,500 rpm limiter.

Radisich and Rouse lined up fourth and fifth quickest, separated by just 0.02 sec, barely 0.20 sec behind the pole position Nissan. The blue and white Fords impressed everyone not just with their straight line speed, but also the way their wide track suspension would soak up kerbs and run so absorbently over bumps, all without the twitching that afflicted so many potential front runners in 1993.

Unfortunately the heat of battle at the sharp end of the field saw both Mondeos dealing out a powerful front drive beating to their Yokohama rubber. Rouse retired with only two laps left to run for this reason and Radisich enjoyed an heroic battle with Championship leader Jo Winkelhock's BMW. Paul did a fantastic job to wrest third place from the German on tyres that could not have been a match for the BMW's at that stage of the race. This GP spectacular would be the last time in 1993 that the factory-backed Fords used the Japanese tyres, thereafter appearing on Michelin.

BMW conductor Jo Winkelhock commented between puffs of his constant cigarette companion, at the finish of an event that had seen Toyota team mates run into each other to allow a Nissan 1–2, 'we struggled today on acceleration. I would be touching Radisich's bumper in the corners, trying to get into his slipstream, but at the end of the straights he would be 20 metres ahead of me.' A fine endorsement of Mondeo's Cosworth competitiveness in its second race . . .

Up to Knockhill in Scotland and a double header run around the tight track. On Michelins the Mondeos qualified fourth (Radisich) and eighth (Rouse) .Whilst Andy was obviously delighted that his engineering skills had put the Mondeo into contention so rapidly, it was obvious he was not so pleased that his chances to add to his incredible total of BTCC victories was

The front drive format paid off pretty quickly: Paul Radisich wins Ford's 200th BTCC event and the Mondeo's first at Brands Hatch in 1993. In pursuit at Paddock are Robb Gravett's Peugeot 405 Mi-16, the championship-winning BMW 318i and Kieth Odor's Janspeed Nissan Primera GT.

not going to be assisted this memorable season by a slower team mate.

The race yielded little reward for the boss, who was out of the top eight point scoring positions on both outings. In the first race Andy collided with Will Hoy's Toyota and was black flagged to repair the damage, losing two laps before he could rejoin to finish. In the second event Andy struggled to tenth, whilst Radisich once again fought through to fifth. Paul showing considerable maturity in these intense BTCC encounters that were second nature to more than half of his opposition.

Oulton Park in early August was a race disaster, the only occasion on which neither car scored points. They qualified well, Rouse 0.01 sec ahead of Radisich, but Andy departed into the gravel traps after just two laps and Paul was eliminated when the drive to the alternator failed at half distance.

Late August brought Team Mondeo/ICS into the spot light at Brands Hatch. Both cars looked strong enough to win all weekend, Radisich qualifying just 0.08 sec from Pole. Rouse was only 0.2 sec behind to take fourth on a grid that featured the first 19 within the same second bracket on the shorter Brands Hatch layout.

On the wink of the green light, Jo Winkelhock did not manage to rocket immediately to the front with the rear drive BMW, breaking a year-long BTCC tradition. Radisich managed to weave his way to the head of the field in the opening moments. Paul stayed there, winning by less than 1 sec over Steve Soper (BMW) on the road. Rouse played his part in the early laps, protecting Paul from the pack, but eventually sank back to sixth, sandwiched by Nissan and Toyota.

That second position materialized as Robb Gravett's Peugeot in the official results, for Soper was demoted by the Race Stewards subsequently. Yes, it was *that* sort of race; no less than 14 drivers (over half the field!) were interviewed by the Stewards after a panel-bashing Round 13. Yet it was a glorious day for Ford, a publicist's dream, with the 200th BTCC race win to complement their maiden Mondeo win.

Team Mondeo continued to perform into the Autumn, consistently at the sharp end of qualifying (Radisich picked up their first pole position at Donington in September). Although they did not win at the round after Brands Hatch, the Mondeos finished second and third at Thruxton to record their best team result.

Donington was a wet to wettish double header that saw Radisich notch another pole and battle for wins with Alain Menu's ragged Renault. The scoreline read one each at the close of play, Paul also coming away with a fastest lap. Andy Rouse was disqualified in the first incident-packed race and finished fourth in the second edition.

Now Ford and Paul Radisich were rocketing up the BTCC points tables. It seemed inconceivable that they could miss the opening three months of the season, and still have Paul in contention for third place in the driver points league. Yet that is exactly what happened, with the best results of the season saved for this blustery but dry finale. The sonorous V6 of the Kiwi dominated proceedings with Pole, fastest lap and a comfortable win over Andy's sister car.

Now the Mondeos, still just the pair of them built, were simply in a different league to the four-cylinder pursuit. It was now obvious that the

Ford could face any 2 litre car, anywhere in the world, provided that the regulations for the forthcoming FIA Challenge at Monza were aerodynamically equable.

Fortunately for their Monza aspirations, early testing at Monza from British-based teams such as Nissan highlighted the fact that the Italian and French-based 2 litres carried extensive underfloor aerodynamics. These were fed by enlarged and flattened 'brake scoops' and had as dramatic effect on lap times as running with another litre on engine capacity. The FIA stepped in and sent a warning letter to the factory teams concerned (primarily Peugeot in France and Alfa Romeo in Italy) *before* the event.

Faced with a level playing field, Team Mondeo presented itself to take on the 2 litre world of BMW (British and Italian Champions), Alfa Romeo, Audi (French Champions) Peugeot, Renault, Toyota, Nissan, Vauxhall-Opel and a lone Mazda. Renault were not present, but otherwise there was the most formidable field of factory and works-backed touring cars ever assembled.

Whilst Rouse and Soper clashed on the opening lap to decimate UK hopes, Radisich drove with the cool speed that has become his hallmark. It was not as easy as the double win result makes it look, for Paul was outdragged at the first start by both GTCC Champion Nicola Larini (Alfa) and Peugeot pole position-squatter, Yannick Dalmas. The Soper-Rouse mess forced a red flag and a second start to the opening 15-lapper.

This time Radisich had it right, beating Dalmas and Larini away. He held on to win at an average of just over 100 mph, beating Alain Cudini's Opel Vectra by 1.15 sec and the rest of the field (headed by Larini) with more than 3 sec in hand.

The second race was all about Radisich and he was never ahead after an initial challenge from Cudini was literally punctured. This time Paul strolled home ahead of the Alfa team's Larini and Philippe Gache, but the gap looked much narrower on paper (0.66 sec) and the average speed of less than 90 mph reflected the interruption of a pace car when one of the eleven BMWs

Winter comfort: a bleak test day at Silverstone and the Mondeo's first public appearance for 1994. It was faster than before, but the incredible 10-manufacturer line up for that season's British Championship meant yet more development work.

present was inverted. Paul took full use of the pace car interlude to play a brake, accelerate, brake game with Larini; Radisich broke away with the decisive advantage for the closing tours of the second 15-lap session.

The rules were slightly different in terms of scoring results, for each driver represented his nation. Thus Radisich and Rouse were not on the same national sides, Paul nearly carrying off a Nations Cup on his own against the assembled Italian and French contenders!

Another one-off event with annual status is the Donington-based TOCA Shoot Out. It does not attract all the teams, having a format that includes reversing grid positions at organizer's discretion/championship points accrued. Then there is the removal of the last car on every lap after a predetermined number have been run, but the 1993 edition sent major car makers scurrying for cover.

The reason? Bold Robert Fearnell of Two Four Sports at Donington had faxed America to see if the new IndyCar Champion, one N. Mansell, would be interested in an end-of-season race in a tin top? Once the cash had been guaranteed, Mansell was on his way back to the faithful with Rouse's personal competition Mondeo. Nigel fitted in Donington amongst a host of personal appearances, including attracting a huge following as he toured the Motorsport Day of the London Motor Show.

Initially Nigel Mansell played down the appearance as 'a bit of fun'. A few offs and spins convinced him to take the business a bit more seriously. A run in Radisich's Mondeo (Rouse stepped down for the weekend: there were *still* only two racing Mondeos in the world) allowed Nigel to see how relaxing the ride through the character-building downhill Craner Curves could be. He 'only' lined up ninth quickest (a considerable achievement given the technique needed to adapt to his first front drive racer), but now he was obviously out for a bit more than that 'bit of fun'.

Whilst Paul Radisich went from the back of the arranged grid to lead David Leslie's Ecosse Vauxhall, Mansell went from misfiring tenth (cured by switching on a second fuel pump) to third, passing no less than Steve Soper on the way. But Nigel M. was right on the limit. Egged on by the 63,000 faithful he had just disposed of an unamused Tiff 'Top Gear' Needell when he came a cropper on the 28th lap.

Exiting the Old Hairpin, Nigel got the Mondeo very sideways. Whether he committed the cardinal front drive sin of releasing the throttle is contradicted by opposing eye witness accounts. Either way Mansell was headed for a very big off when Tiff Needell cavaliered into the Ford. Struck hard in the passenger door, 'Red Five' slammed into the armco that protects drivers from head-on confrontation with the historic Stone Bridge.

Looking at the video replays, or viewing the *Motoring News* front page picture makes you shudder for Mansell. In fact an overnight check in hospital and the bruised Champion was on his way, hopefully making a mental blessing on the strength ARE had engineered into the terminated Ford.

That all meant the race had to be restarted. With six laps and no holds barred for a £12,000 first prize, the touring car regulars waged war. Radisich fell victim to repeated assaults from Steve Soper (who can command unearthly speed down the Craner Curves). The two tin top aces indulged in the kind of spiteful driving that always ends in tears, a spat that continued

Plenty to boast about, including Mondeo mastery of Europe, for Ford in 1993. *(Poster courtesy Ogilvy & Mather, London)*

after the flag finish. The BMW versus Ford dispute let David Leslie win the cash whilst Paul beat Soper home by a couple of tatty seconds in the first burst of temperament seen from the Kiwi.

That was the end of the European season for the Mondeo, but sufficient sponsorship had been raised to enable Paul Radisich to return home and take in a couple of races with Nissan's Australian Champion, Glenn Seton. They had mixed fortunes, Seton crashing in the Wellington Street event they had led convincingly. But the pairing cleaned up the Pukekohe 300 a week later.

It was almost exactly a year since Jacques Nasser, Chairman Ford of Europe, had authorized the budget to race the Mondeo with Andy Rouse Engineering and Cosworth power. Whatever else happens in his career at the top, Mr Nasser can look back on that decision with pride . . .

Men at the Mondeo racing wheel

By the close of 1993 only four drivers had raced the V6 Mondeo Si, but what a quartet! For they included a historic double World Champion and the quadruple British Champion, the man who has scored most BTCC race wins . . .

Developer/driver **Andy Rouse** came to the Mondeo at 46 years of age. He had taken British titles at the wheel of a Triumph (1974), Alfa Romeo (1983) Rover (1984), as well as the 1985 Championship with the underrated Sierra XR4Ti turbo.

Low roofline, high hopes: Paul Radisich (*left*) and Andy Rouse on parade at Silverstone with the 1994 Mondeo Ghia to replace the Si. Even then, the winged Alfas looked like the cars to beat in the Mondeo's second season.

Winner of innumerable class titles and 60 British Championship races, Andy was the protege of Portugal emigrant Ralph Broad (as in Broadspeed). Yet Andy learned his craft with self-built autocross specials in his teens, and went to technical college for a slice of practical engineering theory.

Andy developed into a literal racing engineer whose cars always carry high horsepower and fine handling. The fine manners are a Rouse distinctive trademark, evident when you are fortunate enough to drive one of his cars. He has also driven for Porsche at Le Mans, Formula Ford, and was the 1972 Escort Mexico Champion.

Rouse split his 1993 time between Sheila, their young family (Victoria 15 and Julian, 11) and the Binley, Coventry, business he established in 1981.

Born 9 October 1962, **Paul Radisich** was a 30-year-old gamble when Rouse took him on. His form was mainly Antipodean, but Brits with better memories will recall former *Motoring News* staffer Murray Taylor running Paul with underfunded and occasional success in UK F3 events. Some second places in the 1984 and '85 seasons were brilliantly taken against some of the best in the world.

Both single-seater and saloon car success was racked up 'down under'. Relevant to Rouse was his performance alongside Peter Brock and Jeff Allam in ARE-supplied Sierra RS500s (he was second at the 1990 edition of Bathurst).

By the close of 1993 Radisich+Rouse Sierra was the performance benchmark throughout the 2 litre touring car world. Together they had taken three British Championship races on a reduced schedule, the FIA Touring Car Challenge and had returned to New Zealand in glory to win at Pukekohe in the closing December days of the year.

1992 Grand Prix World Champion and IndyCar Champion of 1993, **Nigel Mansell** needs no further introduction as the epitome of the gritty

Cosworth creativity: Mondeo motor creator Geoff Goddard (*left*) receives the Design Council Award earned by Cosworth Engineering for the AC3000 V8 in March 1994. Straight-talking Geoff is accompanied by (*centre*) Chris Woodwark (now Cosworth MD) and Roy Eastwood of the Midlands Design Council. (*Courtesy the Cosworth Archive*)

racing hero, anywhere in the televised world.

Mansell only drove the Mondeo once, at the end-of-season Two Four Sports Ltd organized TOCA Shoot Out. The weekend fee was reportedly more than any regular British Touring Car driver earned for a season, but he was worth it at the spectator gates.

And what a gutsy drive! Instead of cruising around for the double measure crowd he had attracted (twice the number who attended the Grand Prix at Donington!) Mansell got his head down and launched the Mondeo into third place (past another man who also held a Unipart F3 contract in the '70s: Tiff Needell) before crashing in a terminal 'tank slapper' out of the Old Hairpin.

Fortunately the Rouse Mondeo (yes, the write-off was actually the boss's car!) resisted the ravages of Needell's Cavalier and the Donington bridge. Preserving the world quickest cornering moustache, intact.

Finally, Radisich shared his car in two closing New Zealand endurance events of the year with the slightly younger (28) former Nissan charger Australia's **Glenn Seton**, well known at the time for partnering George Fury.

Proud to be there: the author power steers away from the Brands Hatch pits in April 1994 with the ARE test Mondeo that he assessed for *Autosport*. This Mondeo proved friendly in its long wheelbase handling with the smoothest engine the writer has tried in saloon car racing since the TWR Jaguar V12 for the XJ-S.

The Cosworth V6 connection

To discover more about the racing heart to the Mondeo, I visited Cosworth Engineering at Northampton. Looking back to that impressive 1993 debut was Chief Designer Geoff Goddard, who has tackled everything from 1.5 litre turbo Grand Prix motors to detail YB Sierra Cosworth road development.

Complete with Keith Duckworth twinkle and *bons mots*, Geoff recalled of the Mondeo racing V6, 'When the original Ford approval came through our first task was simply to look at their engine range and advise which was best for this racing category . . . Or, you could say, the least worst! And I do not cast aspersions on any perfectly good road engines, when I say that. For we were looking through very different spectacles at every example of the Ford engine range with a very different purpose to that intended by their designers.

'They all had their Achilles' Heels for racing, but it was pretty obvious to us that the chance to take a 2.5 litre down to 2 litres might leave us with some nice big holes to use.

'Especially in respect of the head porting, valve sizes and bores: in fact we left the bore size as standard and simply ran a proper Cosworth all steel job on the internals (crankshaft, rods and our forged aluminium pistons), plus a correctly scavenged dry sump system. Even at the rev-limited 8,500 rpm [low by Cosworth standards *JW*] things happen quite fast, and we wanted to be sure it was reliable.

'Rouse never did have an engine failure in 1993. The alternator drive that failed was not our idea: we asked for a driveshaft belt. It was not done that way [a camshaft drive was originally specified *JW*] and the alternator drive failed. They have not had trouble since they took drive from the shafts . . .' said Geoff with laughter to belie the deadly schedule met in fielding an effective Mondeo motor.

Cosworth actually came up with an assembled race motor for Ford in just nine days, but why the panic? Surely everyone knew they would need motors earlier than the August 1993 date referred to by Andy Rouse and agreed by Cosworth with Ford in the original contract?

Geoff cut through the usual PR flannel that accompanies any sports

The first of nine racing Mondeos scheduled for 1994, this Mondeo Ghia was wheeled out for testing by late February at Silverstone. By early April Rouse had delivered eight, most to customers in France, Spain and Germany, but there were also three new Mondeos for the team's UK use.

programme and reported, 'It was originally thought Rouse would do the 93 season. Our contract was to run a dyno demo of the developed V6 in August 1993. We were on schedule to do that when, in late March '93, it was apparent that the Mondeo project was hitting heavy weather.

'The car simply was not going to be competitive as it stood in late March 1993. Aside from the front versus rear drive thing, they were still in trouble for adequate power. Peter Ashcroft, then on a retainer to Ford following his retirement, came up with the answer: it was spelt 'COSWORTH'! Peter learned to spell that out more than 20 years ago, when he assembled engines himself and graduated to managerial status having told the Cologne Capri team how reliability might be earned in the racing V6 by recourse to intense crankshaft dialogue with Keith Duckworth.

'Now, remember that although the Mondeo is a reasonable aerodynamic shape it has a *greater* frontal area than any competitor, so it needs bit of grunt to punch it along.' Thanks Geoff, I had fallen for the sleek, low-line bit.

Goddard resumed: 'In late March 1993 myself and Cosworth designer Rob Watkinson started to draw up the racing version of the V6. As I said, we did the usual bullet-proof job people expect from us, but now we were working to hit not just their British GP supporting race deadline, but the Pembrey BTCC round, a fortnight beforehand. The logic was that there would be just a couple of sheep watching if it all went wrong, but in fact, a huge crowd assembled.

'I assure you the motor was from scratch. We had tackled nothing in this speed range before, but once we had the parts to build an engine, it was ready to race nine days later. We just wanted to show that Cosworth can still do a panic job right, if they *have* to.

'As to the specifics, I will say that we retained the Zytek engine management because it was perfectly adequate and it was a small programme to change. In fact it's not even their Formula 1 level of electronics, so there was no need for a replacement in that area. The motor gives good power in the 7,000 to 8,500 range that they need, and that was one inherent benefit we took from a bore designed to serve 2.5 litres.

'We took nothing over from Andy Rouse Engineering, not even their motors. We had Ford deliver an example of each road motor and started from scratch. To support the effort Cosworth attended most races. That meant myself, Rob Watkinson, or possibly development engineer Stuart Lever.

'We built only four engines for 1993, because that was all we had the pieces for. Quite frequently the team had all our available engines, but the idea was that the rebuilds would be at shortish, 800 to 1,000 mile intervals. This was on an insurance basis, because we could not afford to have a failure.'

Geoff admitted candidly, 'We were in such a hurry originally that the 1994 specification was all about tidying things up. The most difficult, and obvious, aspect was the inlet and exhaust system, plus the water and oil plumbing. You will be able to identify the 1994 cars, because they carry more underfloor provision for the exhaust system. We have virtually had to tie a knot in it as we struggled to give each primary exhaust a clear run out of the tight engine compartment.

'Similarly, we wanted a proper carbon fibre cold air box to feed the

Andy Rouse gets in some initial settle down laps for the first of the 1994 Mondeos. Incidentally, German customer cars had to be engineered for a catalytic converter exhaust, and were carrying aerodynamic spoilers by July 1994.

The Mondeo motor racing motor was tidied appreciably for 1994, its 290 plus horsepower seen minus the composite cover employed that season.

Bald back: for the first half of 1994 the Mondeo did without a rear spoiler, but when Alfa Romeo appeared with extended rear wing kits, everyone had to think again . . . The Mondeo with an experimental high level spoiler, designed to make the international authorities think again about 2 litre regulations. For 1995 it was wings for everyone in 2 litre racing. *(Lower picture courtesy Ralph Hardwick)*

induction system. Overall, we've just made things tidier. You can fairly say there is plenty of potential for more power, as we had to hurl things on the motor to get it ready in time for 1993 . . .'

None of that bodes well for Mondeo's flustered rivals, and there was further bad news. First, there would never be the shortages of competition equipment suffered in 1993, for the build order had grown to nine cars plus 12 engines when I called, and it was obvious that a lot more motors would be required.

The second, longer term consideration was that Mondeo *would* be sold in 1995 with the 4x4 system that would allow it to follow the original rear drive plan. With more power available, and Cosworth studying the Ford 24v, DOHC, V6 to see if it had any more potential than the Ford Probe/Mazda motor, there would be no shortage of development potential.

Unprompted, the fiercely independent Geoff Goddard produced this thoughtful tribute to the winning ways of the Mondeo. 'It's not just down to our engine, or any single aspect. I think it's a combination of chassis, engine and driver. The car is stable and it does absorb the kerbs the way that press and rivals have observed but there is something about Paul

Radisich's technique [identified, but I've removed the reference as it is a basic part of Paul's superiority over his 0.001 sec rivals *JW*] that sets him apart from the rest. That helps enormously and was obvious after he had done four laps at Pembrey . . .' concluded our Cosworth guide to the unexpected.

Inspiration? No sign of a Mondeo Cosworth for the public, or any other faster Ford Mondeo as we went to press, but the Americans showed this supercharged 4x4 in January 1994 at both Detroit and Los Angeles auto shows. Engineered by the Ford Special Vehicle Team (with significant input from Ford of Europe's former SVE head, Rod Mansfield), the Mondeo-Profile showcar stood on neat 17 x 7.5 in alloys and was expected to yield 240 bhp.

The Author thanks

ASIDE from those names credited at Ford and Cosworth, can I add my personal thanks to:

- The patient Haynes production team. Especially Darryl Reach (Editorial Director), Alison Roelich (Editorial Department Manager), Flora Myer (anchor editor), and outside specialists Julia Thorley (copy editing), Graham Holmes (design and typesetting), plus Colin H. Paine (line drawings).

- As ever Sheila Knapman and Barry Reynolds at Ford photographic filled in the gaps left by my own and the (separately credited) freelance photographers, including the Cosworth Archive and the rapid service of Ralph and Alison Hardwick.

- Mrs Marilyn Walton filled stomach and spelling gaps.

JEREMY WALTON
July 1994

The road cars

The figures given are those of the manufacturer, or those calculated on manufacturer statistics. Independent performance figures are reproduced in Appendix III.

Ford Sierra RS Cosworth

PRODUCTION: 1986; approximate number built: 5,500; assembled at Genk, Belgium with UK-built Cosworth engine, Borg Warner five-speed gearbox and Ferguson Viscous Coupling rear drive.

ENGINE
Type: Ford Cosworth YBB.
Capacity: 1,993 cc.
Bore/stroke: 90.82 mm x 76.95 mm.
Compression ratio: 8:1.
Max power: 204 bhp at 6,000 rpm.
Max torque: 203 lb/ft 4,500 rpm.
Specific output: 102.36 bhp per litre.
Power/weight ratio: 169.3 bhp/tonne.
Cylinders: four, in line.
Cylinder head: Aluminium alloy.
Block: cast iron.
Valve gear: four valves per cylinder, twin overhead camshafts, belt-drive.
Fuel and ignition: Garrett AiResearch T03, compact air intercooler, Weber-Marelli microprocessor managed four injector injection and ignition.
Installation: Front, longitudinal.

TRANSMISSION
Type: Rear drive, Viscous Coupling limited slip differential.
Gearbox: Borg Warner T5.
Internal ratios: 1st, 2.95; 2nd, 1.94; 3rd, 1.34; 4th, 1:1 direct; 5th, 0.80.

Final drive: 3.65:1, 22.79 mph per 1,000 rpm in 5th.

SUSPENSION

Front: Independent by MacPherson struts, lower track controls arms (TCAs), coaxial coil springs, Fichtel & Sachs twin tube gas damper inserts, 28 mm diameter front anti-roll bar.

Rear: Semi-trailing arms, uniball joints, coil springs in front of axle, separate telescopic F&S gas rear dampers, 14 mm rear anti-roll bar.

STEERING

Type: Power assisted, Cam Gears/TRW rack and pinion, lock to lock: 2.6 turns.

BRAKES

Front: 283 mm, vented discs.
Rear: 273 mm solid back discs.
System: Hydraulically assisted, Alfred Teves GmbH electronic anti-lock action.

WHEELS AND TYRES

Wheels: unique Rial (BBS style) alloys, 7 x 15 in.
Tyres: 205/50 VR (Dunlop D40 was Original Equipment).

BODY

Type: 3-dr hatchback Sierra L with Phoenix-manufactured body kit and rear wing to Ford design, wheelarch extensions, side sills, front bumper/spoiler with flexible rubber extension, twin bonnet louvres, air intake between headlights.

Colour: Originally sold only in white, Moonstone blue metallic and black.
Cd: 0.336.
Construction: Steel monocoque with polyurethane and rubber body additions.
Dimensions: Length, 4,458 mm; width, 1,727 mm; height, 1,377 mm; wheelbase, 2,609 mm: front track, 1,450 mm; rear track, 1,470 mm; weight, 1,205 kg.

PERFORMANCE AND ECONOMY (Manufacturer's figures)

Max speed: 149.8 mph (240 km/h German homologation).
Acceleration: 0–60 mph, 6.47 sec; 50–70 mph (5th gear), 7 sec.
Fuel consumption: 22.8 mpg urban; 38.2 mpg at constant 56 mph; 30.1 mpg at 75 mph.

PRICE AT LAUNCH: £15,950

Sierra RS500 Cosworth

PRODUCTION: 1987; number converted for homologation: 500; converted by Tickworth in the UK from 500 batch of original Belgian-built 3-dr Sierra RS Cosworths, which were stored in UK.

ENGINE

Type: Ford Cosworth YBD.
Capacity: 1993 cc.
Bore/stroke: 90.82 mm x 76.95 mm.
Compression ratio: 8:1
Max power: 224 bhp at 6,000 rpm.
Max torque: 206 lb/ft 4,500 rpm.
Specific output: 112.39 bhp per litre.
Power/weight ratio: 180.65 bhp/tonne.
Cylinders: four, in line.
Cylinder head: Aluminium alloy, inlet tracts of 65 mm instead of 56 mm diameters.
Block: Cast iron, thickwall technique for RS500 only.
Valve gear: four valves per cylinder, twin overhead camshafts, belt-drive.

Fuel and ignition: Garrett AiResearch T31/T04, enlarged air intercooler. Weber-Marelli microprocessor managed four injector injection and ignition replaced by secondary rail and eight injector layout, not programmed for more than four injector operation public sale; many ancillary engine changes for durability/accessibility/homologation reasons.

Installation: Front, longitudinal.

TRANSMISSION
Type: Rear drive, Viscous Coupling limited slip differential.
Gearbox: Borg Warner T5.
Internal ratios: 1st, 2.95; 2nd, 1.94; 3rd, 1.34; 4th, 1:1 direct; 5th, 0.80.
Final drive: 3.65:1, 22.79 mph per 1,000 rpm in 5th.

SUSPENSION
Front: Independent by MacPherson struts, lower track controls arms (TCAs), coaxial coil springs, Fichtel & Sachs twin tube gas damper inserts, 28 mm diameter front anti-roll bar.
Rear: semi-trailing arms, uniball joints, coil springs in front of axle, separate telescopic F&S gas rear dampers, 14 mm rear anti-roll bar, unique alternative trailing arm mount installed for racing homologation purposes.

STEERING
Type: Power assisted, Cam Gears/TRW rack and pinion, lock to lock: 2.6 turns

BRAKES
Front: 283 mm, vented discs.
Rear: 273 mm solid back discs.
System: Hydraulically assisted, Alfred Teves GmbH electronic anti-lock action.

WHEELS AND TYRES
Wheels: Usual 'Cosworth' Rial alloys, 7 x 15 in.
Tyres: 205/50 VR-15.

BODY
Type: 3-dr hatchback Sierra L with Phoenix-manufactured body kit plus RS500 modification, rear wing to Ford design with 30 mm 'Gurney' lip plus lower RS parts secondary spoiler with cutout for upper wing pylon, usual 'Cosworth' wheelarch extensions, side sills, front bumper/spoiler with extra RS500 air intakes (five in total, including official deletion of auxiliary lamps inside flashers — see text) and hard plastic lip/extension spoiler blade, twin bonnet louvres, air intake between headlights.
Colour: Sold only in white, Moonstone metallic and black.
Cd: 0.351 (up 0.015 on original Cosworth).
Construction: Steel monocoque with polyurethane and rubber body additions, plus plastic extensions and secondary wing.
Dimensions: Length, 4,458 mm; width, 1,727 mm; height, 1,377 mm; wheelbase, 2,609 mm; front track, 1,450 mm; rear track, 1,470 mm. Weight, 1,240 kg/2728 lb (up 35 kg on original).

PERFORMANCE & ECONOMY (Manufacturer's figures, except* for an independent)
Max speed: 153 mph (up 3.2 mph on original).
Acceleration: 0–60 mph 6.2 sec (down 0.27 sec on original); 50–70 mph* (5th gear), 10 sec (biggest turbo lagger . . .)
Fuel consumption: 20.6 mpg urban; 33 mpg at constant 56 mph; 24.5 mpg at constant 75 mph.

PRICE AT LAUNCH: £19,950.

Sierra (née Sapphire) RS Cosworth

PRODUCTION: 1988–9; approximate number built: 13,140; also badged without RS and Sapphire in LHD; front engine, rear-wheel drive, assembled at Genk with UK-built Ford-Cosworth engine; rear drive only, BWT5 five-speed.

ENGINE
Type: Ford Cosworth YBB.
Capacity: 1993 cc.
Bore/stroke: 90.82 mm/76.95 mm.
Compression ratio: 8:1.
Max power: 204 bhp DIN at 6,000 rpm.
Peak torque: 205 lb/ft (276 Nm) at 4,500 rpm.
Specific output: 102.4 bhp per litre.
Power/weight ratio: 165.9 bhp/tonne.
Cylinders: four, in line.
Cylinder head: Cosworth cast alloy, 16v, DOHC.
Block: Cast iron.
Valve gear: four valves per cylinder, twin overhead camshafts with toothed belt-drive.
Fuel & ignition: Weber-Marelli microprocessor-managed fuel injection. Garrett AiResearch T03B turbocharger with intercooling, breakerless ignition.

TRANSMISSION
Type: Front engine, rear drive, Viscous Coupling limited slip rear differential, single plate, 240 mm, diaphragm spring clutch.
Gearbox: Borg Warner T5.
Internal ratios: As for original 3-dr and RS500.
Final drive: 3.64:1, 22.8 mph per 1,000 rpm in 5th.

SUSPENSION
MacPherson strut front, trailing arm rear, gas damping, anti-roll bars (28 mm and 16 mm), principles as before, but 1987 specification rear roll bar mounting and unique spring/damper settings.

STEERING
As previous two rear drive models, power assisted rack and pinion.

BRAKES
Four wheel discs, all as before, but Ferodo 3432 pads and Scorpio hub bearing clamp loads (as per recall action on 1986 models).

WHEELS AND TYRES
Wheels: Unique Ford Design 7J x 15 alloys, new.
Tyres: Dunlop D40 205/50 VR, as before.

BODY
Type: Sapphire 4-dr saloon in Ghia trim, but 170 mph speedometer and no tachometer redline, unique body colour-matched front grille bumper/air dam, rear 'hoop' spoiler and side sill extensions by Marley.
Cd: 0.33.
Dimensions: As for 1986 RS Cosworth 3-dr, but length 176 in (4,460 m); width 67 in (1,700 mm); weight 2,750 lb (1,250 kg).

PERFORMANCE AND ECONOMY (Manufacturer's homologated performance figures)
Max speed: 151.4 mph (243.6 km/h)
Acceleration: 0–60 mph, 6.1 sec; 30–50 mph (4th/5th gear) 6.5/11.0 sec.

Fuel consumption: 22.1 mpg, urban; 35.3 mpg at constant 56 mph; 27.7 mpg at 75 mph.

PRICE AT LAUNCH: £19,000

Sierra RS Cosworth 4x4

PRODUCTION: 1990–92; approximate number built: 12,250; assembled at Genk, Belgium using UK-built engine, and Ferguson patented 4x4 transmission with Ford MT75 gearbox.

ENGINE
Type: Ford Cosworth YBJ/YBG*.
Capacity: 1993 cc.
Bore/stroke: 90.82 mm/76.95 mm.
Compression ratio: 8:1.
Max power: 220 bhp at 6,000 rpm (6,250 rpm with Cat).
Max torque: 214 lb ft at 3,500 rpm.
Specific output: 110.4 bhp a litre.
Power/weight ratio: 174.6 bhp per ton.
Cylinders: four, in line.
Cylinder head: stiffened cast alloy.
Block: Modified Pinto/RS500 iron casting.
Valve gear: Cosworth four valves per cylinder head, double overhead camshafts (DOHC) of revised profiles, belt-drive.
Fuel and ignition: Weber-Marelli ignition/fuelling management, Garrett TO3B turbocharger with lead seal for wastegate and enlarged intercooler.

* The YBJ was the red rocker cover Euro 1504 Emission trim; YBG was to the more restrictive US '83 emissions level. Significant 4x4 YBJ/YBG motor changes included: inlet manifold/fuelling rail; replacement cast iron exhaust manifold (no damper); oil and water pumps; cast alloy sump pan; head gasket; first platinum-tipped Motorcraft spark plugs (AGPR 902P) and synthetic oils only.

TRANSMISSION
Type: Front engine, permanent 4WD, Ferguson 4WD/Viscous Coupling patents, 4x4 utilized 34–66 per cent front-rear torque split via transfer box epicyclic centre differential, further modified by Viscous Coupling action, front drive via Hyvo chain, 31 tooth chain wheels, 6.5 in spiral bevel gear free differential and equal length drive shafts, to the rear by gear output shaft, propshaft, 7 in hypoid Viscous Coupling limited slip rear axle, single dry plate clutch, cable operation, 240 mm (9.5 in).
Gearbox: Five-speed Ford MT75.
Internal ratios: 1st, 3.62; 2nd, 2.08; 3rd, 1.36; 4th, 1:1; 5th, 0.83.
Final drive: 3.62:1, 22.24 mph per 1,000 rpm in 5th.

SUSPENSION
Front: Via MacPherson struts, unique RS spring rates, monotube gas damping, thickened (30 mm) anti-roll bar.
Rear: Separate springs and single tube gas dampers, plus 18 mm rear anti-roll bar, spring rates as per previous 2WD Cosworth.

STEERING
Type: Hydraulic power assistance, rack and pinion, lock-to-lock: 2.6 turns.

BRAKES
Front: 278 x 24 mm (10.94 x 0.94 in).
Rear: 273 x 20 mm (10.74 x 0.79 in).
System: Four wheel ventilated discs with Teves ABS electronic anti-lock braking and hydraulic assistance.

WHEELS AND TYRES
Wheels: Unique RS 7 x 15 in alloys.
Tyres: Bridgestone ER90 205/50 ZR 15 on UK cars.

BODY
Type: Sierra 4-dr.
Cd: 0.322.
Construction: Unitary steel with RS polyurethane panels including front and rear spoilers, side sills and bonnet louvres.
Dimensions: Overall length: 4,494 mm (176.9 in); width, 1,698 mm (66.8 in); height, 1,376 mm (54.2 in); wheelbase, 2,608 mm (102.7 in); kerb weight: 1,280 kg (2,816 lb), add 10 kg (22.05 lb) for Cat model.

PERFORMANCE AND ECONOMY (Manufacturer's figures)
Max speed: 150 mph.
Acceleration: 0–60 mph, 6.6 sec.
Fuel consumption: 22.1 mpg urban; 37.2 mpg at constant 56 mph; 30.4 mpg at 75 mph.

PRICE AT LAUNCH: £24,995.

Escort RS Cosworth

PRODUCTION: 1992–; number made (declared at June 1993): 3,061* designed in Britain to marry Sierra 4x4 running gear with Escort outline; development called on truly multinational talents: assembly, Karmann (Rheine), stampings/pressings, Ford at Genk (Sierra origin), Ford Saarlouis; further work by Karmann at Osnabruck.

ENGINE
Type: Ford Cosworth YBT.
Capacity: 1993 cc.
Bore/stroke: 90.8 x 77 mm.
Compression ratio: 8:1.
Max power: 227 bhp DIN at 6,250 rpm.
Max torque: 220 lb/ft best at 3,500 rpm.
Specific output: 113.9 bhp per litre.
Power/weight ratio:181.6 bhp/tonne.
Cylinders: four, in line.
Cylinder head: Aluminium alloy.
Block: cast iron.
Valve gear: four valves per cylinder, twin overhead camshafts, belt-drive.
Fuel and ignition: Garrett AiResearch T3/TO4B, two stage water/air intercooler, Weber-Marelli microprocessor managed single rail injection and ignition, maximum boost, 0.8 bar/11.4 psi sustained, 1.2 bar/17 psi mid-range overboost.
Installation: Front, longitudinal.

TRANSMISSION
Type: Permanent 4x4 drive, epicyclic central differential splits power 34 per cent front, 66 per cent rear, Viscous Coupling limited slip differential action for centre

and rear differentials, single dry plate clutch, cable operated.
Gearbox: Ford MT75.
Internal ratios: 1st, 3.61; 2nd, 2.08; 3rd, 1.36; 4th, 1:1 direct; 5th, 0.83.
Final drive: 3.62:1; 22.28 mph per 1,000 rpm in 5th.

SUSPENSION

Front: Independent by MacPherson struts, lower track control arms (TCAs), coaxial coil springs, Fichtel & Sachs twin tube gas damper inserts, 28 mm diameter front anti-roll bar.
Rear: Semi-trailing arms, bi-directional bushes to rear crossmember and differential mountings with steel plate inserts, coil springs in front of axle, separate telescopic F&S gas rear dampers; 22 mm rear anti-roll bar.

STEERING

Type: Power assisted, Cam Gears/TRW rack and pinion, lock to lock: 2.45 turns.

BRAKES

Front: 278 mm, vented discs.
Rear: 273 mm vented discs.
System: Hydraulically assisted, ITT Alfred Teves GmbH Mk2 ABS electronic anti-lock action.

WHEELS AND TYRES

Wheels: Standard alloys, 8 x 16 in.
Tyres: 225/45 ZR (Pirelli P Zero as OE).

BODY

Type: 3-dr hatchback Escort, assembled by Karmann from Ford Escort and Sierra pressings in steel and '50 per cent' new panels, Sotira-manufactured RTM upper rear wing, Phoenix-manufactured body kit in GRP polyurethane, twin bonnet louvres, further air management includes under engine tray, adjustable front spoiler/splitter.
Cd: 0.38
Construction: Steel monocoque with polyurethane and Resin Transfer Moulding (RTM).
Dimensions: Length, 4,211 mm; width, 1,727 mm; height, 1,425 mm; wheelbase, 2,551.5 mm; front track, 1,453 mm; rear track, 1,472 mm; weight, 1,275 kg (2,805 lb).

PERFORMANCE AND ECONOMY *(Manufacturer's figures)*

Max speed: 140 mph.
Acceleration: 0–60 mph, 5.7 sec; 50–80 mph (5th gear), 8.0 sec.
Fuel consumption: 22.8 mpg urban; 33.6 mpg at constant 56 mph; 30.1 mph at 75 mph.

PRICE AT LAUNCH: Listed at £21,380 (Motorsport or road spec), £23,495 (Lux), £23,976 (Lux plus leather). NB: Significant discounts prevailed in the UK. From June 1994 a second edition with T25 turbo and many modifications (see end of Chapter 10) was listed at £22,535 and £25,825 (Lux). In August '94 a Monte Carlo special edition with OZ wheels, aluminium gear lever, sports steering wheel and celebration decals was offered at the normal Lux price.

---

* At this point, when Ford had won three WRC events in a row, just seven factory works rally Escorts existed; and one of them had just been sold to Snobeck for Bernard Beguin to win the French Rally Championship! Others (two) went to Australia, New Zealand and Argentinia shortly afterwards . . . Ford Motorsport had learned how to win with very low stock levels. A full specification for the works Escort rally car can be found in Appendix II.

Competition car specifications

To give us an overall perspective, we will start detailing 20 years of factory fresh Ford Escort progress. I drove both the 1973 car (several, in fact) and the 1993 machine (Delecour's Corsican winner) and can assure you they were absolutely at the leading edge of works rally car technology in both eras. We follow that nostalgic techno-summary with the 1988 Tour de Corse winner (Didier Auriol), a 3-dr Sierra RS Cosworth tested for the defunct weekly, *Motor*. To balance up the rallying bias (inevitable, as that was the factory emphasis in their preparation at Boreham airfield until the end of 1994), I have detailed a typical RS500 race specification, drawing upon my contemporary experience with the Rouse/Asquith Motorsport examples, a 1991 club racing season with Collins Engineering, and the 1993 track test of the perfectly preserved Brooklyn car that was run for Mike Hodgetts in the late '80s.

Finally, a specification drawn from Rouse Engineering and Cosworth sources to cover such details as they would release on the 1993 Mondeo. I should say thank you to Robin Shute (now at *Autosport*) and Peter Minnis, publisher of *Fast Ford/Heritage* for making me bring much of this material up to date in a disciplined style for their monthly and one-off publications.

Works Escort RS Cosworth, 1993 (1973 works Escort detail in brackets)

ENGINE
Type: Ford Cosworth YBT (BDG).
Capacity: 1994.5 cc (1993 cc).
Bore/stroke: 90.8 x 77 mm (90.4 x 77.62 mm).
Compression ratio: 7.5:1 (11.5:1).
Max power: 360 bhp minimum at 6,800 rpm (245 bhp at 8,000).
Max torque: 404 lb/ft best at 4,500 rpm (160 lb/ft at 6,750).
Specific output: 180.6 bhp per litre (122.9).
Power/weight ratio: 305 bhp/tonne (272)
Cylinders: four, in line.

Cylinder head: Aluminium alloy.
Block: cast iron (alloy).
Valve gear: four valves per cylinder, twin overhead camshafts; belt-drive (same principles).
Fuel and ignition: Garrett AiResearch T3/TO4B, two stage water/air intercooler, water injection. Weber-Marelli microprocessor managed single rail injection and ignition with Ford Motorsport programmed ECU, Pectel monitoring, eight-mode digital readout and electronics co-development. Engine hardware, including replacement pistons, under piston oil cooling sprays, camshafts and lightweight steel crankshaft were assembled by Mountune of Maldon, Essex; maximum boost, 3.0 bar/42.7 psi — standard figure is 0.8 bar sustained, 1.2 bar mid-range overboost (side draught twin choke Weber 45 DCOEs, normally aspirated).
Installation: Front, longitudinal (same).

TRANSMISSION
Type: Permanent 4x4 drive, epicyclic central differential split power in tarmac trim test 58 per cent front, 42 per cent rear (alternative available include 40 per cent front, 60 per cent rear), uprated Viscous Coupling limited slip differential action for front, centre and rear differentials, AP Racing twin plate clutch (rear drive, ZF limited slip differential).
Gearbox: Ford Motorsport MS93, Ferguson hardware (ZF five-speed).
Internal ratios: 1st, 2.071; 2nd, 1.529; 3rd, 1.200; 4th, 0.995; 5th, 0.792; 6th, 0.654; 7th, 0.536 (1st, 2.30; 2nd, 1.8; 3rd, 1.36; 4th, 1.14; 5th direct, 1:1).
Final drive: 4.63 to 3.25:1 available for three axle-installed options — 9 in rear; 8.5 in gear front or 7.5 in front — but final drive reduction gear alternatives (built into gearbox) also homologated: 1.263 to 1.688 (5:1 was normal in the '70s, but 5.3 to 4:1 were amongst five regular homologated alternatives), 19.87 mph per 1,000 rpm tested (12.7 mph was typical!).

SUSPENSION
Front: MacPherson strut principles, totally fabricated, all attachment points can be varied + or - 20 mm, magnesium uprights, alloy lower track control arms (TCAs), compression strut, instant camber and castor adjustment, replacement coil springs, Bilstein gas damping water cooled at spring seat, cockpit adjustable anti-roll bar stiffness (MacPherson and anti-roll bar, all fabricated; compression strut for Tarmac).
Rear: All mounting points allowed + or - 20 mm tolerance, cast magnesium semi-trailing arms, alloy toe-in/out control links, concentric coil springs — standard separate spring removed — telescopic Bilstein gas rear dampers, water cooled to outer body, cockpit adjustable anti-roll bar stiffness (Reinforced four-link live axle, Panhard Rod, usually leaf sprung with Watts linkage and coil spring alternatives for tarmac or race use).

STEERING
Type: Power assisted, competition rack and pinion ('Quick rack'), double, lock to lock, 1.9 turns (unassisted, 2.5 turns).

BRAKES
Front: Tested on 355 mm discs, vented & water cooled, AP Racing piston callipers, cockpit adjustable bias (Typically 259 mm).
Rear: tested on 315 mm discs, vented and water cooled, AP Racing four-piston callipers, cockpit adjustable bias (Typically 259 mm).

WHEELS AND TYRES
Wheels: Tested on Ford/OZ, 9 x 17 in (typically Minilite 5–7 in x 13).
Tyres: Michelin S1 slicks (Dunlop).

BODY
Type: 3-dr hatchback Escort, assembled by Ford Motorsport and including purpose-built TG45 steel integral roll cage structure, standard steel and plastic sections retained (2-dr saloon, bare shell with uprated welds and hoop plus screen 'legs' roll cage by Maurice Gomm, Woking).
Cd: 0.38 (circa 0.46).
Construction: Steel monocoque with polyurethane and Resin Transfer Moulding (RTM) (Steel monocoque plus steel wheelarch extensions and replacement suspension linkage/rear turret fabrication).
Homologated dimensions: Length, 4,211 mm (3,978 mm); width, 1,742 mm (circa 1,740 mm with arches); wheelbase, 2,551 mm + or - 1 per cent FIA tolerance (2,400.3 mm); height (manufacturer's brochure figures), 1,425 mm (1,384 mm); weight, 1,200 kg FIA minimum (1,027 kg).

PERFORMANCE AND ECONOMY
Max speed: 155 mph at 7,600 rpm red line (108 at 8,500).
Acceleration: 0–60 mph, 3.8 sec (6.3).
Rally stage fuel consumption: 6 mpg (9 mpg).

PRICES
Expect to pay more than £150,000 for a good factory Ford today. Value of 1973 car at disposal times would have been in the region of £10,000.

1988 Works Sierra RS Cosworth (GROUP A, Corsican tarmac specification)

ENGINE
Type: Cosworth Ford YBG, Terry Hoyle preparation.
Capacity: 1993 cc (2790.2 cc FIA turbo).
Bore/stroke: 90.82 x 76.95 mm.
Compression ratio: 7.2:1.
Max power: 300 bhp at 6,000 rpm*.
Max torque: 300 lb/ft, 3,500 to 5,500 rpm*.
Specific output: minimum of 155.2 bhp a litre.
Power/weight ratio: 298.2 bhp per ton.
Cylinders: Four, in line.
Cylinder head: Cosworth cast aluminium to Group A tolerances.
Cylinder block: Strength-selected cast iron.
Valve gear: four valves per cylinder, twin overhead camshafts, belt-drive.
Fuel and ignition: Reprogrammed (by Graham Dale Jones/Hoyle) Weber-Marelli fuel injection and electronic ignition management. Group A regulations meant standard manifolding and Garrett AiResearch T03 turbocharger dimensions. Boost substantially increased over the usual 1.2 to 1.5 bar used in competition for our Boreham airfield test session, researching a then non-standard intercooler for the subsequent Sierra 4x4.
Installation: front, longitudinal.

TRANSMISSION
Type: Inline front engine, rear drive, Viscous Coupling limited slip differential.
Gearbox: Getrag homologated Group A rally five-speed, AP 8.5 in plate clutch.

Internal ratios: 1st, 2.34; 2nd, 1.68; 3rd, 1.36; 4th, 1.15; 5th, 1.00.
Final drive: 4.89:1.

SUSPENSION
Front: Replacement MacPherson struts, steel coil springs rated 90 Nm (500 lb/in) over Bilstein gas damping, alloy casings, 325/150 settings, $1^1/8$ in blade-type anti-roll bar.
Rear: Replacement magnesium trailing arms, steel coil springs rated 36 Nm (200 lb/in) over alloy case Bilstein telescopic gas dampers set at 260/110, blade type anti-roll bar, $3/4$ in.

STEERING
Type: Power assisted, competition rack and pinion, lock-to-lock: approx 2 turns.

BRAKES
Front: AP four piston callipers on 330 x 32 mm vented discs.
Rear: AP, 285 x 28 mm vented discs.
System changes: Replacement throughout + Tilton rear line pressure regulator and adjustable front to rear brake bias.

WHEELS AND TYRES
Wheels: Magnesium, Ford Motorsport design/Speedline 8 x 16 in (front); $7^3/4$ x 16 in (rear).
Tyres: Michelin S1 slicks for acceleration runs.

BODY
Type: Hand built, reinforced, 3-dr Sierra Cosworth RS with integral welded roll cage in T45 steel tube, 50 litre 'sprint' fuel tank, externally as per showroom Cosworth.
Dimensions: As per standard 3-dr, save ride height (variable) and weight: 1,106 kg (2,433 lb) (saving 134 kg/295 lb over standard).

PERFORMANCE (For fuller figures see Appendix III)
Max speed: Geared for 185 km/h (115 mph) at 7,500 rpm in 5th.
Acceleration: 0–60 mph, 4.8 sec; 0–100 mph, 10.8 sec.

* Official 1988 Ford reply. Research revealed at least 308–315 bhp and almost 400 lb/ft of torque with a then current Group A intercooler; we had a non-standard intercooler and sharply uprated boost that damp day, so 340–350 bhp would be a fairer estimate. *JW*

Typical racing Group A Sierra RS500 Cosworth

ENGINE
Type: Ford Cosworth YBF, Terry Hoyle/Mountune/Rouse Engineering.
Capacity: 1993 cc.
Bore/stroke: 90.82 x 76.95 mm.
Compression ratio: 7.2:1.
Max power: 520–560 bhp at 2.2 bar boost and 6,000 rpm.
Max torque: Not disclosed.
Specific output: 260.91 bhp per litre (minimum).
Power/weight ratio: 515.87 bhp/ton (minimum).
Cylinders: four, in line.

Cylinder head: Aluminium alloy.

Block: cast iron, thickwall RS500.

Valve gear: four valves per cylinder, solid lifters, twin overhead camshafts, race profiles, belt-drive.

Fuel and ignition: Garrett AiResearch T31/T04, RS500 air intercooler, racing water radiator, Ford Motorsport/Hoyle/Eggenberger hybrid Bosch Motronic microprocessor or Zytek-managed Weber eight injector layout, 2.2 bar regular maximum boost, 2.5 bar emergency button overboost (Rouse/Eggenberger).

Installation: Front, longitudinal.

TRANSMISSION

Type: Rear drive, Viscous Coupling limited slip differential, 9 in Ford cwp, alloy casing.

Gearbox: Getrag, race pattern, Heavy Duty.

Gear speeds at 7,500 rpm on Silverstone GP gearing (Rouse, 1989): 1st, 65 mph; 2nd, 90 mph; 3rd, 112 mph; 4th, 132; 5th, 152 mph.

Final drive: 4.4:1.

SUSPENSION

Front: Independent by MacPherson strut principles all road car components replaced, including front uprights and top mounts; lower track control arms (TCAs), coaxial coil springs, Koni/Spax/Bilstein damper inserts, Ford Motorsport front anti-roll bar, aft of front axle.

Rear: Fabricated and reinforced semi-trailing arms (Eggenberger alternative), solid joints, coil springs over Koni/Spax, Bilstein telescopic shock absorber ('coil overs'), behind axle line, drop-link Group A rallying rear anti-roll bar, Ford Motorsport.

STEERING

Type: Power assisted, Ford Motorsport rack and pinion, lock to lock: 2.5 turns.

BRAKES

Front: 330 mm, vented and cross-drilled discs.

Rear: 330 mm, vented and cross-drilled discs.

System: Hydraulically assisted, cockpit adjustable brake bias, front to rear.

WHEELS AND TYRES

Wheels: BBS split rim, 8.5 x 17 in.

Tyres: Dunlop/Pirelli/Yokohama slicks, 225/430–17 (front) and 240/650 R 17 rears.

BODY

Type: 3-dr hatchback Sierra Motorsport shell, basic construction and roll cage fabrication/installation by teams, installation of 120 litre Premier fuel tank and all fireproofing/on board extinguisher plumbing, plus instrumentation (boost gauge for all, some with turbo exhaust temperature display) and switchgear. All RS500 Phoenix-manufactured body kit in place, plus 30 mm rear 'Gurney' lip, and RS500 front aerodynamics fitted to comply with 1989 Group A regulations, doors trimmed, no floor covering, single racing seat and six-point harness.

Cd: Circa 0.35.

Construction: Steel monocoque with polyurethane and rubber body additions, steel roll cage, Ford homologated plastic extensions and secondary wing.

Dimensions: Length, 4,458 mm; width, 1,727 mm; height, circa 1,277 mm; wheelbase, 2,609 mm; front track, N/A; rear track, N/A; weight, 1,100 kg (down 140 kg on road RS500).

PERFORMANCE AND ECONOMY

Max speed: Over 170 mph on suitable gearing.

Acceleration (Silverstone gearing): 0–20 mph, a month (designed for rolling starts); 0–60 mph, 3 sec; 0–100 mph, circa 7 sec.
Fuel consumption: 3 to 5 mpg.

PRICE AT LAUNCH: £60,000 to £70,000 in 1989 for UK; £100,000+ Eggenberger.

Andy Rouse Engineering BTCC Mondeo (2 litre racing Mondeo Si for 1993)

ENGINE
Cosworth reworked and assembled 60° V6 with DOHC per bank and four valves per cylinder. Ford/Mazda aluminium heads and block casting. Replacement internal components to reduce from designed 2.5 litre to 2 litres (standard bore x shortened stroke, internal dimensions not released by Ford/Cosworth).
Replacement intake manifold and slide throttle fuel injection. Zytek microprocessor fuel and ignition management with Cosworth strategy. Mandatory BTCC 8500 electronic rpm limiter. Dry sump oil lubrication system fabricated by Cosworth, pump driven by tooth belt from front of crankshaft. Thermostatic-trigger for oil cooler (oil cooling auxiliary radiators mounted in front of/adjacent to main water radiator).
Originally had a camshaft extension belt drive for alternator, subsequent driveshaft connection. Unleaded Super grade fuel (98 octane minimum), Mobil 1 oil contract.
Max power: 292–295 bhp at 8,500 rpm (author's estimate).

TRANSMISSION
Type: Transverse engine to front transaxle and drive, AP Racing 5.25 in carbon fibre plate clutch, Rouse/Xtrac sequential six-speed gearbox, non synchromesh. Transaxle incorporated a plate type limited slip differential originally. FFD supplied and assembled Viscous Coupling after five races.

SUSPENSION
MacPherson strut front and strut rear suspension principles retained, but all major components fabricated by ARE to run to BTCC 2.5 in minimum ground clearance rule.
Front: Has two-piece lower wishbone mounting to solid mounted subframe. Front anti-roll bar is linked to the strut casing by adjustable links and is of the cockpit-adjustable, blade, type. Camber, castor, toe in/out can all be adjusted to suit each track. Rouse stub axles carry twin hub bearings, bolt-on steering arms and knock-on wheel hubs. Single nut wheel attachment with four drive pegs and safety clip location.
Rear: Has reworked parallel arms, swung from rear subframe; outboard mounted by equally spaced attachments to the base of the rear hub carrier. Longitudinal links. The adjustable control of camber, castor, toe in/out is through the replacement top mount. Blade-type anti-roll bar also linked to the telescopic shock absorber casing. ARE specify rates for Proflex shock absorbers, replacement road and (front) helper springs. Roll bar (F&R) adjusts via Bowden cable linkage, bell crank and four-position cockpit lever. Roll bar loading, and therefore stiffness, can be altered through a 40 per cent range.

STEERING
(RHD only for first 11 cars.)
Type: Rack and pinion steering, no 1993 power assistance.

BRAKES
Front and rear: AP Racing cockpit adjustable system with 14 in ventilated front and 12 in rears. Six-piston front, four-piston rear, callipers and carbon metallic pads. Ducted cold air supply from front spoiler scoops.

WHEELS AND TYRES
Wheels: Dymag 8 x 18 in magnesium.
Tyres: Initially Yokohama (two races) then Michelin, up to 9 in broad.

BODY
Basic 4-dr Mondeo Si shell in steel, made for Ford Motorsport at the Genk Belgium, Ford factory. Rouse build in TIG-welded roll cage to their own design in T45 steel tubing. Further seam and specialized welding for subframe and suspension pick-up points. Recessed exhaust system requires underbody/front bulkhead channel on passenger side.
Cockpit: Corbeau seat, Mota-Lita steering wheel, six-point safety harness. Stack data-logging display (oil and fuel pressure, rpm, water and oil temperatures). LCD readout includes lap times triggered by track-side transponder. Separate gear selection indicator LED readout. MRTC car to pits radio link. Boot carries lightweight battery, 15 gallon Premier safety fuel tank, aluminium casing for flexible bag construction: twin low and high pressure pumps. 2 gallon dry sump oil tank.

Performance in a civilized suit came with the advent of the 1988 4-dr Sierra Cosworth, which sold in very large numbers.

PERFORMANCE
Max speed: 147 to 150 mph at 8,450 rpm for Silverstone GP/or Thruxton circuits (as reported by ARE/Ford Motorsport).
Acceleration: 0–60 mph, 5.5 to 5.9 secs (author's estimate).

Performance figures

A ll the figures quoted have been taken from independent road tests. Wherever possible these have been taken with permission from the UK London-based weekly *Autocar & Motor* to allow consistent and comparable results.

Sierra RS Cosworth, 3-dr

Mph (sec)	Sierra RSC 204 bhp	Sierra RS500 224 bhp	Securicor RSC 300 bhp	Works RSC 340 bhp
0–30	2.5	2.4	2.2	2.4•
0–40	3.5	3.3	2.8	3.1
0–50	4.9	4.7	3.6	3.9
0–60	6.2	6.1	5.1	4.8
0–70	8.5	8.4	6.3	5.9
0–80	10.4	10.5	8.3	7.5
0–90	13.3	12.9	9.9	8.9
0–100	16.1	16.2	12.6	10.8
0–110	19.4	20.1	15.1	–
1/4 mile	15.5	15.1	13.6	13.3
50–70 (4th)	4.9	5.9+	–	–
Max mph	145*	154*	125/6,900 rpm	115/7,500 rpm
Test mpg	21.4+	– #	–	–
Weight (lb)	2,688	–	–	2,433
Source	*Autocar*	*Autocar*	*Autocar*	*Motor*
Issue	13/8/86	19/8/87	–	1988

* In the light of experience, *Autocar & Motor* dropped the original 3-dr maximum speed quote to 145 mph. This also throws suspicion on the RS500 quote. See the relevant chapter for more details and do not expect a standard RS500 to do more than honestly exceed 145 mph. • Damp conditions.
# Unquoted; in my experience road consumption was 18.9 to 20 mpg.
+ Unquoted; *Fast Lane* (defunct, 1994) result quoted.

Sierra RS Cosworth, 4-dr

Mph (sec)	Sierra (Sapphire) RSC 204 bhp, 2wd	Sierra RSC 220 bhp, 4x4	Sierra 304R* 260 bhp, 4x4
0–30	2.2	2.1	1.7
0–40	3.2	3.4	3.2
0–50	4.4	4.8	4.3
0–60	5.8	6.6	5.6
0–70	8.1	8.6	7.9
0–80	10.1	10.9	9.8
0–90	12.8	13.4	12.2
0–100	15.8	17.1	15.7
0–110	19.5	23.1	19.2
1/4 mile	14.4	15.3	–
50–70 (4th)	4.8	5.2	5.1
Max mph	142	146	–
Test mpg	20.3	21.6	18.7
Kerb weight (lb)	2,660	2,874	–
Source	*Autocar & Motor*	*Autocar & Motor*	*Fast Lane*
Issue	17/2/88	11/4/90	1990

* This was the £32,178 Andy Rouse Engineering complete car conversion that was sold in a limited edition (100-off) alongside a rear drive (302R) in the late '80s and early '90s. Equipped with a smaller (T25) turbocharger it put the accent — successfully — on flexibility rather than outright bhp. It was a thoughtfully engineered car, perhaps the nearest a British specialist has come to the Alpina-BMW approach. I enjoyed driving this car and taking the performance figures, which marked the first time I had measured 0–30 mph in less than 2 sec since the 1984 Porsche 911 and Audi Quattro by Treser. We must hope Rouse does something similar with Mondeo in the '90s. *JW*

Escort RS Cosworth

Mph (sec)	1992 RS Cos 227 bhp	1993 RS Cos/ works Group A 360 bhp
Maximum speed (mph)	137	136*
0–30	2.3	1.22
0–40	3.5	2.06
0–50	4.8	2.71
0–60	6.2	3.80
0–70	8.6	5.12
0–80	10.7	6.32
0–90	13.3	8.11
0–100	17.4	9.90
1/4 mile	14.9/95	12.4/109
50–70 (5th gear)	9.7	–
Test mpg	20.5	6 to 7
Kerb weight (kg)	1,307	1,200
Source	*Autocar & Motor*	*Autocar & Motor*
Issue	13/5/92	21/7/93

UK sales and Cosworth motor production

UK FORD COSWORTH CAR SALES~

Model	1985	1986	1987	1988	1989	1990	1991	1992	1993
3-dr Sierra	10	1,064	1,761	7	–	–	–	–	–
4-dr, 2wd	–	–	–	2,435	2,699	1,093	2	1	–
4-dr, 4x4	–	–	–	–	–	1,227	1,424	1,010	–
Escort, 4x4	–	–	–	–	–	–	–	310	330
Total Cosworths	10	1,064	1,761	2,442	2,699	2,320	1,426	1,321	330
% of all Sierras	–	0.9	1.3	1.5	1.5	1.8	1.5	1.3	–

~ Source: Ford Motor Company and the Society of Motor Manufacturers and Traders.
Total Ford Cosworths, registered UK from 1985–93 (November) = 13,036.

YB Engine family, production and identity

My thanks to Chris Costin, Commercial Engineer, Engines Group, at Cosworth Engineering for making these figures available, January 1994. They record annual production of the YB production engines that powered the Sierra and Escort RS Cosworths, 1986–94. Variant codes, drawn from the Ken Wells publication *Cosworth: Creative Power* and cross-checked at Cosworth, January 1994 is attached. *JW*

TYPE	PRODUCTION SPAN	TOTALS	NOTES
YBB	10/85–7/89	18,990	5,600 for 3-dr; 13,390 for 4-dr. All RWD models; approx 250 excess to build requirements.

YBD	5/87–8/87	525	Recycled engines for RS500, additional to above.
YBG	10/89–12/11/91	12,515	The YBJ was the 'redheaded'.
YBJ	10/89–12/11/91	As YBG	YB to Euro 1504 Emission; YBG was to US '83 emission, green cam cover. Both for 4x4 Sierra. Best year (1990) 7,570 units.
YBT	23/3/92–2/94	5,186	Escort, T04 turbo/Weber inj, 4,078 built 1992, but 788 in '93 and 320 scheduled to '94 end.
YB variant totals		36,691	All but RS500 (add 525 = 37,216).

YB: Cosworth Engineering drawing office codes as used to identify production and competition variants of the 2 litre YB family.

YEAR	CODE	BHP/RPM	PURPOSE
1982/4	YAA	N/A	Cosworth financed 16V head on Ford T88/Pinto block. No turbocharging, intended for TVR + aftermarket.
1984	YBB	204/6,000	Ford commissioned turbo protos.
1985/9	YBB	204/6,000	Production for 3 and 4-dr Sierra RS Cosworth.
1986	YBC	280/6,000	Group A rally engine, developed up to 350 bhp by late '80s.
1987	YBB	224/6,000	RS500, thickwall block, eight-inject.
1987	YBE	204/6,000	Commercial sale for non-Ford road car installations.
1987	YBF	400 +/-	Race RS500; 560 bhp by 1990.
1989	YBG	220/6,000	Two prod emission levels for Sierra 4x4 RSC. See prod.
1989	YBJ	220/6,250	–
1992	YBT	227/6,000	Escort RS Cosworth, see prod. Cosworth also built the Group N Cat YBT for Gwyndaf Evans, '93
1993	YBT/N	280/5,500	–
1994	YBP	227/5,700	Escort RS Cosworth, from 3/94 T25 turbo, Ford EEC IV management.

PS. Group A rallying engines for Ford Motorsport were Terry Hoyle/Cosworth assembly/hardware units, Graham Dale Jones electronics. When the 4x4 Sapphire was being developed, the Mountune era arrived. Cosworth reported Escort Cosworth YBT competition engines as 'consultancy only'. The Corsica-winning works Escort in 1993 was credited with 360 bhp, despite a mandatory 38 mm restrictor. There is also a family of normally aspirated YBM/YBV competition units. They use many production parts to support 315 bhp at 8,300 rpm (YBV, methanol) and 260 bhp/8,500 rpm (YBM, petrol). Uprated YBG heads run 12.8:1 cr, petrol; 13.5:1 for the methanol-munching YBV. *JW*

Index